Lake Baykal

MONGOLIA

DESERT

INNER MONGOLIA

ORDOS

HUHEHOT
(KWEISUI)
KALGAN
CHANGKIAKOW

HEILUNGKIANG

HARBIN

CHANGCHUN
KIRIN
KIRIN

LIAONING
MUKDEN FUSHUN

ANSHAN
ANTUNG

SEA OF JAPAN

PEKING
(PEIPING) CHINWANGTAO
PAOTING
TIENTSIN
DAIREN
PORT ARTHUR

TAIYUAN

CHEFOO

KOREA

JAPAN

YENAN SHANSI

SHENSI

SIAN Yellow River
LOYANG CHENGCHOW

TSINAN

SHANTUNG

KAIFENG

TSINGTAO

YELLOW

SEA

Hungtse
Lake
HONAN PENGPU KIANGSU

Han River HOFEI NANKING

HUPEH ANHWEI SOOCHOW
Tai SHANGHAI
Lake

Yangtze River WUHAN HANGCHOW

ICHANG
SHASI KIUKIANG

Tungting
Lake CHEKIANG CHU SAN
ISLANDS

Poyang
Lake

HONAN CHANGSHA WENCHOW

HENGYANG KIANGSI

FUKIEN

HUNAN FOOCHOW

MATSU
AMOY KEELUNG
KWEILIN KWANGTUNG QUEMOY TAIPEI
LIUCHOW

KWANGSI TAINAN TAIWAN
MAOMING SWATOW KAOHSIUNG (FORMOSA)

MACAO

SOUTH CHINA SEA

EAST

CHINA

N

W E

S

RITTER

TA TA,
TAN TAN

"Fight fight, talk talk..."

TA TA,
TAN TAN

"Fight fight, talk talk..."

THE INSIDE STORY OF
COMMUNIST CHINA

VALENTIN CHU

NEW YORK

W · W · NORTON & COMPANY · INC.

To the memory of my father,

and my brother pei-ling

CONTENTS

PART FOUR *THE TWO CHINAS*

PART FIVE *INTO DEEPER WATERS*

PREFACE

THE PURPOSE OF THIS BOOK IS TO DESCRIBE, ANALYZE AND INTERPRET Communist China to Western readers. To know Communist China one must first know the Chinese Communists. To know the Chinese Communists one must first know the Chinese people and a man called Mao Tse-tung. There is no escape from these prerequisites. By starting from inside and working outward, one is able to make fewer wild guesses about Communist China's internal practices and external postures.

I disagree with the popular conception that the China situation is obscure because we cannot get enough information. Among others, the Chinese Communists themselves have been sending out a tremendous amount of illuminating information day after day all these years. I have unearthed and presented as much factual data as space permits. I have also made interpretations of these facts. The facts are available to anyone who cares and knows how to get them. The interpretations are my own.

In constructing the book, I avoided making it either a pure vehicle of opinion with little factual data, or a mere container of undigested facts and figures unintelligible to the layman. I do not pretend to be "scientifically objective." This is a feat only a natural scientist can achieve, and a claim only a writer relying solely on documents dares to make. In covering the China situation I have witnessed too much despair and hope, too much treachery and nobility, too much hate and love, to study it as mere chemicals in a test tube. My approach is, of course, objective, but my appraisals are frankly subjective and have been inevitably influenced by my own experience, understanding and values.

A brief explanation of terminology is necessary. Although the name of the city should properly be "Peiping" rather than "Peking" (which is an Imperial Chinese name now re-adopted by the Chinese Communists), this book uses "Peking" to designate the political regime *and* the city itself, to avoid confusing the Western reader. My English transliteration of Chinese names is not governed by any single system, but follows common usage and common sense. I have eliminated all phonetic signs which, in spite of the belief of many Sinologists, cannot render the correct Chinese pronunciation anyway. All weights and measures in Chinese and metric units, except the metric ton, have been converted to their Anglo-American equivalents.

My thanks go to far more people than I can name here. They include not only numerous friends and professional associates, but some 600 Chinese—escapees, fellow-travellers and Communists—who talked to and acquainted me with the human side of a complex, viable political situation. Specifically my gratitude is due to Harry and Bonaro Overstreet and Dr. Lin Yutang, without whose encouragement and invaluable suggestions this book might never have been written; to George Lee of Hong Kong, who tirelessly helped me update my research by keeping up a continuous trans-Pacific current of valuable reports from various sources; to Misses Constance Yung, Eva Wong and Nina Bakopanos, whose volunteered help enabled the final manuscript to be finished in record time. But above all, to my wife Vickie, who not only filed and filed, typed and typed, but tolerated and understood my relentless, maddening way of spending my spare moments, month after month, with a typewriter.

With all their help, however, they are not responsible for my opinions.

VALENTIN CHU

New York City
January 1963

PART ONE

EAST-WEST COLLISION

I SCRUTINIZING THE INSCRUTABLE

THESE STRANGE CHINESE. THEY THRIVE ON ALMOST NOTH-ing but swarm all over the place. They wear red at weddings because white is for mourning. They shake their own hands greeting others. They never open a gift in the presence of the giver, and always apologize for bad food after serving a delicious meal. They never name a son after the father for it would be a sacrilege. They say "yes" when they mean "no, I don't." Their writing goes vertically down, and from right to left. Their postal addresses, arithmetic fractions and compass needle point are the exact reverse of the West's. Their women are too modest to show an inch below the neck but think nothing of exposing most of their legs. They use primitive tools to make exquisite *objets d'art*, archaic pictographs to express profound thoughts, and complex philosophies to enjoy the simple things of life. And—they have no chop suey, no fortune cookies, and no laundrymen.

From the days of Marco Polo, China and its people have been an enigma. The Chinese have flashed many contradictory images to the world. Their bland look and piquant epigrams, their disastrous famines and elegant cuisine, their strange tongue and stranger calligraphy, their sages, mandarins, warlords, bandits, coolies, poets, willowy women in slit-sheaths—these have so fascinated the West that describing, analyzing and guessing about the inscrutable Chinese have always been popular sports.

Up to a couple of decades ago the popular Western image of China was a people thriving on chop suey, lotus seeds, opium, and concubines. Between *tong* wars, the Chinese mince-stepped in pigtails and gaudy mandarin robes, and conversed in Confucian analects. Lately the image has changed to a monstrous society of human-insects, creating oil and steel from thin air, lynching their parents with evangelical glee, and multiplying themselves to infinity through amoebic division. Under a poet-dictator whose mind is unfathomable and whose ways are strange, the Chinese are either too dedicated or too helpless to evade their destiny of taking over the world. Soon they will devastate the earth with their nuclear bombs. With the sheer weight of bare flesh, the surviving Chinese will emerge from their rice paddies and inherit this troubled planet.

The variations of the China myth seem endless. But one wonders which is worse: the mysterious China of some years ago or the misunderstood China of today. The cute image of old China was perhaps more harmless, since it was confined to cocktail banter, novels, and Hollywood mythology. But the nightmarish image of new China, used as a serious map to grope for a solution for unprecedented international problems, has turned many sagacious statesmen into Sinophobic nervous wrecks.

The West now realizes that the dust over China has never really settled. In fact, it has been stirred and whirled by unfamiliar winds. In the years to come, Communist China might become the decisive weight tipping the balance of world power. The Western smugness about that ramshackle Celestial Empire has evaporated. In its place is a growing awareness that what the inscrutable Chinaman does behind his beaded curtain may affect far more than the Westerner's laundry. This has created such political tension that everytime someone in Peking sneezes, pundits around the world burn midnight oil trying to analyze whether he sneezed in a Chinese or a Russian accent. Unhappily the eagerness to know is not identical with the ability to understand. More than a decade after Mao Tse-tung and his revolutionaries seized China, the world is still quarreling about Peking's strength, ideological orthodoxy, popularity, and even its morality. It is beyond comprehension that the cataclysmic convulsions involving a quarter of mankind for over a decade could still be fuel for debate instead of food for thought.

East and West have finally met. But the meeting was a stupefying collision that knocked the two silly. Whether the Chinese have a knack of misleading others or others have a knack of misreading the Chinese, the result is the same. The key to the Chinese puzzle is the obscure but powerful magnetic field of the Chinese character, over which political, economic, and social forces slither, clash and coalesce in ways that often fool the Westerner with his scientific analysis and rational logic. To understand the puzzle a rudimentary knowledge of some prominent Chinese traits—not national or racial characteristics but cultural traits—is essential.

The Chinese are the oldest race with the longest and only living ancient civilization. It not only gives them strange manners but an approach to life antithetical to Western ways. China's land characteristics made it a nation of farmers. Confucianism gave it a formidable family system and 2,000 years of egghead governments. Taoism, originating from the philosophy of Laotzu, instilled in them an other-worldliness, and taught them to harmonize with nature in a land where nature is harsh. Several thousand years of agrarian civilization cultivated by ancient sages anchored the people to the land, made industrialization difficult, and created a vast population of cultured illiterates with a small elite of humanistic, artistic scholars. The peasant would not step on a piece of paper with writing, in deference to the scholar. The scholar would not leave a grain of rice in his bowl, in deference to the peasant. Both try to beget many sons, in deference to their ancestors. It is a country where the perpetual necessity is backbreaking farming, and the purest joy is sipping tea and contemplating nature; where a pacifist people periodically surge up in savage disturbance; where unspeakable vulgarity intermingles with unimaginable refinement. The Chinese are a paradoxical people in a paradoxical land.

There is a touch of the Confucian and of the Taoist in every

TA TA, TAN TAN — 6

Chinese. A Confucian is a voracious do-gooder who wants politicians moral, sons filial and widows chaste. A Taoist is a vagabond who, laughing at man's folly, sneaks off to a bamboo groove or a misty lake to be part of it. A Chinese is consciously a Confucian and subconsciously a Taoist. He is a Confucian when enjoying fortune and success, and a Taoist in the face of adversity; a Confucian in public and Taoist when alone. Confucianism without Taoism would make him a stuffed-shirt. Taoism without Confucianism would make him a beatnik. During the past 2,500 years, each time China enjoyed peace and prosperity, Confucianism was in ascendancy. Each time it suffered from adversity, Taoism took over.

The Chinese ideal way of life is expressed by the traditional concept of ultimate contentment: *yu shih wu chen* (no contention with the world). This is a typical Taoist outlook, meaning that the individual is oblivious of such incidentals as wealth, fame, and power. He merges with nature. His desires are in abeyance and his grievances few. He enjoys freedom from any form of government, and has lost his urge to meddle in others' affairs. From this outlook, pacifism is a natural outgrowth. Pacifism is best illustrated by the sayings: "Good iron never becomes nails; good men never become soldiers," and "The superior man uses his mouth; the inferior man uses his fists." The scarcity of fist fights in China is only equaled by the profusion of verbal quarrels. The typical street brawl in China is quite different from the Western variety. The participants usually create much noise and heat, and strike poses of imminent assault. But they rarely end up touching each other. Each tries to provoke the other to strike first, for the one who starts a fight is always considered as the unreasonable one.

Even in the Chinese underworld, the favorite form of gangster warfare is the drinking of "talk-tea." Over the tea cup the disputants usually settle their differences by arguing it out, by pulling rank, or through the arbitration of higher bosses. When the argument is settled or redress made, the whole affair ends with a feast, at which the victorious and the vanquished toast and apologize to each other. In this way a "war" is fought and nobody loses face. Violence is the last resort.

The popular belief is that a belligerent person is seldom the strongest, and a really strong person needs not be belligerent. A saying goes: "Among the strong, there are always the stronger." One of the most popular types of Chinese fiction is the *wu hsia* stories, in which valiant heroes, often outlaws expert in shadow-boxing, help the poor and the weak and punish the bullies and the powerful. A typical *wu hsia* hero is not a brawny muscleman quick on the draw, but a meek, lean man slow to anger. He quietly walks up to the villain and in courteous words tells him to desist from molesting the heroine or the frail scholar. After he is laughed off or pushed around three times, he strikes the villain down. An important code for the men of strength in China is "Courtesy first; hostility second." Such a pacifist and unobtrusive attitude is a major factor in the absence of Chinese juvenile delinquency. It is also the paradoxical reason for periodical violence in China's history. Because the docile people dislike physical violence, they let aggressive elements make a mess of the country, until as a last resort they rise in violent revolt.

In personal relations or warfare, the Chinese are usually careful not to push the other party to the wall because "a trapped animal fights." They try to block up all other directions but leave a graceful exit for the opponent—in the direction they want him to go.

The most prominent Chinese trait stemming from the Taoist philosophy is resilience. Throughout Chinese history resilience is linked with survival and life, inflexibility with destruction and death. The only way to survive and eventually overcome an over-whelmingly stronger force is to be soft—penetratingly soft. By yielding elastically to brute force, one diverts the blow, conceals one's real strength and preserves the chance for a comeback. The Kingdom of Yueh in the fifth century was conquered by the Kingdom of Wu. The defeated King of Yueh endured unspeakable humiliation from his conqueror but never lost sight of an eventual revenge. He slept on straw and daily licked a piece of gall to remind himself of the bitterness. He did it for twenty years, while slowly rebuilding his nation, until one day he rose up and vanquished the King of Wu. Since then, *wu hsin chang tan* (sleeping on straw, tasting gall) has been a motto to every Chinese. This historic anecdote embodies the attitude that enables the Chinese to endure seemingly impossible hardships with infinite patience and with temporary submission to insults and humiliations in the hope of eventual retaliation. They tend to think in terms of generations, for they say: "To hurry is not to reach the destination." Because they refuse to be impatient, they often reach places the less patient could not. Life under adversity has made the Chinese a stoical people. They are seldom disheartened by adversity, which they believe strengthens the character. They say: "Genuine gold fears no fire."

Such wisdom and philosophy at times border on cowardice and selfishness. One of the popular self-preservation mottoes is: "Each sweep the snow in front of his door; never bother about the frost atop other roofs." Whatever happens outside the family or clan is a matter in outer space—remote and irrelevant. Public spirit and civic pride have been alien to the Chinese.

The saying "A wise man makes his own decisions; an ignorant man follows public opinion" denotes a truism now rapidly going out of fashion in the West. It expresses the Chinese fondness for individualism and dislike for the band-wagon. It does not look so, but beneath that shell of ceremonial conformity is a very free-wheeling mind. The Chinese are hopelessly undisciplined and disunited. They chide themselves as "a tray of loose sand." They love freedom, but their concept of freedom is not the political freedom to vote or to tell the government what to do, but the personal freedom of being left alone by the government. This comes from Laotzu's ideal government—a government that does nothing. In China, even a bad government can often last a long time, if it does not interfere with the people.

Individualism and the belief in the purest form of freedom

make the Chinese extremely tolerant. In China people of conflicting religious, political, or moral beliefs often merge in business,
friendship or marriage without noticing such differences. A man
may disapprove his friend's gambling or amorous dalliance, but he
would not breathe fire and brimstone nor form a society to convert such wrong-doers. He comforts himself that there may be
extenuating circumstances, or that he will get his retribution some
some day. Anyway, one is human and must answer to his own
conscience. Even more fundamental than the Confucian code of
conduct is Confucian humanism: each man is guided by the still
small voice within—a sort of moral inertial guidance system. The
worst indictment for a Chinese, even for a bandit, is to say that
he has no conscience.

Moderation is another Chinese trait. The Chinese are taught to
think about failure at the time of success, and think about success
at the time of failure. And the Chinese love of introspection makes
them reticent and unobtrusive. Compared to Westerners most
Chinese are introverts. Few of them are bombastic or flamboyant.
Partly because of this the Chinese language is extremely terse.
It tosses a fertile seed and lets the listener cultivate his own blossoms. Imagine an entire language consisting of expressions similar
to "know-how," "cook out," "easy come, easy go," "like father, like
son," or "*que sera sera.*" Reticence is used not only to conceal
mediocrity, but to camouflage wisdom, as a classical saying puts
it: "Great wisdom resembles stupidity." The Chinese ideal of a
competent man is "Still as a maiden; swift as a rabbit." They are
not only intensely private individuals but believe that "Into the
mouth go diseases; out of it come troubles." One seldom catches
a Chinese putting his foot in his mouth, which is usually covered
with his hand.

The classical saying, "Knowing what it is, but not why it is"
points to the Chinese preference for intuition to logic. The Chinese
abhor any attempt to cut up the universe and stuff it into a filing
cabinet. They dislike to analyze the shapeless and classify the
indivisible. They prefer to reach a solution by insight rather than

by deduction. Their culture produces more philosophers, artists and writers than mechanics, statisticians and lawyers.

Centuries of trial and error taught them that in human relations the shortest distance between two points is seldom a straight line. It is rather the line of least resistance. If their goal is the north, they usually start in any direction but north. Strategic retreat is their favorite way of advance. They are detour artists in business, friendship, courtship and war.

The Chinese are great tongue-in-cheek talkers and between-the-line readers. They put forward the obvious, about which they may not care, together with the obscure, which they really want to convey. They do this as a matter of courtesy, or in order to by-pass resistance, or for the sheer love of *double-entendre*. Other people use words to state their thoughts. The Chinese often use them to camouflage thoughts. They prefer to convey meaning by implication, by suggestion, by the hidden hint. In their language as well as in their painting, or poetry, or an opera actor's gait, or Peking's palatial landscaping, one finds the meaningful space, the pregnant silence, the dynamic pause.

The Chinese are subtle sensualists who enjoy delectable food, rich clothes, exquisite art objects and gentle wine. Some unjustly call them hedonists, which they could never be because of their philosophy. Strongly attached to kin and friends, they are a very sentimental people but not often emotionally demonstrative. Hence they appear bland and inscrutable to strangers. This is a secret well worth knowing for any Westerner trying to understand the Chinese. Their deceptively apathetic look hides a vulnerable heart. They are susceptible to the changing moods of flowering peach blossoms, falling leaves, or raindrops beating on banana leaves. Some of the most exquisite love poems are found in Chinese classical verse, which is sensuous but not sensual, impassioned but not passionate.

They are persevering, diligent, thrifty, aloof to strangers and warm to friends. They pay less respect to legal than to unwritten human laws. Hence China has been full of minor legal infractions but few serious crimes. The traditional businessman scorns a written contract but unhesitatingly honors a verbal agreement.

These traits do not wholly comprehend the Chinese personality, of course. Some of them are dying out. But by and large they provide the framework for Chinese life and behavior. The Chinese tend to be patient, serene, self-sufficient, at times a little wise, but often unaggressive and diffident. On the whole a highly developed Chinese personality is like aged wine, mellow but potent. It has "no contention with the world."

II THE RED CHINESE PUZZLE

YEARS AGO EVERYONE SCOFFED AT A POSSIBLE MARRIAGE between Communism and the Chinese mind. Yet today the world is faced with the reality of Communist China. It seems that the Chinese mind has accepted, perhaps reluctantly and helplessly but nevertheless accepted, Communism.

But Red China is no child of marriage. It is the offspring of an ideological rape. The bastard child has many psychological conflicts and no integrated personality. The West, having never encountered the type before, does not know how to cope with such a novel personality. It is at once annoyed and intrigued, repelled and charmed.

The collision between Communism and the Chinese mind has produced ceaseless and subtle chemical reactions on both sides. The Communists combined their ideology with Chinese tactics, thereby making Chinese Communism, or Maoism, more palatable —and deadlier. On the other hand, rigid Communism has driven the people into their favorite sanctuary—Taoist philosophy—and has resulted in an apparent yielding under brute force.

These two groups, the Maoists armed with Marxist doctrine and the people armed with Taoist philosophy, but both using typical Chinese tactics, have been staging one of the most bizarre struggles in human history. The subtle give-and-take, the nondescript parries and thrusts, the antithetical footwork of the opponents are always incomprehensible, often imperceptible, and at times misleading to the rational West. Sometimes the ballet-like shadow-boxing is so incongruous that to the uninitiated it looks almost like love-play. It is precisely this battle that is making the deceptively simple Chinese situation a viable and irritating dilemma of historic proportions.

By now the world is aware of the results of this struggle—the virtual paralysis of Red China—although few can follow this exotic chess game. How is this struggle carried on? Have the Maoists succeeded in breaking up the traditional fabric of this ancient race and reweaving it into a Marxist motif? Or will the yielding softness of the Chinese eventually prove to be Mao's undoing?

Communism is idealism gone haywire. It is a tragic, hopeless attempt to reach the Beautiful via the Ugly. Its destination is a utopia of absolute freedom, absence of war, and complete withering of the state. This is why it puts stars in the eyes of the world's dreamers. But its journey to this utopia is peace through war, freedom through slavery, and democracy through dictatorship. Thus terror, hunger, treachery, and death become the necessary stopovers. The tragedy is that Communism, in searching for an idealistic end, has become marooned on macabre means.

Since it is based on the dogma of the unanimity of masses, Communism brooks no heresy. But since mankind is never homogeneous and at times is heretic, a Communist regime survives only by ceaselessly suppressing the dissident, the individualistic, the free-wheeling. Jailers must be watched by other jailers. Conflicts must be sustained by more conflicts. In the Communist universe, space is delineated by layers of control, time is clocked by waves of purges.

Communism is Fascism turned feminine. It does not attack democracy brusquely as Fascism does. Instead it pays lip service to democracy but is specifically tailored to work through the fissures of democracy for its eventual disintegration. At a distance Communism is all things to all men. It offers economic equality to mutineers from capitalism. It whispers freedom to liberals outraged by authoritarian governments. It flaunts patriotism before the nationalistic, dedication before the devout, and revenge before the oppressed. But at close range it is something quite different. It is a classless society trampled under a super-class. It is a worker's paradise where capitalist exploitation is replaced by state exploitation. It is an enormous factory powered not by incentive but by fear. It promises equality, freedom, and peace; it gives equality in privation, freedom of the insane, and the peace of death.

Because their long civilization has developed persistently in the area of humanities, the Chinese are past-masters in practical psychology. Their strategy in human relations is unexcelled. But their highly humanistic philosophies instill an inner moral sense which prevents them from being a ruthless, crafty people. Discard the moral Chinese philosophies but retain Chinese tactics to serve an alien, inexorable ideology, and one gets a wily system unencumbered by conscientious scruples. This new product may look and sound Chinese, especially to the non-Chinese, but it is really not Chinese. Mao Tse-tung has done exactly this. He had some tremendous initial success with his Maoism, but this very success is responsible for many novel and unexpected obstacles now facing his regime.

One of the best jokes from behind the Bamboo Curtain is about Mao Tse-tung and the cat. Stalin's ghost is discussing with Mao the different paths to Communism. Mao asks what is the Russian way of making a cat lick its own behind. Stalin says he would push the cat's head backward, but Mao takes a cat and sprinkles pepper liberally on its rump. Soon the cat is frantically licking itself. Mao says with a touch of pride: "We Chinese never use force. We use persuasion." By this persuasion Mao has turned China into a nation of volunteers. The Chinese volunteer to inform on their friends, volunteer to denounce their parents, volunteer to have their property confiscated, volunteer to fight the Americans, volunteer to do slave labor. They volunteer not to eat, not to sleep, not to love. And the *yang-kuei-tsu* (foreign devils) say with awed admiration that Communist China has become a nation of fanatics.

The Maoists are more ingenious than their Russian tutors. Mao's greatest contribution to international Communism is not in revising it—which he does at his pleasure—but in flavoring it with Chinese sweet-sour sauce. Many of Mao's recipes are inspired by his favorite readings in ancient Chinese military science and in popular fiction. He tested them during his guerilla war days and now applies them with infinite variations to domestic and international situations.

All good military leaders in Chinese history loved *ruses de guerre*. They thought of war in terms of a chess game. They much preferred to win battles by avoiding head-on assaults, by using feints, traps, bluffs, counter-bluffs and similar tricks. One of Mao's stratagems in dealing with a much stronger force is derived from a dictum of Suntzu, a fifth-century military theorist. This trick in Mao's own words is: "Enemy advances, we retreat. Enemy retreats, we pursue. Enemy encamps, we disturb. Enemy tires out, we attack." This is the quintessence of guerilla warfare. Time and again, Chiang Kai-shek's overwhelmingly stronger and better-equipped "bandit-suppression armies" found themselves fighting elusive, shadowy guerillas who melted into the mountains and came out to create disturbances at night, or found themselves pouring heavy fire on phony pillboxes cluttered with scarecrows and remote-controlled firecrackers exploding in empty kerosene cans. Mao would never fight a stronger enemy head-on. He would not fight if the enemy expected a battle. He would not fight if the terrain was unfamiliar or unfavorable. Truly he was faithful to his boast that he never fights an uncertain battle.

Later when his army grew to a size fit for regular battles, Mao developed his best-known strategy: *Ta ta, tan tan; tan tan, ta ta* (fight fight, talk talk; talk talk, fight fight). Two little words. Yet they express enough slyness for the undoing of Mao's many enemies. By a skillful interspersing of sudden battles and phony truces, Mao averted countless military debacles with his reasonable offers to talk at the psychological moment, and ended many fruitless talks with unexpected military actions. Today the Chinese Nationalists are sadder and wiser, but others have yet to realize this. Of course once Mao grows stronger than the enemy and has set the stage, he will carry out a *coup de grâce* even if the enemy prefers talk.

Another ancient trick called *li chien* (sowing discord) has been refined into one of the most deadly weapons of Communism. Mao used it with flying colors domestically in the guise of the United Front, and internationally in the guise of neutralism. In his own words, his main strategy in dealing with the West is: "Our tactical principle remains one of exploiting the contradictions among them in order to win over the majority, oppose the minority, and crush the enemies separately." By isolating one enemy at a time and mesmerizing the rest into neutrality, he can progressively eliminate a whole flock of opponents with the unwitting help of the neutrals—his enemies of tomorrow. In the indoctrination of a Chinese Communist, the man is always told never to forget that today's friend may be tomorrow's enemy.

The Maoists mix Marxist dialectics with Chinese double-talk, which is found even in legal statements. One famous example from the imperial judicial courts is the judge who would say: "This is legally unpardonable, but humanly forgivable," when he gave a not-guilty verdict, and: "This is humanly forgivable, but legally unpardonable," when the verdict was guilty. The florid Chinese language, so delicate in nuances and rich in literary allusions, can seldom be translated into English without losing significant overtones. Many statements from the Peking government seem to point in several directions at once, especially in their original Chinese versions. When the Chinese Communists describe something as "basically fulfilled" they hint it is *not* fulfilled. When they want to admit a mistake publicly, they always praise the bad job first. In spite of the heavy-handed Teutonic style of Marxist expressions, a typical Peking statement is a mixture of Chinese linguistic floss and Communist dialectics, often deliberately made fuzzier for special effects and future switches.

The combination of deliberate Chinese tactics, unconscious Chinese mannerisms and platitudes, and Marxist Machiavellism have resulted in such strange phenomena as the two-way language and transcendental statistics of Maoism. These alone have at times swept the coolest Western observers off their feet. What makes the picture even more misleading is the behavior of the Chinese people under pressure. In Communist China things are seldom what they appear to be. In understanding what has been happening in China, it is well to remember that in the weakness of the Chinese lies their strength. It is easy to extract a false confession from a Chinese, but hard to give him an effective brainwash. It is easier to conquer China than to govern it. The Chinese are usually weak as a nation but tough as a race. These are a lot of paradoxes. But the Chinese are a paradoxical people.

III OLD DRAGON
IN NEW WAVES

TO MOST PEOPLE, CHINA IS A BIG COUNTRY SOMEWHERE AT the far end of the world. It is populated by a fast-breeding, slow-moving people whose customs are exotic and minds inscrutable. To the Chinese themselves, China is a cultural entity, a way of life transcending the spatial and temporal demarcations of a nation. This unique psychological idiosyncrasy is at the root both of their national indolence and their periodical upsurges. It is also the recondite, self-renewing dynamism which at times enables the Chinese to surmount impenetrable historic barriers and at times mess up their own country.

The Chinese are intensely aware that they are the heirs to the world's oldest living culture—a culture that has been flowering in recurrent splendor for 5,000 years in virtual isolation from all other major civilizations. They call their own country *Chung Hua* (The Central Splendor) or *Chung Kuo* (The Central Nation) —an island of elegance surrounded by an ocean of barbarism. Such exaggerated pride is not without reason. Marco Polo did not rave over nothing. The Chinese were responsible for some of the world's major achievements many centuries ago. They invented the compass, the rocket, gunpowder, printing, paper, chinaware, and the use of silk. They hand-dug the world's longest artificial waterway, the 1,286-mile Grand Canal, and built the titanic Great Wall.

China has had many forms of government. It had the world's first police state in 221 B.C., complete with slave labor, book-burning, and thought control. It had the world's first socialist regime in 8 A.D., with price control, land equalization and government monopolies. For some 2,000 years China practiced a unique government which used national competitive examinations to select its high officials from scholars for their moral concepts and literary and artistic sensibilities.

China has been expansionist. During the Han Dynasty (206 B.C.–221 A.D.) it annexed parts of Annam and Korea, defeated the fierce Huns, pushed its military and diplomatic influences westward as far as the Persian Gulf, and once defeated the Roman Legion. Its prestige was so great that to this day the Chinese still call themselves "Sons of Han." The Chinese empire was further extended overland under the Tang Dynasty (618–907 A.D.), and overseas under the Ming Dynasty (1368–1644), when the Chinese fleet made seven expeditions to the South Seas, the Indian Ocean, and the eastern coast of Africa, and exacted great homage and tributes from maritime Asia.

Greater and more lasting achievements, however, are in the non-utilitarian sector of its civilization. Chinese porcelain, jade, and embroidery are treasured by the world's connoisseurs. Chinese cuisine is considered by gourmets as the ultimate sophistication of the palate. Chinese painting and calligraphy are visual poetry. Chinese literature, which is really untranslatable into other languages, is perhaps the most esoteric among the world's classics.

Scholarship is worshiped by the Chinese, including the illiterates. No nation in history has had a greater respect for scholars, a respect that bordered on fetishism. For thousands of years no Chinese would discard a piece of paper with words on it, or use it to wrap things. It was carefully collected in special receptacles and burned, like a flag. The greatest status symbol in China was the title of *han lin,* awarded to the top scholar of the land at the imperial examinations which all could take and which were often won by poor, self-educated candidates. As early as the Chou Dynasty (1122–255 B.C.) China had a national university in its capital and numerous schools in its villages. The university's enrolment reached 30,000 around the time of Christ.

In human relations, the Chinese built up a social order which for thousands of years was known for its stability, and a family system that characterizes all their social behavior. But it is in philosophy that the Chinese civilization really flowers. Some 500 years before Christ and 100 years before Socrates, Confucius was teaching kings and peasants his great doctrine of humanism. In that era competing rulers sought advice from scholars and thinkers on their political and moral conduct. This stimulated and helped create the Hundred Schools of Chinese thought, covering practically all the ideologies known to men. Notable among their teachers were the humanist Confucius and Mencius, who taught benevolence, tolerance, and harmony as fundamentals of all human relations; the sophist Motzu, who taught pacifism and universal love; the Taoist Laotzu and Chuangtzu, who taught naturalism and individualism; and the Legalist Hanfeitzu, who taught totalitarianism.

China entered its Golden Age during the first two centuries of the Tang Dynasty (618–907 A.D.), when it was the greatest country on earth in area, population, government, and intellectual and aesthetic cultivation. During that period the government was enlightened and liberal, the officials were moral, and the people were happy and prosperous. Foreigners flocked to China to share its culture. Some of them were eagerly employed as government officials. Others studied in the national university, which had 8,000 foreign students. The Chinese used foreign goods and adopted foreign ideas and customs. In addition to Buddhism, which came in earlier, freedom of religion permitted the introduction of Nestorianism, Zoroastrianism, Manichaeanism and Mohammedanism. The people, including the peasants, led a leisurely and refined life, enjoying freedom of thought and belief, and such recreations as boat-racing, lantern festivals, picnics, chess, flower-arranging, tea-drinking, and wine-sipping. Literature, poetry, drama, music, singing, sculpture, and painting reached their zenith.

The long history of China was not marked by uninterrupted peace and culture. There were many periods of political corruption, civil strife, and foreign invasions. But the Chinese racial and cultural stamina was such that each chaotic period was followed by a spirited resurgence. Through intermarriage with the invading barbarians, the Chinese ethnically stayed young and culturally engulfed all lesser civilizations which came into contact with them. The cycles of decay, intrusion, assimilation, and rejuvenation worked in a self-perpetuating rhythm.

China under the Ching (Manchu) Dynasty (1644–1911) reached another peak during the seventeenth and eighteenth centuries. But as it entered the nineteenth century conditions began to deteriorate. The population had increased rapidly, creating serious economic problems. The imperial examinations had degenerated into a mere mouthing of classical clichés and the writing of rigid, stylized essays. The government had turned effete and reactionary, and persecuted scholars who expressed discontent. Corruption was everywhere. Unemployment, banditry, piracy, and peasant revolts grew. Once again China had reached the low point of its metabolism. Once again the periodical decay had set in. But this time something happened that shook China to its core.

It was the momentous head-on collision between the East and West. The traumatic encounter set off a chain-reaction whose reverberations rattled China throughout the past century, and are now felt by the rest of the world. During the nineteenth century, contacts between China and the West increased rapidly. China was weak and senile, but the West had become virile and aggressive. European powers, looking for new colonies and new markets, scanned the horizon and spotted the Sick Man of East Asia. The incompetent Manchu regime, still clinging to the traditional Chinese scorn of barbarians but completely ignoring the power of modern technology, repeatedly rebuffed Western diplomatic and trade overtures. This isolationism was partly a reaction to Britain's policy of shipping opium into China. The illicit trade was so lucrative that by 1838 six million pounds of opium were imported annually into China by British clippers. After repeatedly protesting in vain, the emperor sent an imperial commissioner to Canton where he seized a large quantity of opium from the British and burned it publicly. The result was the Opium War of 1840–42. China was defeated and forced to cede Hong Kong to Britain, open five ports to foreign trade, legalize opium and grant diplomatic equality and trade privileges to the British. These privileges were soon shared by other powers, including the United States.

The Opium War opened the floodgates of foreign aggression. Repeatedly the European powers, joined by emergent Japan, sent their gunboats, troops, diplomats and merchants to China, demanding or helping themselves to territory and special privileges. Russia took immense slices off Manchuria, Mongolia, and Sinkiang. Britain got Hong Kong, Kowloon, Burma, Sikkim, and numerous titbits of Tibet and Southwest China. France grabbed all Indo-China. Japan annexed Korea, Taiwan (Formosa), the Ryukyu Islands and the Pescadores Islands. Between the Opium War and the end of the nineteenth century China lost a total of 3,670,000 square miles of its territory and dependencies, equivalent to three Indias or almost all of Europe.

On top of this the powers zoned off the best parts of major ports as concessions, where they set up their own governments, courts, police and troops, and enjoyed extraterritoriality. The Europeans further seized control of China's maritime customs and postal service. They operated freely Chinese railroads, factories, mines, shipping, and commerce. Their gunboats patrolled the China Coast and penetrated the inland waters. Their low-duty manufactured goods flooded China's cities and choked its economy. Chinese fortifications were razed. Chinese coolies were kicked and well-bred Chinese pushed around by arrogant Europeans. An apocryphal story says that a signboard was once erected in a Shanghai park reading: "Chinese and dogs not allowed." And everywhere it was opium, opium and opium. Each time the

Chinese balked at what they called "unequal treaties," more territory was seized, concessions exacted or indemnities demanded. At the turn of the century the powers were ready to partition the decrepit empire. China was only saved by the American "open door" policy and the wranglings of the powers themselves.

Never in history had any big, technically independent nation lost so much sovereignty and suffered so much humiliation. To the Chinese, whose ethnic pride and cultural jingoism had always been high, the experience was unbearably shameful. Their Celestial Empire had been the heart of the cosmos. The Chinese way of life had been the ultimate goal to which all other civilizations aspired. Now came these "red-haired devils" from across the sea with their obscene manners and swift gunboats, who at every encounter turned out to be superior—in brute strength if not in cultural refinement. It was unfortunate that China's contacts with the West then were drastically different from those of earlier times. Earlier, visitors from the West were mainly learned travelers like Marco Polo and missionaries like Matteo Ricci. They dealt with elegant scholars and enlightened mandarins of a resplendent civilization. But during the nineteenth century most Western visitors were Colonel Blimps and opium-laden merchants looking for a fast pound. They dealt with incompetent bureaucrats, obsequious compradores, ignorant amahs and unprincipled smugglers—the scum of a decadent society. These latter Westerners further were in the habit of equating industrialization with culture and humility with cowardice. And their scorn knew no bounds. It was natural that foot-binding and the pigtail became symbols of a backward and degraded people. This shocked the once proud Chinese so profoundly that mandarins, scholars and peasants alike were stirred into action.

Toward the end of the nineteenth century some mandarins like Li Hung-chang tried to modernize the nation by building factories, railways, and arsenals and sending officials and students to study in the West. Scholars like Kung Yu-wei and Liang Chi-chao, with the support of Emperor Kuang Hsu, tried to graft Western technology onto the traditional culture by a comprehensive modernization of the nation's education, government, commerce, and communications. But their reform movement was cut short by a palace revolution of reactionaries and eunuchs, abetted by the Empress Dowager, who imprisoned the emperor, seized the throne and diverted funds ear-marked for a modern navy to rebuild the Summer Palace, earlier burned down by English and French troops. Popular discontent, however, soon erupted in the violent anti-foreign Boxer Rebellion of 1900. This organized riot, sponsored by grassroots secret societies with the blessings of the Empress Dowager, attempted to oust all foreigners from China and laid siege to the Legation Quarters in Peking. But the rabble, equipped with magical talismans and obsolete weapons, was routed by an allied expedition of British, American, German, French, Russian, Japanese, Italian, and Austrian troops; the result was the most humiliating of all unequal treaties.

By then many Chinese realized that the only salvation lay in ousting the corrupt, incompetent Manchus and toppling the monarchial system. As early as 1894 a group of young overseas Chinese in Honolulu formed the revolutionary *Hsing Chung Hui* (Society for Rejuvenating China), which eventually became the Kuomintang (National or Nationalist Party). Their leader was the young doctor Sun Yat-sen, who was later to be known as the "Father of the Chinese Republic." After a couple of unsuccessful attempts, the young radicals finally overthrew the Ching Dynasty in an uprising that began on October 10, 1911 (The Double Tenth).

In spite of the initial elation, the republic did not fare well. The attempts of the inexperienced, idealistic revolutionaries to establish a parliamentary democracy were sidetracked by reactionaries, restorationists, and warlords. This disunity whetted the appetite of Japan, which became the leading aggressor in China during the ensuing decades. Japan had extended its influence into China after its victory in the Russo-Japanese War of 1904–05, which was fought on China's soil. On May 9, 1915, a day later observed by the Chinese as the Day of National Shame with flags at half-mast, Japan further forced China to accept an ultimatum known as the Twenty-One Demands. During World War I Japan seized Tsingtao from the Germans, who had grabbed it earlier, and extended its control into the rest of Shantung province. Although China later joined the war on the Allied side, the Versailles Conference completely ignored its hope of recovering Shantung.

The Versailles Conference touched off an unprecedented explosion of pent-up emotions in the awakening Chinese intellectuals. On May 4, 1919, angry professors and students of the National Peking University staged a demonstration, demanding that the weak-kneed government punish "traitors" responsible for the Versailles and the Twenty-One Demands debacles. This demonstration immediately spread to many cities, and was joined not only by intellectuals, but professionals, merchants, clerks, and workers. Just as the Double Tenth marked a change in China's political structure, May Fourth marked a change in its intellectual consciousness. Frustrated by continued foreign aggressions, disillusioned by a republic in name only, and inspired by the liberalism of the West, many educated Chinese felt that perhaps the ultimate culprit of China's woes was not the imperialists but its own obsolete concepts and values. They had had enough of national humiliation, enough of self-satisfied classical scholars, enough of ceremonial rituals, enough of feudalistic families and obedient sons and chaste widows, enough of Confucius.

The May Fourth Movement marked a drastic re-evaluation of China's revered philosophies and tradition, and a search for new ways and new values. Among the leaders of this movement were many Chinese intellectuals educated in England, France, Japan, and the United States. They felt a tremendous thirst for Western democratic ideas and scientific methodology and were variously influenced by European humanitarianism, naturalism, romanticism, realism, Marxism, and the philosophical writings of John Dewey and Bertrand Russell, who visited China at that time. Eventually the movement headed along two different paths. The liberals stuck mainly to the 1917 "Cultural Renaissance" in the creation of a new form of literature, *pai hua*, (or the vernacular) as opposed to classical writing. The leader of this group was Hu Shih. The radicals went into politics. They either joined the Kuomintang or formed the Chinese Communist Party, whose founder, Chen Tu-hsiu, was a prominent May Fourth leader who boldly attacked Confucian teaching and all its latter outgrowths as the slavish morality of a decadent society.

After its formation the Chinese Communist Party had several years of honeymoon with the Kuomintang until a split during the latter's Northern Expedition led by Chiang Kai-shek, who ousted the warlords and for the first time unified modern China. In spite of the Kuomintang-Communist split and isolated but unsuccessful warlord rebellions, China under the Nationalists began to enjoy relative peace and prosperity. The progress so alarmed Japan's militarists that they moved to squash it. In 1931 Japanese troops staged a surprise attack and seized Manchuria. In 1932 they attacked Shanghai, and in 1933 invaded Inner Mongolia and North China. In 1937 the Sino-Japanese War began in earnest, resulting in Japan's seizure of coastal China and the Nationalist retreat to Chungking. Then came Pearl Harbor. And Hiroshima.

At Japan's surrender China emerged as a victor, but a befuddled victor. Economically it was exhausted by years of war. Politically it was a nation divided, the Communists having gained much territory and strength. Diplomatically it was disillusioned by the secret Yalta agreement, which granted special privileges to the U.S.S.R. at China's expense. China was virtually forced to cede Outer Mongolia as an independent state and much of its sovereignty in Manchuria to the Russians in the subsequent Sino-Soviet Treaty of Friendship and Alliance. To the Chinese, Yalta opened the old Versailles wound, because for the second time after a world war China as a victor was "sold out" by its allies. Many Chinese became skeptical of the democratic system when they felt that Western democracies still engaged in deals characteristic of the old imperialistic power-play. Psychologically China itself had still not found new values to replace adequately its discarded old ones. The flowers of Western political and social ideas hastily and inadequately grafted on had not thrived.

On the eve of its conquest by the Communists, China was an unhappy nation. It was an old dragon, still confused, still impotent, still resentful, floundering in the new waves from the West.

PART TWO

THE INSTANT PARADISE

PART TWO

IV

GATE OF HEAVENLY PEACE

ON THE TERRACE HIGH ABOVE THE MASSIVE, ANCIENT *Tien An Men* (Gate of Heavenly Peace) of Peking stood a group of uniformed dignitaries in caps and berets. Behind them soared a green framework pavilion with yellow dragons, red-lacquered pillars, saffron-yellow tiles, and giant pomegranate-shaped vermilion lanterns.

The *Tien An Men* on October 1, 1949 became an unforgettable landmark in the long history of a great nation. Behind it were the magnificent "Forbidden City"—and 5,000 years of halcyon splendor and turbulent upheavals. In front of it, on the sprawling *Tien An Men* Square, marched 300,000 people—and the new hopes, promises, and glory that stretched beyond the Altar of Heaven 10,000 years into the future.

The whole of China seemed to be there as the lava of humanity flowed slowly along the wide Changan Avenue into the Square. Soldiers precision-stepped with newly captured automatic arms. Tanks, armored cars, and cavalry units rumbled on while planes droned overhead. Blue-clad workers paraded with new-found pride. Chest-heaving athletes in T-shirts and sneakers carried huge banners that fluttered in the brisk winds. Girls in pink flowing gowns danced with silk scarves. There were college professors, primary pupils, artisans, peasants, housewives, and white-whiskered old men. Flower floats, drums, placards, pennants, streamers were interspersed by brass bands playing the Communist national anthem, *Guerilla's March*. As the marchers approached the reviewing stand, they saluted the Communist revolutionaries atop the Gate, across the gently curving moat spanned by five marble bridges. For Mao Tse-tung and his comrades, it was a long way from the loess dust of Yenan to the imperial pomp of *Tien An Men*.

October 1, 1949, marked the spectacular birth of a new China under the Communists. It was the beginning of a new era for an ancient people, a beginning that disturbed, frightened, intrigued, and inspired the rest of the world. It was a glimpse of the promised land through the Gate of Heavenly Peace. Each year since then this scene has been re-enacted, with the marchers first walking, then running, and finally staging a Great Leap into Mao's Instant Paradise.

Who are the Chinese Communists leading one quarter of the human race in this epic parade? The Chinese Communist Party with its seventeen million members today is the biggest in the world. When it was founded in 1921 it had fewer than sixty members. The founders included college professors, mandarin scholars, land-owning intellectuals, but not workers or peasants. When it became an armed party it absorbed ex-warlords, soldiers, and underworld elements. It was also joined by peasants, workers, and, in later years, disaffected intellectuals.

Although the Communist movement is theoretically based on the proletariat, China's Communist Party had to be based on peasants, who constituted 80 percent of the population, because the proletariat constituted less than 1 percent of the population even when the Communists came into power. Today the composition of the Party is roughly 70 percent peasants, 14 percent workers, 12 percent intellectuals, and 4 percent miscellaneous elements. As peasants are distrusted by all Communists and intellectuals too often tend to think for themselves, the Chinese Communist Party in recent years has been trying to depress the percentage of peasants and has vacillated in its treatment of intellectuals. The real authority in the Party is with a small group of powerful men, mainly of the formerly poor and landed intellectual, mandarin, and warlord classes. Except Chen Yun, a former typesetter, there is no worker in the inner ruling circle.

Wielding supreme power over all is the Party's chairman Mao Tse-tung, son of a peasant grain merchant, Confucius-hater, idealistic student of Marx, fanatical disciple of Stalin, mystic, and shrewd politician who rode into power on the vast peasantry of China. Assisting Mao is his heir apparent Liu Shao-chi, gaunt, steely-eyed Chairman of the Communist government, expert labor agitator and the Party's foremost theoretician. Ranking next is Premier Chou En-lai. Known to the West because of his role as the Party's professional glamor boy, he is a charming, able administrator but not a policy-maker. An expert in dealing with non-Communists, Chou's greatest distinction is his ability to emerge unscathed from toppling cliques time and again. For this he is nicknamed *pou tao weng* (a heavy-bottomed Chinese doll which rolls and tosses but always recovers its balance). Next in command is benign-looking Marshal Chu Teh, vice-chairman of the Party and member of the Politburo. Chu was an old-fashioned warlord who gave up his concubines and opium when he became a Communist.

These four head the hierarchy of the Chinese Communist Party, whose vast membership carries out their orders with iron discipline and unquestioning obedience. Although the Party is heterogeneous in composition, it is run on a basic Stalinist pattern with Chinese trimmings. From 1949 when it came into power, it has been creating one political spectacle after another through incessant nation-wide campaigns. The results produced have been traumatic and at times controversial to the outside world. But what exactly has been done to the silent, teeming millions of China? How exactly do they feel about this regime?

"The Chinese people seem to have entered an age of legends," said the *People's Daily*, Communist China's official mouthpiece, looking back a decade after the founding of the Communist government. "The Greek mythology of ancient times was only a tale, a dream, an ideal. Today in the Era of Mao Tse-tung, heaven

is here on earth. . . . Each prophecy of Chairman Mao has become
a reality. It was so in the past. It is so today."

This remark was supported by the impressions of thousands of
independent, honest visitors from all over the world. A Canadian
newspaperman after visiting China in late 1960 said: "At certain
moments one thinks one is really dreaming. Is this the China which
in the past had been miserable and backward, the prey of foreign
powers . . . a giant forever asleep? Is this the people which used
to be described as careless, gentle, poetic, but incapable of pulling
itself together? . . . And what an incredible thing: China become
clean, well-ordered and without flies . . . China where everybody
works with pride for a unique goal. . . . We ask ourselves, is there
anything which China cannot produce?"

It is virtually impossible and often thankless for the skeptics to
express their doubts, for the circumstantial evidence in favor of
the Instant Paradise is too overwhelming. The dazzling achievements made by Peking may sound like a dream. But the dream is
buttressed by statistics, official reports, pictorial magazines, motion
pictures, enthusiastic words from penitent capitalists, happy peasants, self-criticizing professors, and things actually seen with
their own eyes by foreign visitors.

In 1949 Dean Acheson ridiculed the Chinese Communists' promise to solve the problem of feeding the people and predicted that
no government in China would succeed in doing it. In the same
year Mao solemnly declared: "The Chinese people will see that,
once its destiny is in the hands of the people, China will, like
the rising sun in the east, flood the earth with its brilliant rays,
swiftly washing away the dirt left by the reactionary government,
heal the war wounds and build up a new, strong and prosperous
people's democratic republic of China which will be true to its
name." A decade later Premier Chou En-lai with intense pride
noted the two remarks and challenged: "Whose prediction has
come true?"

The Chinese Communists, according to their own claims, had
during the first decade made flying leaps at the speed of "one day

is equal to twenty years." Steel output was increased 75 times. "The most basic characteristic of our steel-making is high speed. ... Such high speed for ten continuous years ... has never happened in history." Electric power was increased over 8 times. "From the interior to Sinkiang throughout the whole country, in mountain areas and in the plains, in cities and in villages, the masses are setting up power-generating stations, and these are now as numerous as the stars in the sky." Coal production was increased over 9 times, and cotton yarn 4 times. At the beginning of the decade China stood 26th in the world's output of steel, 9th in coal, 25th in electric power, 5th in cotton yarn. By its end China was 7th in steel, 3rd in coal, 11th in electric power and 2nd in cotton yarn.

A significant thing was: "While we are developing industry, we have not forgotten to develop agriculture." China became the world's greatest food producer by 1952. Food grain output in a decade was increased by one and half times. Since the communes "the overwhelming majority of those who lack labor power are being provided with grain or meals free of charge. The old hard life in which they had to worry about where their food would come from will soon become a memory of the past."

While manna and blue birds were raining from the red sky, all over China the Communists built railroads, highways, bridges, dikes, dams, canals, factories, schools, cultural palaces and workers' dormitories. Illiteracy rapidly disappeared. School enrolments zoomed up. Science, publishing, drama, dancing, cinema, music were popularized. Beggars, gangsters, prostitutes vanished as quickly as flies, mosquitoes and rats. Per capita income was doubled. The people not only enjoyed a more comfortable living, but also various freedoms guaranteed by the Constitution. When the communes were introduced the family and society went into a transfiguration so complete that even aesthetic and olfactory values were changed. Students collecting fertilizer said, "We begin to have feeling towards manure," and "What was considered beautiful a month ago is now ugly, and ugly things begin to look beautiful."

On the tenth anniversary of People's China, Chou En-lai, enumerating Chinese achievements in the pamphlet *A Great Decade*, posed a pertinent question: "We would like to ask the rightist opportunists who think that greater and faster results will not mean better and more economical results, and that the launching of mass movements in industry will lead to a mess or cause more loss than gain: What is your explanation for all this?"

His question was not without some irony, because three years later, in 1962, the Chinese Communists were very busy trying to answer this question themselves.

V THE MAD
STATISTICIAN

THE CHINESE COULD HAVE BEEN GOOD MATHEMATICIANS. They were constructing the right angle, approximating the π value, and toying with integer numbers long before Euclid and Archimedes were born. They were writing mathematical textbooks when Greece was still under barbarians who knew no weights nor measures nor script. They invented the first calculating machine—the abacus—still used today. The Chinese could have been good mathematicians—if their affinity for arts and mysticism had not got the better of them. As it happened, their indigenous science, medicine, and mathematics are a hodgepodge of amazing truths and naive nonsense.

During the first decade of Communist China a new phenomenon arose. China was suddenly transformed from a land of approximations and unknown quantities to a nation which at the slightest pretext sprayed the world with a profusion of statistical bullets. Here was a nation still inscrutable, but now apparently measurable. It was a game of mutual convenience: the Peking statistician dished out numbers; the foreign observer dutifully swallowed them—once in a while with a grain of salt. A shiny image of New China was thus built up, mostly with statistics.

The smooth give-and-take, however, was jarred considerably in August 1959 when the Chinese Communists sheepishly conceded that due to their "inexperience with the bounteous harvest" of 1958, they had made a "slight variance" of over-counting 125 million (metric) tons of grain, 2 million tons of soybeans, 1.2 million tons of peanuts, 3.08 million tons of steel, 1.2 million tons of cotton, 20 million pigs, and 23 million acres of new forest lands. This drastic statistical revision for 1958, the first year of Mao's Great Leap Forward,* was unprecedented in the world's history. It was followed by comparatively modest production figures for 1959. For the past couple of years, however, Communist China has not issued any production statistics except those for steel.

What happened? Was the Peking abacus over-oiled? Were the Chinese Communists deliberately fooling the rest of the world? Were they trapped by their own hoax? One has to dredge up facts and figures from the murky depths of official and press statements during the last fourteen years in order to understand how the black magic of Red statistics worked, and why it backfired.

Actually long before 1958, Peking's statistics often showed glaring discrepancies not spotted by those who religiously quoted them. Some examples:

In April 1954 the *People's Daily* said that China's 1950 trade with the Communist bloc as a whole was 26 percent of its total foreign trade. Five years later, it said the 1950 trade with the U.S.S.R. alone was 30 percent of its total foreign trade. This was a case of the part being bigger than the whole.

The Vice-Minister of Forestry said in 1958 that during the First Five-Year Plan 33.6 percent of the timber was used in the building industry. A year later the official periodical *Geographical Knowledge* said it was 59.68 percent.

The newspaper *Ta Kung Pao* reported in March 1957 that 48 million square meters of housing was built during the period of 1953–1956. The *People's Daily* in December said it was 65 million. The official periodical *Planned Economy* in 1958 said it was 80 million.

The Minister of Education reported that 60 million illiterates were learning to read and 11.99 million students were in high

---

* A frenzied, unplanned production "leap," ordered by the Chinese Communist Party for the whole nation, in industry, agriculture, science, education and the arts, lasting from 1958 to 1960.

schools in 1958. The figures of the National Statistical Bureau were 40 million and 9.99 million. It was a discrepancy of 20 million illiterates and 2 million students.

During the great Yellow River flood of 1958, the *People's Daily* repeatedly said that at the flood crest at Huayuankuo, in Honan, the maximum flow was 21,000 cubic meters per second, and that the 1933 crest flow was 22,000 cubic meters. (Actually old records say the 1933 crest flow was 23,000 cubic meters.) A year later the official technical periodical *Water Conservancy and Power* elevated the 1958 crest flow to 22,300 cubic meters and downgraded the 1933 crest flow further to 20,600 cubic meters. This manipulation of figures made it possible to claim that the 1958 flood "broke all records."

The *People's Daily* said in January 1958 that China had 12,036 standard farming tractors in 1957. The "Communiqué on Fulfillment of the First Five-Year Plan" said in April 1959 that China had 10,177 tractors in 1957. The same year the official booklet *Ten Great Years* gave the 1957 figure as 24,629.

Red Flag, the Party Central Committee's official mouthpiece, said in 1958 that the province of Heilungkiang had 6,200 units of farming tractors that year. In 1960 it gave the 1958 figure as 580 units.

Sometimes the discrepancies can only be detected through calculation. Coal production in 1955 was claimed to be 93.6 million tons; and 1956, 105.9 million tons. Later the official *Hsinhua News Agency* said that in 1956 each coal miner produced 1.7 tons coal per eight-hour shift, and that each produced 13 tons more than in 1955. A session on the abacus shows that Peking's dry statistics are all wet. If these figures were true, then on the national average a Chinese coal miner worked only 66 days a year, or that an eight-hour shift was 44 hours long.

The consensus in the West is that very little is known about how Communist China collects statistical data, balances its equations, and arrives at the final figures. Actually many telltale symptoms are available to any skeptical statistician. Even those figures not contradicting each other are often extremely vague. Percentages are a favorite. Lump sums are not broken down. Categories are not defined. Indices often have no items, not to say weights. Price bases and base periods shift about erratically, sometimes clashing head-on, sometimes disappearing altogether. Cost and labor are excluded from accounting. The distinction between consumer and producer goods is not by items but by ministries. The concept of gross national product is nebulous; that of national income is even more so.

Some Communist statistical methods are unique. When they say nine standard tractors, they may actually mean nine tractors, or fewer than three. Like the Russians, the Chinese Communists count tractors by standard units of 15 h.p. But unlike the Russians, who also give the number of physical units, the Chinese call a 45-h.p. tractor "three standard tractors" without apologies.

The all-important collection of food grain data is even more devious. Instead of measuring crops in barns as most nations do, Communist China uses estimates of the pre-harvest crop as final figures. But a pre-harvest crop is often a pre-calamity and wishful crop. Such estimates are theoretically made by the sampling method, but the samples chosen are usually better-equipped state farms and high-yield land. And estimates are made by Great-Leaping Communist *kanpu*,* sometimes from the top of their heads. Thus in the method alone there is built-in statistical inflation.

Up to now no one really knows how big China's population really is; for twenty centuries it has been the target of gross approximations, learned but contradicting estimates, and rigged censuses. According to old estimates, the population remained quite constant between fifty and sixty million from the time of Christ through the seventeenth century. It was 140 million by the mid-eighteenth century, 300 million by 1795, and 400 million by 1835. At the beginning of the nineteenth century, estimates by

---

* *Kanpu* is a Chinese Communist term for military, government and Party functionaries of any rank. It is roughly the same as the cadre.

Western and Chinese authoritative sources ranged widely from 19.6 million to 333 million. During the Nationalist rule on the mainland, estimates by Protestant missionaries, the Post Office, the Maritime Customs, the Ministry of Interior and the Statistical Office varied from 441 to 486 million. The United Nations Statistical Yearbook gives the 1948 population as 463.5 million.

The Chinese Communists in their 1952 *People's Handbook* give the figure of 486.6 million, and in their 1953 atlas, 548.6 million. Their 1953 census gives the total Chinese population as 601,938,035. Deducting that of Taiwan and overseas, the mainland population was allegedly 582,602,417. It is the 1953 total figure of 600 million that has been popularly used, and it now has been upgraded to 700 million.

Actually the two censuses in recent times are both unreliable. A census started by the Manchus in 1910 gave the figure 330 million, now known to be deliberately rigged down. The 1953 census by the Communists was taken by 2.5 million untrained activists whose main duty was distributing election cards for the People's Congress. The head-counting was done on the county level, uncheckable by provincial or central authorities. The actual method of calculation has never been published. The annual population increase rate was gathered not from a long-term survey nor from an extensive area, but from an instant check-up covering 30 million people in the Ninghsia province, 29 cities and a sprinkling of counties and villages elsewhere.

It is significant that Chinese experts on statistical science took no part in the 1953 census. This was revealed at a conference on May 27, 1957, when the census results were criticized by leading experts like Chen Ta, Wu Ching-chao and Li Ching-han. Chen Ta is the internationally-known, foremost authority on China's population, who has studied the problem for 30 years. He said that the census method was "impossible to produce scientific results." Remarking on the government claim that very few mistakes were made in the census, he said: "If this is true, it is a most extraordinary thing."

A more intriguing question is whether the 1953 census figure is the only exception in accuracy and authenticity, or whether it was obtained in the same style as all other statistics. It is impossible to prove one way or the other, but an educated guess is that the figure was grossly inflated for political reasons. Communist China's population was probably below 500 million in 1953, and is below 600 million at present. It is conceivable that extensive genocide and famine may have even resulted in a slight decrease. For practical reasons the generous estimate of 600 million is used in this book. But whatever the true figure, China's population is tremendous and will remain its main problem.

If Peking's statistical equations are a strategic secret, its mode of data collection is not. In 1950 the State Administrative Council issued a decree asking from Party and government organs weekly, ten-day, monthly, quarterly, semi-annual, annual and unscheduled special statistical reports. In 1953 it followed with another decree, demanding more numerous and more frequent detailed statistical data for anything and everything done by the myriad minuscule cells of the sprawling administration. In statistically advanced countries such demands would be mere bureaucracy, but in amorphous China, they bordered on mathematical fantasy.

So avalanches of statistical forms descended upon every city and village in China, creating spectacles unmatched by any advanced or backward nation. The variety is incredible. The Statistical Office of the then Liaotung province in one year sent out 316 types of statistical questionnaires, consisting of 11 daily, two tri-daily, 31 five-day, 31 ten-day, 89 monthly, 31 quarterly, five semi-annual, eight annual, and 108 special reports. A government committee in Shansi issued four sets of economic questionnaires totaling 74 pages and 6,307 items. The set on agriculture had 114 items of instruction totaling 10,000 words, just to tell the illiterate peasants how to fill in the forms. Ssuhui county, Kwangtung, was required to report 227 kinds of figures every three days. Aside from the main statistical items, the peasants must report such figures like the *number* of insect pests and the *number* of insect eggs destroyed. Every three days the number of pigs, sheep, rabbits, chickens, ducks, and geese in *each* peasant household must be reported.

There was much duplication. Of the 104 varieties of agricultural statistical questionnaires released in Lintung, Shensi, one item was duplicated in 44 places. Many forms received in a single area are completely identical, except from different authorities. Sometimes one single subject is investigated time and again. In a municipal district in Peking, one subject was statistically investigated 18 times during a single year.

Many questions asked are unanswerable. Yet they must be answered. Village *kanpu* are required to compile price indices for each village—an unnecessary elaboration not even done in statistically advanced United States. Mat-shed theatres are required to report the percentage of class composition of the audience. Bank branches are required to report the political categories of depositors. A propaganda office in Minhou, Fukien, demanded from each neighborhood the number of slogans posted in the streets, the number of people who saw them, with breakdown into males, females, industrial workers, peasants, *kanpu* and students. Similar questions took up more than half of the 260 items in the form. A health bureau near Canton asked for "The number of deaths and the number of people who may die."

Information asked one day is canceled the next. A *kanpu* in Hopei province said: "Countless questionnaires are required today and discarded tomorrow. We are all confused." A women's league in Szechwan sent out a form on marital, political, and production statistics for women, setting one month as the deadline for the county leagues. The county leagues set a one-day deadline for the town leagues. The town leagues, which received the form at noon, set a midnight deadline for the village leagues. As a harassed *kanpu* bewailed: "The special districts demand; the counties press; the districts push; the villages hurry. The top-dogs yell for the forms; the under-dogs break their legs running."

At times deadlines pre-date issuing dates. An insect pest investigation form issued one year in Chingyang, Kansu, demanded that all district offices send in the returns by July 2. But the district offices received the form on July 13.

No organization big or small can escape from these statistical orgies. The Hsing Yeh Aluminum Factory, a kitchenware plant in Shanghai, was required each month to file a total of 28 different statistical reports consisting of 90 forms, with duplicates ranging from 2 to 20 copies. The factory had a grand total of 15 laborers, and two clerks who doubled as cashiers, accountants, purchasing agents, delivery men, and contacts for banks and revenue bureaus. The Tientsin newspaper *Ta Kung Pao* commented on this case: "This is not an isolated phenomenon. . . . The condition of clerks rushing around to fill in statistical reports is ordinary and ordinary." It added that in bigger factories the situation was "of course worse."

Canton's *Southern Daily* said: "Investigating forms have become a rampaging calamity in the villages. Why can we not think of a remedy to save the situation?" The *People's Daily* said: "The State Administrative Council has repeatedly issued directives prohibiting the indiscriminate issuing of investigation forms. But they were all ignored." The *Tientsin Daily* said: "Statistical forms have developed into a disaster. After years of clamor and noise, we saw a moment of improvement, then a relapse into chaos. It is getting more and more serious."

With the Party demanding impossible figures and impossible deadlines, the *kanpu* have to find a survival trick. The trick, typically Chinese, was succinctly put by a Shansi *kanpu*: "Our mouths are like flowing water. Our mind is like an old account. What they want, we supply." The *Hsin Hua Monthly* officially concurred: "The leadership, in order to fulfill its duty, wants even mythical figures." One popular saying in the villages on production statistics is well known: "Harsh demands from above; blind fabrication from below."

The faking of statistics, judging from Peking's reports, became the rule rather than the exception. During the 1956 cooperatives campaign, village *kanpu* elevated farm price assessments, equated inferior grain with first-class grain, included undistributable items like pasture animals in distributable columns, delayed the refund of agricultural loans and left little or no fund for next year's production. As a result, peasant income all over the nation increased on paper and decreased in reality, and agricultural financing turned into furious disorder. Some collectives in Szechwan increased their production by 15 percent, but their books showed 50 percent. In nine Anhwei counties, 1,223 collectives or 60 percent in that area faked reports. In a Shansi county 87 percent of the collectives faked reports. Many kept two sets of books. Some 50 Kirin collectives had either illegible account books or no books at all. Yet they all produced statistics. Half of the collectives in Hupeh, Kwangsi and Hunan faked reports. In some counties not a single collective sent authentic reports.

Faked statistics covered not only agricultural production, but the number of people in labor brigades, the amount of coal mined, steel produced, cloth woven, irrigation canals dug, mineral reserves prospected, food rationed, farmland flooded, flies swatted and counterrevolutionaries executed. For example, it was discovered in 1957 that in Noho, Manchuria, 1,700 new wells were said to be dug. The actual number was 700. Also the actual amount of manure collected was half of that claimed. In the same year 9,000 *kanpu* were sent by the State Economy Committee to check warehouses in China. They found that out of 274 state enterprises, 147 falsified records of steel stocks.

By the 1958 Great Leap, the statistical tidal wave had engulfed the whole country. As a result, statistics first became creative, then destructive. It was a nation-wide practice to push them up at any cost. Food grain was mixed with gravel and sprinkled with water. Manure collected in fertilizer drives was adulterated with sand, mud, and water. Cloth was heavily sized, stretched and ironed by textile mills to increase the yardage. Barbers were praised for lightning haircuts. Hospital doctors were judged not by the way they treated the patients, but by the number of patients treated.

Machine factories were reluctant to make spare parts which did not count much statistically; the result was the idling of many industrial and farm machines. Books printed in a hurry carried numerous correction slips, and corrections of corrections.

Factory workers, according to the *China Youth Press*, "are always calculating whether it is worth it. If it is worth it, they will willingly pay fines for making waste products, since they can more than make it up with the extra wages from increased quantity." Peking claimed to have trained 400,000 instant "geologists" who trotted all over China and sent in competitive reports on the mineral reserves they discovered. Yet in a more sober moment the *People's Daily* lamented that not a single geologist, of the type known in the West, graduated from universities between 1953 and 1958. Only a few hundred have been trained since.

Falsification of statistics has been double-pronged. They are faked at the grassroots to fool the Party, and also at the top by the Party to fool the world. Caught in the middle are the few genuine statisticians who believe statistics should not be pure fiction. In 1955 the deputy head of the National Statistical Bureau said that the majority of his staff were old *kanpu* and young students who "know nothing" about the areas they covered, and "the leading members of the statistical bureaus have not studied statistical theory and have no professional knowledge." The technical periodical *Statistical Work* had to publish an article to explain to the professional statisticians the meaning of percentage.

In 1957 at a statistics conference, it was revealed that all the leading Chinese statisticians were ignored by the regime. They were either idle or had changed professions. At another conference in April 1959, the statisticians used typical Chinese discretion and subtlety to criticize the Party's statistics. They knew what was coming, for even as the conference was in session, a report was issued in the name of the National Statistical Bureau containing the wild production figures for 1958. Hsueh Mu-chiao, then head of the Bureau, backed by the statisticians, said that if their statistics could not fully satisfy the Party, "they could be supplemented conveniently, but attention must be paid to preventing at each and every stage the addition of figures." He urged that long-standing scientific methods should not be lightly altered. "The precision of statistical data," he said perhaps wistfully, "should approach as much as possible to reality."

Four months later, when the 1958 figures had to be revised, the statisticians were proved right, but they were chastened as "right-ist opportunists" because they had proved the Party was wrong. Hsueh was removed as chief of the Bureau. The apprehensive new chief, Chia Chi-yun, at a later conference had to parrot the Party line. He was glad that "the aloofness of statistical work from politics had been overcome." It was entirely wrong, he said, to check production figures. He further made these strange remarks: "Statistical work has abandoned the idea that statistics are for statistics' sake which is narrow dogmatism. . . . Some of the sta-tistical data have been used by the rightist opportunists as a weapon in their attacks against the Party. This is a very painful lesson. If statistical material does not express a clear political idea, but merely reflects real conditions, then obviously it will be used by the enemy. What a dangerous thing this is!" He defined the purpose of Peking statistics: "Statistical work is a weapon of class struggle and political struggle. Our statistical reports . . . certainly should not be a mere display of objective facts. . . . Statistical work must be something which when the Party is using it, does not cause embarrassment and annoyance." Whether Chia was praising or subtly insulting the Party, he gave an unmistakable assessment of the reliability of Chinese Communist statistics.

Faked at the bottom by hard-pressed, ignorant *kanpu*, juggled in the middle by reluctant statisticians, twisted at the top by ideo-logical fanatics, statistics from Communist China are often figura-tive, psychological, and surrealistic. While a person who auto-matically quotes such statistics will find himself in a mathematical never-never land, one who completely ignores them will fare no better. It is only through patient detective work that one can get glimpses of the truth through the statistical fumes.

Communist China's industrial growth figures, for example, have been a favorable measurement for Western economists. But they are deceptive. The 1952 gross industrial output was 250 percent that of 1949, surpassing the pre-1949 peaks in most of the important items except pig iron. The progress was impressive only on the surface, for in 1949 most industries were at a standstill after years of war. The gross value of industrial production was said to have increased by 140 percent during the First Five-Year Plan. Even if this figure was not fabricated, it is statistically misleading. For it includes also the cost of raw materials and intermediate products consumed in the industries. Thus the more raw materials were wasted, the higher became the gross value. The 66 percent increase in the 1958 gross value of industrial output was even more misleading. For that year Peking added in the output of the handicraft industry, which had always been considerable in China but which was never included in earlier calculations. Furthermore, the fad of making advanced machinery of dubious quality that year threw the picture all out of perspective. These new products were priced according to test-manufacturing expenses, thereby inflating the gross value of heavy industry.

How much of the world's past and present appraisal of Red China, based mainly on statistics, really makes sense? Can mere figures indefinitely feed the people, trade for imports, and prop up an increasingly grotesque economy? The answers to these questions struck home in Peking in late 1960 when, after three years of the Great Leap, agriculture, transportation, construction, heavy and light industries wheezed to a virtual standstill.

But the guiding light of this mathematical mumbo-jumbo is Mao Tse-tung who, with a librarian's penchant for cataloguing and a peasant's disdain for scientific exactitude, with his Marxist dogmatism and mystic romanticism, has become the Mad Statistician of Peking.

VI HOW TO EAT
WITHOUT FOOD

IN THE THIRD CENTURY B.C. THE RULER OF A CHINESE
kingdom sought advice from the sage Mencius. The king had been
vigorously shifting his people and resources all over his country
in an utmost effort to govern. Yet his people were not prosperous.
He wondered why.

Mencius said to him: "If the seasons of cultivation are not inter-
fered with, the grain will be more than you can eat. If close-knit
nets are not cast in the pools and ponds, the fish and turtles will
be more than you can eat. If axes enter the hills and forests only at
the proper time, the wood will be more than you can use." But
instead: "Your dogs and swine eat the food of men, and you curb
them not. People are starving by the wayside, and you open not
your granaries. When people die, you say: 'It is not I; it is the
year.' What difference this is from stabbing a man to death and
saying: 'It is not I; it is the weapon'?"

Twenty-two centuries later Mao Tse-tung, the ruler of another
Chinese empire, has been vigorously shifting his people and resources all over his country in an utmost effort to govern. When
people die, he says: "It is the natural calamities." But he too,
perhaps, is wondering why.

It *is* something to wonder about. How could Communist China,
whose food increase during the first decade was allegedly seven
times its population increase, have a famine?

In 1958 Peking won the world's admiration by announcing that
its food and cotton output had more than doubled since 1957.

Mao Tse-tung himself prophesied: "Feats never imagined by mankind will come true. Agricultural productivity several times, a dozen times and even several tens of times the present productivity will result." Soon Peking was swamped by reports from the provinces, claiming harvest crops had shot up from 6,000 to 30,000 to 400,000 pounds per acre. Over 26 million acres each allegedly yielded more than 6,600 pounds of grain. One state farm said that 8 million pounds of cabbage zoomed up from a single acre. An apple tree in Manchuria had 12,175 apples dangling from its boughs.

While the quota-makers in Peking deliriously and repeatedly raised the year's food target to catch up with the farmers, Mao announced a "Three-Three System" which anticipated the national average yield of food grain soon and easily to reach 20,000 pounds per acre. (The national average yield that year in agriculturally underdeveloped United States ranged from 1,644 pounds of wheat to 3,137 pounds of rice per acre.) China's crop land—hitherto insufficient for food alone—was to be reduced to one-third its area, leaving one-third lying fallow and another third for orchards, pastures, forests and fish ponds. Under the magical system, even when the population reached 700 million there would be plenty of food for everyone. The press was full of pep headlines like: "Marxism Can Produce Food," and "We Have Broken Through the Barrier of Scientific Superstition." It seemed that China had catapulted itself into a state of intolerable bliss.

This was 1958—the Year of the Miracle.

Then came the moment of truth. The bumper harvest was checked and it was discovered that the fantastic increases took place only in statistical reports. This admission had to be made because great shortages, unheard of even in China, emerged in staple food, edible oil, vegetables, meat, tea, silk, cotton, hemp, tobacco, bamboo, timber, along with manufactured goods. This resulted in a drastic cut in rations and the sending of millions of city people to work on the farms.

Even according to the revised figures, the food situation in

China did not make sense. Between 1949 and 1959 Communist China's food had increased by 150 percent, while its population only by 22 percent. There should have been enough reserve to forestall a famine even with severe natural calamities. Yet all symptoms showed otherwise. The 1959 food output was allegedly 270 million tons. After deducting 50 million tons for seeds, fodder, and industrial use, there should have been 50 pounds of milled grain per person monthly for the 600 million people. But that year a person actually got only 30 pounds. What happened to some 90 million tons of the 1959 food? The 1960 food output has never been officially announced, although it was hinted that the 1960 grain production was 150 million tons. If this were true, each person should get 23 pounds a month. But since late 1960 most have received about 17 pounds.

The huge amount of missing food was not exported. China's food exports fluctuate around 1½ percent of its total output. The exports could not have reduced its food appreciably, even though they betray the regime's inhumane attitude. Neither did this portion go into the granaries, as stored grain each year amounts to about the same as exports. Judging from Peking's decision to mortgage its precious foreign-exchange earnings for imported food, whatever grain was stored must either have been near exhaustion, or was not stored as claimed. The explanation lies elsewhere. Communist Chinese agriculture while searching for a breakthrough has resulted in a breakdown.

The land of China, equal to 17 times that of France or slightly bigger than the United States, is not ideal for agriculture. It is more mountainous than the United States, Soviet Russia, or India. Almost 70 percent of its land is over 3,000 feet above sea-level and only 15 percent is under 1,600 feet. It has a variety of climate ranging from subtropic summer to Siberian winter. Arable land on the China mainland amounts to 264 million acres or only one-tenth its total area. Of this 30 percent is good soil, 40 percent is of medium quality and the rest is inferior. Four-fifths of China's population have to toil on one-tenth of its land in order to maintain a subsistence level. In Soviet Russia half of its population works on one-eleventh of its land to make a meagre standard of living. In the United States, one-eighth of its population farms one-fifth of its land to create a national overweight problem and pile up great surpluses.

The trouble with the Chinese is that the fecundity of their soil can never match the fecundity of their loins. In their land it is easier to breed than to feed. Each year more babies are born in that country than the combined population of Norway and Sweden. No matter how one looks at contemporary China's problems, he will eventually reach the bedrock dilemma of population versus food—a deceptively elemental situation that cannot readily be solved by modern agronomy or exotic ideologies.

Too little arable land and too big a population are not the only problems. In China a year without natural calamities is a year for thanksgiving. All this has not discouraged the diligent Chinese peasants, who have not harnessed nature but have adapted themselves to it. For centuries every square foot of arable land has been cultivated with loving care. What is even more remarkable is the ingenious way every product raised from the earth is utilized.

The staple food in China is grain: rice in the South, wheat in the North, and miscellaneous grains like millet and kaoliang (sorghum), and sweet potatoes in poorer regions. Rice and wheat husks are used for fodder and fertilizer. Straw is an important village fuel, and is used to thatch roofs and to reinforce the mud-lime mortar of village walls. Its ashes serve as fertilizer, cleansing powder, and bedding for animals and poultry. Grain stalks are made into brooms. Shaohsing, the yellow wine of China, comes from rice. The fragrant, potent Chinese liquor kaoliang is distilled from the grain.

Soybeans are the cow of China. Soybean milk rivals cow's milk in nutrition. Bean curd is a nutritious food for the poor, and is cooked in a hundred ways. From soybeans comes also the ubiquitous gourmet condiment soy sauce. The best type takes six or seven years to age, and requires as much art in its preparation as good French wines. Bean oil is a popular cooking oil and goes into soap and paints. It also lights grass-wick lamps in villages where electricity is unavailable and kerosene is expensive. Bean waste is an important fodder and fertilizer.

China's leading meat is pork. Lard is used for cooking. Pigskin is not only tanned as leather, but is prepared in many intricate ways as a tasty food. Bristles are a noted export item. Pig bones go into toothbrushes, hairpins, and art carvings.

Bamboo is the steel of China. It is the skeleton of village huts, the scaffolding of construction projects, and the universal material for fences. It is built into pavilions, memorial arches, bridges, piers, ladders, sedan chairs. The universal bamboo pole is a carrying pole for coolie loads, and a steering pole on sampans and junks. Split bamboo is woven into baskets, suitcases, dustpans, bed mats, and screens. Bamboo is the elastic spring in boxes and the stem of writing brushes. It is made into furniture, lamps, flower vases, cups, tea trays, chopsticks, fishing rods, umbrellas, fans, picture frames, mahjongs, smoking pipes and musical instruments. Bamboo shoots are a table delicacy.

Like rice, wheat, kaoliang, soybean, and bamboo, cotton is another necessity. To the Chinese peasants, cotton is not only their wool and nylon but also their stove in winter. Cottonseed is used as a fodder and a fertilizer. The oil pressed from it is used for cooking. Cotton stalks and pods are made into paper and serve as fuel.

Most Chinese drugs are made from herbs. The list is endless but these examples show how intimately China's agriculture is intertwined with the daily life of the people. The humbleness of these items is only equaled by the sophistication of their utilization. It is said that the Chinese are the only people who developed an advanced civilization almost exclusively through vegetables.

Today as in the past, agriculture is the basis of Chinese economy. Nearly half of the raw materials and almost all the capital investment for the country's industrialization must come from agriculture. The greatest economic task for generations to come will be *industrialization without starvation*. This single issue more than any other will decide the success or failure of any political regime in China.

Into this picture stepped Mao Tse-tung and his Agrarian Reformers in 1949. They wanted to feed and clothe the poor peasants, and at the same time industrialize and make China a strong nation. What have they accomplished in the past fourteen years in agriculture—their immediate objective?

The agriculture of Communist China, along with other facets of its economy and social condition, went through the most violent convulsions known to mankind. The end justifies the means in the Communist philosophy, and right after they gained control of the country, the Communists rapidly pushed their agrarian reform programs in the form of land redistribution.

One of the popular fallacies about China is that the Chinese peasants suffered from a landlord system analogous to that of Medieval Europe or Tsarist Russia. Neither of the two main features of feudalism—the restriction on the free sale of land and the attaching of labor to the land—had been found in China for several hundred years before the Communists' arrival. Mao Tse-tung's claim that half of China's farmland was owned by absentee landlords was not authenticated by other sources. Instead, studies by independent Chinese and Western scholars placed 70 percent of pre-Communist China's farmland as owned by the farmers themselves. More than half of Chinese peasants owned fully all the land they tilled. Another 30 percent had their own land but rented additional crop land. Furthermore, one-third of the farms were smaller than 1.6 acres and only 8 percent bigger than 8.4 acres. Farm sizes in pre-Communist China supported the fact that more people owned less land than in Tsarist Russia or present-day United States. The average Chinese farm was only 3.5 acres, or only one-sixtieth of the then average American farm of 215 acres. Through generations of inheritance even these small farms were subdivided into tiny half-acre plots scattered over the hillsides within the villages. Sun Yat-sen, "Father of the Chinese

Republic," put his finger on the crux of the problem when he said that China's ailment was not unequal distribution, but general poverty. China's agricultural problem was not so much one between man and man, as one between man and land.

The real purpose of Mao's land reform was political rather than economic. China had virtually no proletariat, and with Mao basing his revolutionary theory on the peasants, he had to use the landlords as a sin-offering. Many peasants who owned as little as two or three acres of land, which they tilled themselves, were included in the estimated 5 million "landlords" liquidated.

The slogan of "land to the tillers" was not an end but a means for the Chinese Communists. An embryonic collectivization emerged in 1952. This elementary collectivization was a relatively cautious, gradual preparation for the ultimate full collectivization dreamed by all Communists. The policy line at that time was: because of China's weak industrial base, simultaneous industrialization and collectivization was impossible. Therefore collectivization was to go on moderately and through an indefinite period while industrialization was taking place.

Up to this point, Communist China's pattern of collectivization was not unlike that of Soviet Russia, although it was already far more rigid and severe than that of East Europe. But in July 1955 Mao in a major policy speech overruling unnamed but powerful Party moderates, whom he ridiculed as "women with bound feet," ordered a headlong plunge into full collectivization. Under this system of "advanced cooperatives" the peasants did not even own their land in theory, and their income was based on labor only. They thus became full-fledged serfs under a single landlord, the state.

In summer 1958 came the communes, which were supposed to maximize labor and minimize waste. As things turned out, the communes threw agricultural administration into chaos, damaged the land, and heightened the passive resistance of the peasants. As a result the nation's agriculture has reached a state where the main concern of the Peking regime is to get enough food for the population.

The Chinese peasants have always been at the mercy of their eroded mountains and capricious rivers. China's history records 1,397 serious droughts since Christ was born. Floods have also been disastrous. The Huai River, draining an area equal to six Netherlands but having no mouth of its own, flooded its valley 979 times in 2,200 years. The mighty Yangtze River, the world's third longest, in whose valley nearly half of China's population lives, had 242 floods and droughts in 265 years. From mythical times the Chinese have been trying to tame the Yellow River, known as "China's Sorrow." This 2,900-mile river, with a basin equal to Italy, Switzerland, and Norway combined, devastated its plain 1,500 times in 3,000 years, and made nine major changes of its course, swinging its mouth in wild arcs up to 500 miles long. Adding dust storms in the arid Northwest, typhoons along the coast, insect pests everywhere, and rare but severe earthquakes, the lot of the Chinese peasants has been inseparable from natural calamities. As the Chinese peasants get three quarters of their food directly from their own land, when famine strikes it always means hunger and often starvation. One million people were killed in the 1887 flood alone. Some 800,000 lost their lives in the great earthquake of 1556, and another 246,000 perished in a similar disaster in 1920.

After many centuries of exploitation by a vast farming population, China has very little natural vegetation left. Its forests consist of only one-tenth of its total area, about 80th on the list of the world's countries on a percentage area basis. The water-holding capacity of the soil is therefore extremely poor. Excessive run-off is thus a major cause of floods. Another major cause is the breaching of dikes. The Yellow River, the world's siltiest, deposits on its delta enough silt to fill up one and a half Empire State Buildings daily. For hundreds of miles it flows between dikes on a river bed high *above* the surrounding countryside with the silt raising the bottom continuously. A single breach could empty the entire river onto the flat Yellow Plain for as far as the eye can see. Such floods sometimes stay for as long as a year.

Many other rivers in North China have similar skyway river beds between precarious dikes. Floods in this area are incredibly destructive. The most frequently flooded area is northern Kiangsu and Anhwei, where the flow of the lower Huai River often increases to fifty times its dry-season volume. Another frequently flooded area, mainly due to uneven rainfall, is along the Yangtze River in the vicinity of the Great Lakes region. Sometimes a week's rain over the basin of a single Yangtze tributary is equal to several weeks' water over Niagara Falls. And when too much water goes to one place, there is bound to be too little elsewhere. Drought occurs oftener than floods, is more destructive, more extensive, and lasts longer.

It is tempting to conclude that since the Chinese live in a land of catastrophes, the recent catastrophe is just one of those things. This is not so. Peking has been *playing up* the natural calamities but *playing down* the famine. But the present famine is due not so much to sudden dramatic blows from nature as to a bureaucracy efficient in control but lacking in common sense. A sizable portion of the floods and droughts during the past few years have been aggravated and at times directly caused by a decade of pseudo-scientific methods in farming, irrigation and soil treatment.

One ominous feature of this famine is its almost continuous expansion in area year after year since the Communists came into power. The total area of farmland hit by natural calamities in 1950 was only 13 million acres. It was 29 million in 1954; 38 million in 1956; 78 million in 1958; 107 million in 1959; and 148 million in 1960. The 1961 and 1962 calamity areas have not been announced but they appear comparable to those of 1960. This is not a common Chinese famine, which usually affected a couple of provinces for a short time. It is not a momentary lack of food, but a pernicious exhaustion of the land and the people—the cumulative result of over a decade's abuse of nature and human nature.

At the beginning, the Chinese Communists envisioned a titanic program of farm mechanization on the Russian and American scale. But unlike Soviet Russia and the United States, which have vast plains and thinner populations, China's huge population concentrates densely wherever the land is arable. Most of the farmland is in the form of cut-up wet paddies or terraced hillside plots where modern tractors would be paralyzed. The United States has 5 million and Soviet Russia 1.7 million tractors. China has fewer than 33,500, with some 6,700 in disrepair. This is less than 4 percent of the requirement as estimated by Peking. In October 1959 the *People's Daily* had to admit soberly: "It is too early to talk about general mechanization. We have no oil, too few animals. Steel is expensive. The cost of machinery is prohibitive."

Attention was then turned to "semi-mechanization," which means improved animal-powered farming implements. The glamor star of "semi-mechanization" was the Double-Wheel Double-Share Plow—an ordinary all-metal plow pulled by animals. With tremendous publicity, Peking turned out 3.5 million Double Plows in 1956 and 6 million in 1957. But this heavy plow got into difficulty in wet paddies and terraced fields, which constitute China's most important farmland. It was badly manufactured. Many brand-new plows had missing parts. Soon peasants all over the country refused to use what they called the "Sleeping Plow." Peking on one hand accused the peasants of "hostility toward innovations" and "backward conservatism," and on the other announced a new, lighter model every six months.

Even if the Double Plow were successful, the question would arise as to who is to pull it. China had 87 million work animals in 1955. Due to abuse, sabotage, and lack of fodder the number was reduced by 2 million in 1959. This caused the Communist Youth Corps magazine *China Youth* in an article "Beware of Buffalo Extinction" to ask: "Who is to pull the plows three years from now?"

Lately, the regime has been encouraging the use of traditional small farming implements. The quality of the newly made small implements is revealed by a *People's Daily* editorial in 1960. It recalled wistfully the pre-Communist days when "a hoe would last three generations—the property of the man who used it, repaired it and cared for it." Today a hoe often does not last one season, especially when it is made of the "steel" from the backward furnaces. Today the peasant no longer owns it, repairs it or cares for it. These small implements are "lost, wasted or destroyed . . . left scattered in the open air in the fields where rains and winds ruined them."

Mechanization having failed as a panacea, attention was turned to fertilizer. Each winter since 1957 tens of millions of peasants and city residents have been staging a technicolor spectacular that was a sight to the eye as well as a kick to the nose—the fertilizer drive. With gongs and drums beating, with red pennants fluttering in the scented breezes, brigades of men and women sang and marched in military fashion to convoy the secret weapon of Communist China's agriculture. In wooden buckets, bamboo baskets, tin cans, earthen pots, slung from bamboo carrying poles, in makeshift carts pulled by children was the excrement of China's 600 million human beings and 265 million farm animals, sewage silt, garbage, river mud, peat, green meal, fumigated earth, chimney ashes, brackish water and industrial waste.

This bizarre gold rush falls into perspective when viewed with the realistic situation. Communist China produces less than 3 million tons chemical fertilizer a year, while its requirement is at least 10 times that amount. But to build enough modern fertilizer plants or to import fertilizer requires money, which Peking was unwilling and is unable to spend. China therefore still has to depend largely on compost. By the use of night soil, China's population daily return to the earth more than 700 tons of phosphorus, 1,200 tons of potassium and a large amount of nitrogen. Peking estimated that the night soil from 300 million adults each year is equivalent to 9.6 million tons of chemical fertilizer. Evidently, such a source cannot be discarded at present. Hence the high drama of the fertilizer drive.

However, human and animal excrement, green compost, and

river mud have been used by the Chinese peasants for forty centuries. Through their nonscientific, empirical ways they have learned to make use of every bit of these natural fertilizing agents. For thousands of years the night soil from Chinese cities has been collected avidly from each house every morning free of charge by specialized merchants. Caravans of "honey carts" in streets and fleets of "honey boats" in canals then take the cargo to the countryside for the farmers, who also erect free lavatories along country roads for the same purpose. The Chinese word for "manure" is composed of three characters, meaning "rice," "field," and "common." The Communist-inspired drives for compost, therefore, do not increase the total fertilizing strength, but only the total tonnage—by throwing in all unlikely adulterating ingredients. Peking's *Science Journal* once warned against the indiscriminate mixing of organic compost with inorganic matters. Chemical reactions from mixing ashes and alkali with manure often cause the loss of nitrogen content. Many cases of crop collapse and burning were reported due to bad handling of fertilizer.

In summer 1958 after the Party took over direct control of agriculture, close-sowing and deep-plowing were practiced extensively. Nearly half of the crop land was soon cultivated this way. Such methods should be practiced with discretion and careful coordination with fertilizing. But they were practiced indiscriminately; as a result many plants weakened, collapsed or died, and the soil was debilitated. By the fall of 1959 Peking conceded: "What we gained was not up to what we lost."

Further damage was caused by a battle of crops. In the early years the Communists assaulted agriculture, fisheries, animal husbandry and forestry simultaneously. The resultant reduced food crop caused a reversal of policy: concentrate on food crops, lay off subsidiary activities. So hundreds of thousands of acres of cotton, hemp, kaoliang, bamboo, tea, and mulberry, peach and orange trees were razed to turn into unstable, unfit, ill-conditioned fields for wet rice, wheat and potatoes. In agricultural China, more so than in any other agricultural country, every valley, every plain

has its peculiar combination of soil, climate and economic require-
ments, which cannot be altered without massive use of chemicals
and modern equipment which are simply not available. Peasants
have already adopted the best crops for the most profitable use.
For example, in a silk-producing area near Canton the peasants
engage in fish culture as a sideline. They use the waste from the
silkworms to feed the fish, then dig up the fertile mud from the
fish ponds to fertilize mulberry trees, the leaves of which are fed
to the silkworms. Everything is used. Nothing is wasted. But when
the mulberry trees in a village were razed by zealous Party robots
to plant rice, the entire cycle of peasant economy was disrupted.

Plowing too deeply, sowing too closely, planting too early, using
the wrong crops or wrong seeds, employing too much or too little
or inadequate fertilizer, and not allowing certain fields to lie
fallow—these reasons alone, even if there were no natural calamities, dealt the harvests a severe blow.

As for the calamities themselves, the 1959 locust disaster was an
example of the Party bureaucrats' attitude, even though they estimate that *every year* insect pests damage 10 percent of the country's grain, 20 percent of the cotton and 40 percent of the fruits.
In early April, peasants in Honan discovered some young locusts
and reported to the commune *kanpu*. But the *kanpu* scolded the
peasants: "Right now the corn and soybean have just sprouted
and the wheat will ripen soon. We don't even have enough people
for weeding and fertilizing. How can we divert labor for insect
pests? This is reversing the urgent and the unimportant." The
peasants appealed to the county Party commissar. They were
again pushed aside: "Little ghost and big fright! You saw an
insect and you bring us a heap of blind words. We shall have an
insect-destroying campaign someday anyway. Why make the fuss
now?"

Two months later the crops in two counties were eaten up by
locusts in one night. Immediately the provincial Party secretary
pushed the panic button and issued a set of "Regulations Pertain-
ing to the Swift Extermination of Locusts." During three days in

mid-June, 1,250,000 peasants were hurled into the sea of locusts for an epic extermination battle. By then it was too late. Crops, grass, and leaves on a million acres in 48 counties in Honan were wiped clean. The locusts then invaded the neighboring provinces of Anhwei, Kiangsu and Shantung, damaging nearly 5 million acres of farmland in 179 counties.

In these provinces peasants from six to eighty were pressed to fight locusts. Airplanes were used to spray insecticide. But the spraying, done with frenzy and inexperience, killed 100,000 farm animals.

Water conservation seems to be the only practical major means to improve agriculture with China's limited means. In quantity China's water is plentiful, but in distribution it is lopsided. Every year 668 cubic miles of water flow over mainland China's 3.6 million square miles of land, averaging 12 tons of water for each person daily. But three quarters of this water is in the Yangtze valley and south of it. North China has less than 5 percent.

Irrigation in China is an old science. River taming and canal digging are traced as far back as the eighth century B.C. The total mileage of canals in pre-Communist China was estimated at 300,000, including the world-famous Grand Canal. Patterns of irrigation throughout the centuries have become very complex and detailed, differing in each region and river valley. The Yangtze and Pearl River deltas are almost entirely man-made landscapes interlaced with intricate canals. In mountainous Szechwan the peasants convert terraced rice fields into winter reservoirs for spring use. The vicinity of Ninghsia is a canal-fed oasis in the Ordos Desert of Inner Mongolia. In arid Kansu, pebbles are piled thickly on fields to retard evaporation, and 40-foot water wheels have been scooping water from the Yellow River for hundreds of years. The Chinese have done notable work in irrigation, but not enough for their modern needs; and while the Nationalists had some great plans, most of them were never carried out.

Came the Communists, who claimed that during their first

decade they increased the irrigated area from 40 million to 180 million acres. It used 40 billion man-days to dig 105 billion cubic yards of earth, equivalent to 450 Panama Canals or a wall 3.3 feet high and wide girdling the earth 2,000 times. This work consisted of the building or repairing of some 60 large reservoirs, 1,000 medium ones, 4 million small reservoirs and canals, 74,600 miles of dikes, 15 million farm weirs and 10 million wells. A colossal network of canals covering the entire China Plains was started in 1958 to bring water from South to North China.

The official statistics are impressive. One imagines millions of Chinese peasants, ant-like, faceless, infinite in number, digging and hauling all over the land, disciplining the rascal rivers and salving the fields with gentle moisture. It is possible to rationalize that the misery of millions forced to labor today might bring *some* good to other millions who will inherit the land tomorrow. But the fact is that China's water conservancy has done more harm than good.

Until 1957 Peking had concentrated its water conservancy in big hydroelectrically oriented dams. Many of these expensive projects were ill-planned or badly constructed. The largest, most important project was a TVA-type system to regulate the Yellow River, the world's trickiest, and its tributaries, so that by the time the river passed the vicinity of Kaifeng and reached the flat Yellow Plain its flow would be controlled. When the project was initiated, Peking proudly announced that the Yellow River would be tamed forever, and that by autumn of 1961 its lower reaches would be "crystal clear." The key of this system was the mammoth Sanmen Gorge Dam, to be built at a point just before the river leaves the mountains. To protect it, 59 high dams were to be built in the upper river. By 1956 half of the high dams were built. That year the floods came, destroying or silting up almost all of them. Despite a Chinese specialist's warning that they should re-examine the whole plan, the Sanmen Gorge Dam, with a one-million-kilowatt power plant, was started the next year. The dam was planned, model-tested, and supervised by the Russians. Due to structural defects, its design and construction had to be altered time and again. In 1958 another flood came, and 70 percent of the swollen water came from *below* the Sanmen Gorge. An official technical journal, *Water Conservancy and Power*, then admitted that even after the completion of the project, major floods cannot be prevented. It is not known whether this blunder was made by politicians in Peking or experts from Soviet Russia, as Chinese engineers have never been confident about mere dams across the Yellow River, whose idiosyncrasies have been recorded in Chinese history books for the past 2,000 years, and whose valley is called the worst erosion area in the world.

Another one of Communist China's hydraulic engineering prides is the much-publicized Futseling Reservoir in Anhwei. This reservoir was completed with Russian aid in 1954 amid great fanfare. Then came the Huai River flood, which inundated the entire plain it was supposed to protect. Five years later the reservoir was still not functioning, because the sluice gates turned out to be heavier than designed, and fears were expressed that they would not open when it was filled with water. A similar fate befell the Yungting Reservoir Tunnel near Peking, opened with a loud blast of propaganda. After the hosannas came the flood, inundating 7 million acres and washing away 2.6 million houses. Then there is the Tahuofang Dam, one of the country's biggest reservoirs, near Fushun in Manchuria. After a year's work on the dam, construction had to be halted in 1954 when it was discovered that the structure "had the consistency of rubber."

Some of the mistakes are almost unbelievable. During the dry season, fields in many areas could not get a drop of water even though the reservoirs were full. It was discovered that nobody was ordered to build water conveyance systems for these reservoirs—no sluice gates, no canals, no ditches. The *People's Daily* in June 1959 summed up the situation of the large-scale projects: "There are reservoirs without water, reservoirs with water but without aquaducts. . . . A great number of flood-prevention works which have to be renewed yearly were not done, or even if they were started, were not finished." *Water Conservancy and Power* further reported that a number of hydroelectric dams were leaking badly, that many reservoirs "look all right as long as water is not let in," and that on some of these projects equipment was installed but no power could be produced.

Medium and smaller works have fared even worse. Peking reports admitted that during the floods of 1956 and 1957, Shansi province lost 1,000 dams and 3,500 culverts and drains. Kansu lost 1,600 dams. In Kwangtung the 1959 flood ruined 27,000 large and small water conservancy structures. Between 1950 and 1954 Peking built or repaired 26,000 miles of dikes in China "to a level that never could be topped by any flood." The 1954 flood in the Yangtze and Huai rivers areas alone collapsed 15,534 miles of dikes. By 1962 about 60 percent of medium and small conservancy structures were believed to have collapsed.

Water conservancy is a complicated science. It requires detailed study, careful surveys, and over-all planning. It involves intimate knowledge of river flow, flood history, silt content, topography, soil characteristics, ground-water tables, weather patterns, and the needs of surrounding areas. But Peking has no over-all plan. Technical direction often does not fit the actual working condition. Quality is always less important than quantity and speed. For larger projects the steel and cement available are never enough. For smaller projects, only earth and stone are used. Everywhere substitutes and shortcuts are favored—and praised as "technical innovations."

The dam fiasco touched off an orgy of canal-digging in 1958-1959. Peking finally realized that the much-vaunted big dam projects, which had so impressed foreign visitors, often turned out to be mere monuments to stupidity. So in 1958, it turned its attention from big dams to regional irrigation projects consisting of medium and small dams, wells, and, especially, canals. In August 1958 the Party Central Committee announced a stupendous project: a network of canals criss-crossing the entire China Plains and linking the three great rivers, the Yellow, the Yangtze, and the

Huai. The canals were to be of five sizes, ranging from small irrigation canals to large ones accommodating 3,000-ton ships. The canals would serve as inland waterways, as a gigantic reservoir, and as a water-regulating system to bring water from South to North China.

When the plan was announced millions of peasants had already been digging for months. By early 1960 half of the canals in some provinces were completed. But after months of confused experience, the small canals were found inadequate. They were too numerous, creating problems for future farm mechanization. They were too small, so that they served little use at times of flood or drought. The village *kanpu* in charge of the digging were unclear about the measurements, and they varied greatly. In the winter of 1958 the plan was revised. Small canals already dug were abandoned or filled up. Medium and large canals were dug at relocated sites.

The frenzied canal digging created problems undreamed of in the Communist philosophy. As every square foot of agricultural China has been used for cultivation, the canals took away much of the valuable farmland. They leaked badly, in many cases with 60 percent of the water escaping. In many areas where the ground-water table was near the surface, deeper canals drained the land, thus creating an artificial drought. In other areas, mainly in dry North China, where the ground-water table is low and the soil is unleached, water leaking from the canals raised the ground-water table, thus accentuating capillary action through the lime-rich earth. This brought up harmful salts and alkalies from the subsoil that formed a crust on the soil surface after evaporation, thereby turning formerly dry but good farmland into badlands. Such effects are slow but pernicious. By 1959 the *People's Daily* sensed something was wrong: "During the past one or two years, the alkalization of much soil in many irrigated areas in the North is spreading." But the canal digging went on. In 1960, the same paper again reported that saltpetre, which normally appears only in serious drought, had affected millions of acres of farmland. In

April 1961, the *Kuang Ming Daily* said: "Arable land is continuously shrinking and alkali soil spreading." In August 1962, the Party's authoritative mouthpiece *Red Flag* reported that nearly 20 million acres of farmland in Manchuria and in North, Northwest and Central China had turned alkaline, and that the peasants were unwilling to till the swiftly alkalizing farms which soon became barren land, thus reducing the already limited arable land of the country.

In a country like China, where the water balance has already been upset by centuries of intensive cultivation and overpopulation, the best place to store water is not behind big dams nor in sloppy canals, but underground near where it falls. Not surprisingly, Peking also had some grandiose plans along these lines. The great vision, which today is no longer mentioned, consisted of a number of bold reforestation projects, among which were two "Green Great Walls." One was to be a 1000-mile protective windbreaker, starting from the China-Korea border, winding along the China Coast, and ending at the mouth of the Yangtze. The other, equally long, was to be a forest screen to shield against the sand from Outer Mongolia. It was to start from the vicinity of the Old Silk Road in Kansu, cut across the sand dunes of the Alashan Desert and the Ordos Desert in Inner Mongolia, and end at the great bend of the Yellow River.

A great campaign began in early 1956 to "green up China in 12 years." It would be easy: "If everyone of the country's 500 million peasants plants two trees each year, we shall have one billion trees in a single year." In twelve years, Peking believed that it could change its arid land, barren hills, and deserts into 160 million acres of sylvan delight. So millions of school children were ordered to plant trees all over China. In most cases the entire program consisted of digging holes, inserting cuttings or saplings, and watering them for a few days. Then the human sea surged in other directions on other campaigns, and the trees were left to die of thirst.

While reforestation surged up and died off, deforestation grew more systematic. Besides forest fires and tree diseases, artificial deforestation has been on the increase, especially since 1958. Farm cooperatives and communes have set their cattle to graze on saplings, or chopped down roadside trees or whole forests for timber or to "open virgin land." During the 1958 steel-making campaign many mountains were stripped bare for fuel. In one swoop a commune in Kwangtung close-shaved 13 forest-covered hills. Timber industries in forest areas, led by quota-conscious *kanpu*, competed with each other in cutting down big and small trees without replanting. Even saplings were not left to protect the soil, which soon became barren. Since the 1958 Great Leap the Chinese Communists have been too busy making steel, digging canals and fighting calamities to worry about reforestation. But deforestation is going on more than ever, reducing the already poor moisture-capturing capacity of the soil, extending erosion areas, heightening excessive run-off of rain water, and worsening floods and drought for generations to come.

The foolish squandering of resources and manpower on big haphazard projects before 1958, and the wanton canal-digging since then, deteriorated the water and soil in China's richest farming regions. It is no coincidence that the worst droughts of the past several years have been found in the very provinces where millions dug canals from 1957–1959. The water-distribution system of the entire China Plains was supposed to be reshaped by these projects. It certainly has been. The hydrologic cycle in China is now upset by faulty water conservancy and deforestation. Soviet Russia talks of changing nature. Communist China has unwittingly done it.

The lessons, repeated many times in every province, finally hit home. Minister of Water Conservancy Fu Tso-yi, who boasted in 1952: "The danger of disastrous floods which were a scourge to the Chinese people for thousands of years has been fundamentally removed," told the Congress in 1959: "For the past two years, since I have been sick, I took little part in actual work. This is therefore what I wanted to say about water conservancy and power." A government directive that year admitted: "The quality of many engineering works is bad, and thus they do not fulfill their function." The *People's Daily* in 1960 said: "Irrigation is an art which demands study." Minister of Agriculture Liao Lu-yen confessed: "Water conservancy has been in name only." The Party Central Committee's official mouth-piece *Red Flag* lamented: "Irrigation and drainage facilities were unsystematic, administrative techniques improper, land was damaged by wrong ways of irrigation, and soil became alkaline."

While food coming out of the earth is decreasing, crops already harvested are spoiled and wasted. For centuries, wasting food was a moral sin in China. Under the Communists, much food is unnecessarily spoiled. Many granaries are haphazardly built. Others are converted from decrepit temples or ancestral shrines. Some are without doors and windows although all have fences or walls to prevent theft. An investigation one year revealed serious conditions in grain storage in seven provinces. In Kwangsi, of the 740,000 tons of grain inspected, 83 percent was spoiled by worms. Grain stored in one granary in Shensi was 30 percent mildewed and 40 percent sprouting. In 1958, 700,000 tons of corn in Kirin was found to contain 30 percent moisture, and 70 percent of 5 million tons of grain had to be fumigated. The *kanpu* in charge of food supply in the communes are nicknamed by the peasants: "Five Don't Knows." They don't know how much grain is harvested, don't know how much is eaten, don't know how much is in the commune kitchen, don't know how much is stored in the granaries, and don't know how long the store will last. When the famine became acute in late 1960, a *People's Daily* editorial revealed that the total amount of grain stored in Communist China was not known. It launched a national campaign to weigh the stored grain, explaining: "We shall only know the real situation if we weigh and clearly account for the food grain collected." Since then Peking has been importing grain. The real situation, apparently, is now known.

The efficiency of China's farm labor, low in the old days due to a lack of modern means, is lowered further by Peking's administrative epilepsy. The Chinese peasants have always worked hard without being told. Each knew what to do and how to do it with the limited means they had. Today, they are told how to plow, when to sow, and what to plant. They are pressed into a robot army maneuvered with human-sea strategy and commando tactics. In the winter of 1955, many millions were "volunteered" into constructing dams and dikes. Next summer, when it was found that subsidiary farm work had slumped to half its normal amount, they were shunted back to the fields. To remedy the situation the Party in some provinces ordered up to 40 percent of the peasants to stick to subsidiary farm work, even though drought was spreading. Great quantities of rice and sweet potatoes were damaged by the drought when left unharvested. When this was discovered the peasants were hurried back to plant more food crops. Meanwhile, the half-finished dams and dikes left by the peasants were damaged by floods. In 1958 some 60 million people were told to make village steel. This created a labor shortage on the farms. In many places fertilizer was not put into the fields and rice was not harvested in time. In Hopei province 40 percent of the crop land that should have been sown was not. In North China cotton and potato picking were not done on time. Elsewhere 650,000 tons of tobacco leaves were plucked but unsorted. The damp leaves started to spoil. For three winters up to 70 million peasants dug canals. Then they turned to fighting flood and drought. The number of calamity-fighters in recent years exceeded 10 million in each of the seriously affected provinces. When the fertilizer drive was on, 80 million had to forage for manure. When there was a coal shortage, 20 million were sent to local hills to dig dubious coal.

This madcap use of farm labor created another unnatural disaster: the "weed calamity"—a term coined by the Chinese Communists to denote fields unplanted or unattended, which are covered with weeds. The weed calamity began in 1959. By the fall of 1960 weeds were reported in at least 13 provinces from northern Manchuria to Kiangsu, covering one-fifth of China's farmland. In many areas weeds were taller than the crops. In Shantung one-third of the farmland was covered by weeds, which in places grew so thick that "man cannot walk into the fields." So the Ministry of Agriculture sounded another alarm to fight the weeds. Peasants, city dwellers, students, civil servants, and even soldiers were ordered to forsake whatever they were doing and hand-pick the weeds in the fields. In Hopei province six million were mobilized; in Shantung, more than seven million. In Liao-ning two-thirds of the students and civil servants from the cities were diverted to the countryside. In Shansi, half of the total farm labor was used.

While weeds plagued the farmlands, grazing grass and hay became increasingly short in the pasture lands of nine provinces. By 1961 some cattle-raising communes found the shortages had reached as much as 75 percent of the fodder required. The *People's Daily* repeatedly indicated that the reasons were natural calamities topped by spoilage due to lack of peasant incentive. But it seems that the more the peasants work under the Party's blundering policy, the less they produce. And the less they produce, the more they have to work. The end result is this unique famine.

At present an ordinary resident in show cities like Peking and Shanghai gets a small ration in rice or flour of inferior quality, plus a monthly allotment of about half a pound of pork, three ounces sugar, and three ounces edible oil. For a few vegetables, he has to line up as early as 3 A.M. Eggs, poultry and fish have virtually disappeared. The peasant in the communes gets much less: usually two bowls of semi-liquid gruel or paste made from bad cereals, gritty flour, or sweet potatoes for each meal.

Since 1959, Communist China has officially ordered the eating of rice husks, bean waste, potato leaves, pumpkin flowers, wild plants, and algae. During the past few winters, each province sent a half to three million peasants and city residents to forage for wild plants in the hills. Newspapers praised the high nutritive value of wild plants and recommended recipes for these and other novel foods. Rice straw, soaked in lime solution, dried, ground into powder and mixed with flour, is made into cakes served in restaurants upon surrender of ration coupons.

China's streets and villages used to be cluttered with friendly dogs and cats. Today dogs and cats have virtually disappeared. So have such common birds as sparrows, pigeons, crows, and cuckoos. Some 2.2 billion sparrows were systematically exterminated as predatory birds in a nation-wide campaign. But the killing of this bird was banned when an upsurge in predatory insects resulted. The appearance of a wild rabbit or a crow in China today is an occasion for a mass hunt for extra food. Vegetables, such as sweet potatoes and turnips in suburban fields, must be guarded throughout the night, or they will be stolen by city people who raid the fields and sometimes eat the loot on the spot. Beggars openly wait by restaurant tables for leftover food. Often they grab food from the patrons. Policemen merely shrug at such petty crimes. The black market is growing, supplied by corrupt Communists who control food supply centers. These rings sometimes have their own sampans and armed escorts. Communist China used to ban food parcels from Hong Kong and Macao, then permitted a limited number. In late 1960 they lifted the restrictions. Immediately the tiny Hong Kong post office was buried under a daily avalanche of 50,000 food parcels from frantic relatives. By mid-1962 more than 200,000 parcels were sent daily. The little British colony now has 1,000 firms specializing in sending food parcels to China. Hong Kong Communist newspapers not long ago eagerly quoted a Japanese visitor to China who said: "I did not see any hunger in Peking." On the same pages where this story appeared several firms advertised to deliver food parcels to China "Fast, Fast, Fast!" and with "Rocket Speed!"

A normal man in Asia requires a minimum of 2,300 calories of food daily. In food-short India, according to a United Nations survey, the daily average food intake is 2,000 calories. In pre-war China it was 2,234 calories. In Taiwan it is 2,310 calories. Most of the peasants in Communist China, who must work long hours at hard labor, have been getting about 1,000 calories.

Like most Asian countries, China has always had its public-health problems. Modern doctors number only one to every 10,000 people. Except in big cities, people have to depend on the traditional herb doctors, who are good at certain ailments but inadequate for contagious diseases and surgery. In certain rural areas diseases like schistosomiasis (a chronic intestinal disease with enlargement of the liver and spleen), hook-worm, and beri-beri were common. But the bulk of the population have fared well through a strong immunity and wise eating habits. Except for fresh fruits, the Chinese never ate uncooked food. Water was always boiled and food eaten piping hot.

During the first few years of their rule, the Chinese Communists did try to improve public health. Notable were the campaigns of fly-swatting, rat-exterminating and street-sweeping, which were amply reported by foreign visitors. But since the mid-fifties and especially since the Great Leap, conditions have changed drastically. Drinking water in the communes is no longer boiled because of the fuel shortage, although in many villages water is often taken from polluted creeks and ponds. Manure, green compost, and garbage are handled indiscriminately with bare hands during the fertilizer drives. Newspapers often praised fertilizer heroes who, as a dedicated gesture, refused to wash their hands after handling manure. Collective working and living without adequate sanitary precautions resulted in widespread food poisoning and epidemics.

According to recent refuge information, one out of three or four peasants have dropsy. People are used to peasants working in the fields suddenly collapsing and dropping dead. Industrial and traffic accidents have jumped up due to malnutrition. A government technician from Nanchang said that in his bureau one-fifth of the civil servants had liver inflammation or infectious hepatitis. A nurse from Peking said one-tenth of her colleagues were hospitalized. Hospitals in all cities are full of patients suffering from hepatitis and other diseases, but only serious cases are admitted. Although tuberculosis is spreading widely, patients of this disease are not even treated because it is less alarming than other ailments. Many women have stopped menstruating. Many babies are born dead. Families of people who die in cities have to make reservations at the busy crematoriums. Those who supply firewood get priority.

These grisly eyewitness accounts are supported by the official press in its guarded but nevertheless revealing stories. In July 1959 the *Honan Peasant's Daily*, a provincial paper not even allowed outside Honan but sometimes smuggled to Hong Kong, revealed that many peasants died from malnutrition plus overwork that summer. During two summer weeks that year, 367,000 peasants collapsed and 29,000 died in the fields; 60,000 peasants collapsed after six days and nights of flood-fighting with little sleep or rest. Other smuggled papers revealed that during similar periods 7,000 peasants died in the fields in Kiangsi, 8,000 in Kiansu and 13,000 in Chekiang.

Epidemics have been increasing in China since 1959, although little is known about them outside. The Communist press at first successfully covered up the situation but subsequently has been making partial admissions of "seasonal contagious diseases." The Minister of Health reported that during 1959 a total of 70 million cases of schistosomiasis, filariasis (parasitic worms in the blood), hookworm, and malaria were treated. The Vice Minister of Health said that influenza, measles, diphtheria and spinal meningitis were spreading at water conservancy sites, in commune nurseries and primary schools. The People's Congress in April 1960 revealed that kala-azar (infection of the liver, spleen, and bone marrow, especially those of children) was spreading; that ke-shan (a disease caused by infected water) erupted rapidly in Inner Mongolia; and that the Great Leap was causing serious chemical poisoning in industrial cities. In a circular that year, an emergency public health committee urged better handling of manure, garbage, and dirty water, and warned that careless handling had spread "all kinds of diseases."

Actual epidemic conditions have never been publicly reported. They can only be gathered from press reports about large numbers of public-health teams rushing from cities into unnamed rural areas on short notice. In the spring of 1960, some 500,000 city residents in eight provinces were sent to the countryside on emergency public health missions. In the summer of that year 110,000 were sent to the villages in Szechwan, 60,000 in Hunan, and 2,000 teams in Fukien. At the same time an unnamed alarm was sounded in Tientsin, where 3 million were checked by many hastily trained "epidemic spotters."

These teams consist mostly of students and civil servants, including the entire faculty and student body of medical schools. They are all labeled "medical workers," although their work is mainly to assist in the simplest sanitary measures. One team helped to build 51 primitive lavatories for a commune. Another supplied reed covers for the doorless tents of construction workers on the sub-zero Wei River banks. Others inspected commune dining halls, tidied up fertilizer receptacles, installed crude filtering facilities for polluted water. Special achievements were praised: at one construction site where 3,000 peasants lived, "not a single case of contagious disease was found"; in a county in Anhwei "no epidemic has broken out since the end of 1959." One commune kitchen in Peking received a citation because no contagious disease had ever originated there. The repeated mention in the press of rats, flies, mosquitoes, water fleas, manure parasites, and the word "rest" as a cure told much that was not said.

According to refugees, cholera killed 30,000-50,000 in 1961 in Kwangtung alone. After the cholera spread to Hong Kong, Macao, Indonesia and North Borneo, Peking finally admitted the epidemic to the Geneva Red Cross. Today Peking is worried, not so much about the people's suffering as the loss of manpower. The basic rule was sternly laid down by the *People's Daily* late in 1959:

"The point of departure is production. It must be our unwavering determination in fighting pests and extinguishing diseases that this work shall be subservient to production. . . . Public health as a purpose in itself—a bourgeois way of thinking—should not be permitted."

Agriculture in China *can* be modernized and the lot of the peasants *can* be improved in spite of natural limitations. But because of these limitations the process can only be a tedious one without any dramatic overnight returns. A strong, stable regime with a level-headed plan could have, through sane and just economic measures, effected a land redistribution. The vast number of small, cut-up farm lots should be integrated into bigger farms of a size more economical for cultivation. Only when this is done can one talk about mechanization. Even then, careful research will be required to devise lighter, water-resistant farm machines that fit the peculiar terraced fields and wet paddies of the country. There is tremendous long-range work to be done in soil research, afforestation, and water conservancy. This can be done either through fast foreign aid and investments, or through a long-term development of light industry, making use of agricultural raw materials without depriving the people of their food and livelihood. To convert a sophisticated agrarian civilization into a modern industrial one requires more than mere revolutionary fervor.

VII BACKYARD FURNACES—
AN EXERCISE IN METAPHYSICS

To CREATE THE INSTANT PARADISE, PEKING BELIEVES IN instant industrialization. A highly industrialized nation is based on rich mineral resources. China, however, is poor in all the major minerals except coal. It has enough iron for present needs but very little oil and uranium. With the best development, China can never compete with the United States, the U.S.S.R., or Western Europe in heavy industry. But to meet its modern needs China must industrialize. The problem is how.

The iron and steel industry, being the backbone of industrialization, has been given top priority by Peking. It is claimed that China has 12 billion tons of iron ore in reserve, sufficient for an annual output of 100 million tons of iron and steel for the coming fifty years. Much steel is needed for industrial and agricultural machines, trucks, ships, power plants, and armament. But during the First Five-Year Plan, China's machine industry used only 30 percent of the domestic steel, as much machinery had to be imported. During the Second Five-Year Plan, while the need for machinery increased, imports from the U.S.S.R. decreased. Thus the need for steel became more acute. Considering its size, China has very few railroads, which nevertheless must shoulder 80 percent of the long-distance domestic transportation. To have as many railroads as the U.S.S.R. had in 1937, China needs 6 million tons of rails alone, not to say steel for locomotives and other accessories.

Under these circumstances, Mao Tse-tung personally devised

the famed backyard furnaces. Believing that mind could overcome matter and that science was "useless superstition" in face of
mass fervor, he used the human-sea tactic to make up for the lack
of technology and equipment. The whole thing was in essence an
exercise in metaphysics, reminiscent of ancient Taoist alchemy
with modern trimmings.

The backyard furnaces, a novel idea undreamed of by old-
fashioned blacksmiths or modern steel-makers, began in the
summer of 1958 when Peking threw everything into the melting
pot to forge a poor man's steel empire. Some 80 million farmers,
factory workers, civil servants, students, housewives, children,
barbers, cooks, watch repairmen, ivory carvers, and cobblers were
ordered to dig ore, smelt iron, and make steel. Tiny, crude mud
furnaces mushroomed all over China in villages and on barren
hillsides, in crowded city squares, factory and government compounds, military barracks, beautiful gardens, and humble back-
yards. The official *Hsinhua News Agency* depicted an inspiring
if incongruous scene: "Molten steel . . . flows from furnaces operated in barber shops, laundries,* photo studios and stores." By
November the Chinese landscape had a touch of Dante's Inferno,
with 60 million people toiling day and night beside 2 million do-it-
your-self furnaces, and 20 million people marching into the hills
to mine iron ore and coal. The women of Chengchow built 93 furnaces in the streets. In Paotow, 70,000 students were sent on
mining expeditions. One team of 2,300 marched 150 miles. Possessing a total of 30 shovels, the youths had to dig iron ore with
their bare hands in 20-degree-below weather. To carry back the
ore, they used school bags, caps, clothes, and ropes. Throughout
the country, pots, pans, kettles, kitchen knives, incense urns, win-
dow grills, door clasps, staircases, nails, screws—everything made
of iron—were requisitioned for the furnaces by "treasure-hunting"
teams.

---

* Despite the world-famed Chinese laundrymen abroad, before the 1958
communes, China had no commercial laundries except a few shirt laundries
introduced from the West.

After revising the production target upward eight times in eight months, the National Statistical Bureau announced that in 1958 China produced 11.08 million tons of steel and 13.69 tons of iron, more than double the output of 1957. Peking declared with pride: "The capitalist countries needed seven to thirteen years to double their iron and steel production. In China, we need only one year." The achievement was attributed to the "daring thoughts, daring words and daring acts" of the masses breaking through "old superstitions that the smelting of iron and steel belongs only to the aloof few." Mao Tse-tung's own comment bordered on the mystical: "Many things seem quite strange. Sometimes we don't have them, or very little of them. But when we do want them we get plenty. . . . We have doubled the food production this year, and may again double it next year. Steel is just the same."

But the elation was short-lived. The 80 million amateurs, driven by the Party to forage for anything that resembled black rock and throw it into furnaces the size of bath tubs, created some strange products. Due to the coke shortage, unwashed and untested anthracite and charcoal were used for fuel. As coal in China, especially that south of the Yangtze, has high sulfur content, and as 70-80 percent of the sulfur in iron comes from coal, the "indigenous pig iron" produced contained 4 to 60 times more sulfur than the standard permitted in the West. Sulfur in iron cannot be eliminated in modern Bessemer converters when it is made into steel, much less in backyard converters at low temperature.

Much of the primitive iron was sent to Peking's modern converters and became "steel." Some of it cracked in the rolling mills. Some of it survived the rolling and was made into machinery, which soon disintegrated. The big steel centers were not only getting bad iron, they were also starved for raw materials that were being diverted to the amateur smelters. During the height of this drive railroads gave top priority to iron and steel transportation. But as coal had to be moved from north to south and agricultural products had to be moved everywhere, the sudden

change of the transportation pattern resulted in a massive traffic
jam. In late 1958, 34 million tons of coal, 4 million tons of village
iron and large quantities of industrial raw materials, grain, and
consumer goods were stuck without transportation. With more
than one-tenth of the population diverted to the furnaces, farm
production slumped. In the cities people found no one to cut
their hair, cobble their shoes or repair their plumbing.

Many of the primitive earthen furnaces turned into mud piles
after a few days' rain. A furnace in Honan was nationally publicized because "it can operate even in rain or cold weather."
Many thousands were maimed or killed by exploding furnaces.
In Peking alone, sixteen hospitals set aside special wards and
doctors to treat steel-making casualties but, as the *Peking Evening News* reported, "within a few days after the forming of the
emergency network, these hospital beds became insufficient."

By early 1959 Peking was forced to make a total retreat from
the backyard furnaces. The *People's Daily,* which earlier had condemned critics who said the project was useless, wasteful, and
backward, and had insisted that the "indigenous steel" was good
enough "even for ball-bearings," admitted that the stuff was
"neither steel nor iron . . . worth not a cent." It further conceded:
"Production in the factories became chaotic," and "We must face
the problems frankly: last year's small furnaces could not produce
pig iron." Hsia Yi-hun, a delegate to the People's Congress, while
dutifully praising the Great Leap, described what had happened
around the backyard furnaces as "remote from reality." Thus
ended the most wasteful and backward project in industrial history. It required fifty to sixty man-days to make a ton of pig iron,
which turned out to be of little use.

In 1959, Communist China scrapped the 2 million backyard
furnaces and started to remedy the situation, but only partially.
A couple of thousand of the better furnaces were retained for use,
and called "small high furnaces." Ores, coke, and coal were to be
washed "if possible," and the washing was to be improved by
using water troughs instead of buckets. Pig iron containing not

more than 0.2 percent sulfur was allowed into the converters (a low standard); that with 0.3 to 0.5 percent was to be de-sulfured (an expensive re-processing); and that with higher content must be returned to the furnace. There was complete silence about "indigenous steel." In 1961 the total capacity of "small high furnaces" was double that of the modern furnaces, but the pig iron produced from them was of dubious quality.

Apparently, even pig iron and steel from the most modern centers in China often fall short of standard. Peking admitted recently that the ordinary Bessemer converter process "at present is still not perfectly mastered." One problem is the quality of raw materials. Party *kanpu* are now ordered to check ores and pig iron at the sources, but most of the checking is done empirically, without any chemical analysis. Shanghai's modern mills, which produce about one-tenth of the country's steel, get their pig iron from thirteen provinces. It would be an impossible task to use modern analytical methods to check the varying qualities of pig iron from each province, town and furnace. Thus the steel made from local pig iron still contains one to three times more sulfur than the regular standard. Anshan, the leading steel center, although it produces its own pig iron, must rely on raw materials supplied by seven hundred big and small enterprises from fifteen provinces. Even in this best-equipped center, iron ore from distant places was often thrown into the furnaces unchecked. Only in 1961 did Anshan send men to the port of Dairen to check the ore before it was transported to the furnaces.

In 1958 Peking claimed the ability to produce more than 500 types of steel and more than 6,000 kinds of steel parts. Despite the statistics, China can only mass-produce ordinary carbon steel and silicon and manganese alloy steel. In Shanghai, silicon steel and seamless steel tubes are made from inferior pig iron, so that flaws and blowholes appear in the products. The Third Steel Plant there, which has the reputation of producing many first-class products, was found to waste 297 pounds of pig iron in producing every ton of steel in 1959. In 1961 its workers were dumbfounded when taken to the rolling mills to see the steel ingots they had produced disintegrating under the rollers.

The Anshan situation is similar. Besides inferior pig iron from its own furnaces, products sent to its rolling mills were often mixed up, so that heavy rails erroneously treated had to be used for other purposes, and light rails had to be made from seamless steel tubes. In 1961 silicon steel from Anshan was found to contain too little silicon and too much carbon. In a major steel plant in Chungking, it was found that 47 percent of the pig iron was wasted during the first quarter of 1961. When manganese was put into the furnace, sulfur rose to the surface. The surprised workers finally discovered that the manganese used was impure.

Alloy steels, containing precise quantities of chromium, nickel, tungsten, manganese, vanadium, molybdenum, silicon, or copper, are essential in making modern machinery, precision instruments, and structural materials. China does not have enough electric furnaces; much of what little alloy steel it produces has to come from converters, in which it is technically difficult to regulate the alloy composition. The problem is made more serious because of inferior raw materials, technical shortcuts and unscientific management. On the whole, Communist China's iron and steel industry has progressed quantitatively, but qualitatively it has been a costly experiment.

China's coal reserve is abundant. Early European geologists estimated the reserve as 1 trillion tons. In 1945 the National Geological Survey placed the reserve at only 284 billion tons, an estimate believed to be more accurate. Peking, however, still clings to the 1-trillion-ton figure. Its *Geology Monthly* claimed that an annual coal output of 1 billion tons could last at least fifty years. Pre-Communist coal production reached a peak of 62 million tons in 1942, about the same level as the Communists reached in 1952 before the First Five-Year Plan. Annual production was said to have reached 130 million tons in 1957; 270 million tons in 1958; 348 million tons in 1959; and 400 million tons in 1960.

If these figures are reliable, there should not be the serious coal shortage that has developed since 1953, even counting the increased industrial demand. Paradoxically, vying with industry is civilian coal consumption, which has increased because traditional fuels like firewood and dried straw, grass, and plants have been diverted to other uses. A major factor in coal shortage seems to be the steady decline in coal quality, first revealed in 1953, and the natural result of the emulation drives, which force ever higher quotas on the miners. The situation was so bad that 100-pound stones were often found in coal delivered to industry. In 1955 the coal delivered by four leading mines alone contained 820,000 tons of rock. Rock content of coal from the famous Fushun mines in Manchuria reached 40 percent of total production that year. Ash content also rose sharply, as in the coal from these leading mines: Huainan, 21 percent; Pinghsiang, 24 percent; and Peipiao, 38 percent. The worst was the Lungfeng mine in Fushun. According to Peking's *Daily Worker,* from 1952 to 1955 its production increased by 96 per cent, but rock content increased by 209 percent.

The *People's Daily* lamented that though the quantity of coal had been increased, the damage done to the state economy was grievous. The Ministry of Coal Industry, having no intention of becoming the Ministry of Stone Quarries, issued an urgent order in late 1955 that if a single piece of rock with a diameter bigger than 5 inches was found in a carload coming out of any mine, that carload must be declared waste coal. Since some mines paid the miners partly with waste coal, the miners deliberately produced this type of "waste coal."

The situation got worse in 1956. The shocked *People's Daily* reported that in one delivery of 200 tons of coal, 100 tons were stone. The Ministry of Coal Industry said that in spite of repeated instructions and warnings, "the low quality of coal, a problem of all the past years, has not been improved." Po I-po, then chairman of the State Planning Commission, told the People's Congress that rock and ash content in coal were "steadily rising." In 1959 the Ministry warned that if ash content rose 1 percent that year, it would equal to a drop of 2.86 percent in pig iron production; and if rock content rose 1 percent, it would equal to 2 million tons of rock in 70,000 railroad cars cruising all over China throughout the year.

Inferior coal not only creates bad iron and steel, but also wastes transportation space, increases industrial accidents, and causes a chain-reaction of qualitative deterioration in other industries. The situation was so serious that, in June 1959, six national conferences were held in an attempt to arrest the downward trend in the quality of steel, coal, coke, machinery, metallurgy and consumer goods.

When the Great Leap was proclaimed and millions were told to scratch for coal, the increase of ash and rock content was accelerated. In Szechwan, where the coal seams are less than 1½ feet thick, a large number of people manually scraped for coal in 2,200 "indigenous mines." The total number of these mines numbered 100,000 in 1958 but because they had no ventilation and pumping facilities, deep digging was impossible even where the seams were thick. It was this kind of coal which ended up in the backyard furnaces. The best kinds, reserved for export, still appeared not good enough, as with the coal offered to Japan. In 1961 the Yamata Steel Company said coal samples from China were too high in ash and sulfur content. The Japanese found that coking coal offered them was of "unexpectedly poor quality."

During the Great Leap, normal management, safety measures, surveys and planning, were not practiced even in major coal mines. Due to a timber shortage in 1959–1960, pit-props were made of concrete, bamboo and waste timber glued together. The number of accidents that resulted was never reported, but by 1961 there was a desperate search for old-fashioned timber to prop up the roofs of the biggest, most modern mines in Kailan, Fushun, Fengfeng, and Fushin. In many provinces, shock troops for "emergency tree-cutting and timber-transportation" were organized, and the only railroad in Fukien was set aside to transport pit-props.

In 1957 the *Daily Worker* revealed that money earmarked for simple safety measures was spent on machinery to increase production, that miners in Fushun were forced to work sixteen hours continuously, and that "many miners suffer from tuberculosis, rheumatism and other diseases." The situation grew worse during the Great Leap. After repeated accidents the Chiaotso mines checked and found "8,800 factors of industrial accidents." Liaoyuan mines in Manchuria abolished the system of returning leftover dynamite and fuses to the warehouse, so that unattended explosives littered inside the mines caused many explosions. A girl student who escaped from a mine in Meihsien, Kwangtung, reported that in December 1958 mine tunnels, up to two miles long without pit-props, collapsed after heavy rains. Of the 45,000 people in the mines, 30,000 were entombed. In 1961 the *People's Daily* belatedly disclosed that in 1960 a serious gas explosion occurred in a Fushun mine "when material conditions deteriorated and at a time of mental depression," putting the mine out of action for five months. Such conditions hint at the reason why coal production in modern mines, even according to official statistics, decreased quantitatively from 1958 through 1960. The situation had not appreciably improved by 1962.

Despite optimistic claims of great "possible reserves" which so far have not been proved, China is apparently an oil-poor country. At present it has three major oil fields in remote Northwest China, and several small ones in other provinces operated by primitive methods. The most important oil field is Yumen, Kansu, first developed under the Nationalists in 1939, when production was small because of the war. Great enthusiasm was voiced by the Communists when they took over, but, as they subsequently revealed, Chinese and Russian experts did some faulty drilling into the domed strata, causing natural gas to escape and oil to remain underground without pressure. Water-injection, an expensive method, was used in 1954 but discontinued a year later. Many problems face the Yumen field, which is at the edge of the Gobi Desert. Oil wells need much water but Yumen's annual rainfall is only 4 inches. It is bitter cold in winter so that freezing, dust and paraffin (15 percent) in the oil often combine to clog up the wells. By 1956 Communist fervor seemed to have waned. As the *People's Daily* said: "People are desperate and feel that the whole work was badly planned and was built up in a haphazard way." From 1953 to 1957 many efforts were spent in drilling, but progress was slow due to technical errors and poor machinery. Because of the high expenses involved, in oil development, normally only the best equipment is used. But as in other industries, Peking used substitutes. In 1957 some 2,400 tons of discarded equipment was renovated and put back to use, including 43 percent of the drill-heads. During the Great Leap 13,000 skilled workers and 18,000 tons of equipment were inexplicably diverted from Yumen to other oil fields. Left to "mass management," Yumen's production slumped. Some wells stopped flowing "owing to a neglect of management." This condition was not remedied until late 1961 when routine management was re-established and 400 repairs were made in a single month. Peking's *Daily Worker* then reported that with the improvement the workers were now careful not to put an unclean pipe or an unfit pump to a well.

Another major oil field is Koramai, Sinkiang, near the Russian border. Production began in 1958 with a daily output of 1,400 barrels. It has a 91-mile pipeline to a small automatic plant in Wusu. Progress has been slow, and since 1961 reports about Koramai have dwelt mainly on the bitter weather and the hardships of the workers, who had to forage for wild plants for food. The third major field is Lenghu, in the Tsaidam Basin in Chinghai. Its wells are shallow but the oil is good, yielding about 4,300 barrels daily. It is still being developed, with five small refineries in the area.

Much of the oil produced in China is synthetic oil distilled from shale. The biggest synthetic oil plant is in Fushun, Manchuria, first built by the Japanese, and another new plant has been built in Maoming, Kwangtung. China has much shale, but its quality is inferior. During the Great Leap, Peking claimed the construction of "1,000 synthetic oil plants," most of which were sheds with a stove and a blower. Some even dispensed with a blower, using a fan instead. Except in the few modern plants, the product is not true synthetic oil made through the hydrogenation process, but primitive dry-distillation from peat, pine roots, birch bark, and coke. In 1960 the emphasis was still on the "indigenous plants" but by 1961 a discreet silence fell over them. Mention was only made of the few modern plants.

Despite great demand, Communist China has produced and will continue to produce very little oil. Most of the oil is in Sinkiang, Kansu and Chinghai, three remote provinces where water shortages, sub-zero winters, and transportation create big problems. There are no extensive pipelines, except a very few short ones which must be heated in winter. Peking is unwilling to invest much in the oil industry because of its slow returns and the expert technology required. In 1961 China produced a total of 17.63 million barrels of oil, only 0.67 percent of the United States total.

Many efforts have been spent on power plants, which are faced with similar problems and plagued by the same Great Leap confusion as in the case of steel and oil. Little information on Peking's power capacity has been published in the past several years, probably due to the acute power shortage and the deteriorating quality of coal, which produces three-fourths of China's electric power. There is great potential in hydroelectricity because of China's mountainous terrain and swift rivers, and the Communists have been trying to build power plants at most of the dam sites. But these plants require huge investments, and their benefits can only be reaped many years later. For its instant needs, Peking is forced to rely on thermal electric plants using coal. Thermal plants are less costly and can be built faster, but they require more elaborate machinery and superior alloy metals, both of which China is unable to produce in quantity. Furthermore, they consume a vast amount of coal. In the long run thermal plants are more expensive. Thus after thirteen years, Communist China is still in a dilemma whether to give priority to thermal or hydroelectric power plants.

Besides setbacks caused by jerry-built reservoirs, Peking suffers from shortages of steel, cement, skilled labor, and power equipment. As a result, many dams are without power plants. Many power plants have generators installed but without other essential electrical accessories, thus producing a fraction of the planned power or no power at all. The net result is that hydroelectric plants are operating at less than 70 percent of capacity—when there is enough water. Uneven rainfall during the past few years has brought additional woes.

During the Great Leap, Peking also promoted "indigenous methods" to "create electricity by the whole population." In 1958 the masses were said to have built 4,334 "hydroelectric power plants." But they had a total capacity of 130,000 kilowatts. Many of them were turned by wooden wheels beside hillside streams. They were still used in 1960 but completely abandoned the next year. A nation-wide shortage of electricity was reported in late 1958, resulting in severe economies in lighting and adding a visual gloom to the cities. The situation grew so serious that low-quality coal had to be used in many thermal plants. In 1961 the generators in Fushun, a major coal-producing center, had to consume briquettes—a mixture of coal dust, mud and ground rock. It is a scientific mystery how, with this method, the amount of coal required to produce each kilowatt-hour of electricity was allegedly reduced time and again.

In power production figures alone, Peking has made considerable progress; the output increased nearly 10 times between 1949–1959. However, this increase is still less than half of that achieved by the Japanese in Manchuria between 1933–1943. Actually, percentage increases are misleading, as it all depends on the absolute figures of the base period. A better measurement is per capita power consumption. In 1959 Communist China produced 41.5 billion kilowatt-hours. For a population of 600 million, the consumption was 69 kilowatt-hours per capita. Compared to per capita power consumption of some other areas in the same year, Nationalist Taiwan produced 4.9 times, Japan 15.5 times, the U.S.S.R. 18.4 times, Great Britain 33.4 times, and the United States 64.7 times that of Communist China. Cheap and abundant power for Communist China is still in the remote future.

The machine industry appears impressive at a cursory glance, but it is actually the weakest link in Peking's industrialization. China had 63,000 workers in its machine industry in 1947, 300,000 in 1949, and 3 million in 1960. The development of the machine industry would be rapid in modern China under any regime, but the crucial point is *how* the industry is developed.

Communist China has some 100 machine factories built or enlarged with Russian aid, plus many small ones. It has been making a large quantity of machines. It has also been making precision and heavy machines. The two phenomena, however, are strangely unrelated. Essentially, Peking is using old-fashioned methods to produce large numbers of simple machines, and meanwhile exerting very expensive efforts in test-manufacturing modern machines. For a country with a flimsy industrial foundation and low technology, this is a laudable effort but economically costly.

A certain number of serviceable machines are made, such as automobiles, tractors, simple airplanes, ships of a few thousand tons, electric generators, equipment for steel mills and machine tools, but most of their key parts are imported. Again, the industry is bedeviled by the Great Leap human-sea movement—making lathes with cement, or substituting cast iron for steel and wood for iron. In 1958 all factories were encouraged to produce machines to fulfill high quotas, increase the gross product value, and forget about spare parts. In 1959 the painful discovery was made that, as the *People's Daily* said, all kinds of machines were made without the slightest possibility of standardization. Machines either had no spare parts or the parts would not fit. Factories modified designs without prior experiments. Workers checked raw materials and products "without supervision by specialized engineers."

Looking at the whole picture, before 1957 Communist China

made some industrial progress not unlike that of Soviet Russia's forced industrialization, although its objective conditions were quite different from those of Russia. By comparison those years were more sensible, even though shortages and dislocations began to emerge by 1957. However, the Great Leap, marking "three years of bitter struggle," created a grotesque economic situation. The Leaps in agriculture and steel-making had to be called off by 1959, but those in many other economic sectors continued as late as the end of 1960. In 1959 direct results of the Great Leap were already felt, but indirect, delayed chain-reactions grew and multiplied through later years.

The agricultural Leap resulted in sharp slumps of food grain and economic crops. As 50 percent of Peking's fiscal receipts, 70 percent of its exports and 80 percent of its light industry depend on agriculture, the farm debacle not only created shortages in food and consumer goods, but seriously affected the entire industrial chain. Raw material shortages, inferior iron, steel and coal, transportation mix-ups, and continued "indigenous methods" resulted in a chaotic situation even by Peking's own admissions. In early 1959 the *People's Daily* and Shanghai's *Sin Wen Daily* each ran seven editorials sounding alarms on raw material shortages.

The situation appeared critical by 1959 when 20 million people were mobilized for a "Little Autumn Harvest" to dig up wild plants and grasses for ersatz food, edible oil, fibers, starch, chemicals, and medicine. From South China to Inner Mongolia city residents were organized to collect waste paper, rags, broken glass, hair, fish scales, worn shoes, and even used match-sticks to feed industry. Wooden crates and bamboo baskets appeared at street corners labeled "Treasure Bowls," to receive waste articles. As the thrifty Chinese seldom throw anything away, the drive was not too successful. Nanking had a scavenger factory producing articles from discarded objects and refuse. Even its furniture and tools were entirely patched up from broken pieces.

The consumer industry has suffered the most. Rubber factories tried to use water in rubber cement. Match factories used an unnamed substance to replace sulfur, and resin to replace paraffin. Shoe factories tried to make shoes out of fish-skin. In Canton, nine factories used discarded rubber articles to make "Resurrection Rubber"; a medical equipment factory used iron for copper and wood for plastics. Refusing to release raw materials to the consumer industry, Peking ordered "self-help" instead. This practice was unique. In Shanghai, coal briquette factories sent workers to Soochow to dig mud to mix with coal dust; vacuum-bottle factories sent workers to the next province to chop down bamboo for bottle shells; factories under the Bureau of Light Industry sent 50 trucks 1,000 miles to Inner Mongolia to dig up sodium salts. Workers complained vociferously, quoting a Chinese proverb: "Without rice even an ingenious woman cannot make meals." But the Party insisted: "Under Party leadership, meals can be made without rice. . . . There are difficulties, but they can be overcome with sky-zooming zeal."

By 1959 consumer goods, estimated by Peking to number 100,000 items, became extremely scarce. Among those listed by the *People's Daily* as short in 20 major cities were sugar, cloth, raw cotton, cigarettes, kitchen utensils, tableware, scissors, brushes, umbrellas, straw mats, stationery, furniture, shoes, light bulbs, soap, and articles made of wood, bamboo, rattan, grass, and metal. The *Daily Worker* reported a curious story about the Party secretary of the Wuhan Metal Construction Company who sent scouts all over the metropolis to look in vain for a lock for his desk drawer. His own factory and other hardware plants had ceased making unimportant daily articles and now concentrated on big machines.

More serious have been the shortages in important industries. Factories have had not enough iron, steel, cement, fuel, bleaching powder, caustic soda and industrial acids. In Canton, a tractor factory used low grade carbon steel for medium grade, and medium grade carbon steel to make axles; an automobile factory had nothing to make ball-bearings with, but 20 tons of scrap steel from a dockyard saved the day. According to the *Liaoning Daily*, the Dairen Dockyards, one of the biggest, suffered from acute shortages in more than 40 important items, including steel, copper plate, pig iron, coke, fuel oil, plastics and soldering alloys. Trying to build a crane for its own use, the dockyard could get neither the necessary major items nor the 760 small pieces of insulating material.

The situation was aggravated by bureaucratic management and the low morale of the workers. Factory management is elaborate. A chemical plant in Hopei had fifteen workers but eighteen administrators, including five managers. A big steel mill in the same province had forty-nine administrators for every hundred workers. Under the mill's six managers were more than 700 Party *kanpu* occupying 20 offices, plus 1,100 labor welfare workers. In 1959 in Anhwei, 400,000 transport and mining workers were sent to the farms. They were first diverted to the backyard furnaces in 1958. When that project collapsed, the province's transportation and mining were already in confusion. To avoid paying wages with no work available, the Party simply fired many of them, but not after a few ideological sessions to make "those leaving feel pleasant, and those staying feel secure."

Production fervor lasts only as long as the presence of Party overseers. The *Daily Worker* recounted a representative case: in a Chungking coal mine daily production rose from 3,700 to 4,600 tons when the *kanpu* went down the shafts to watch the miners. When the *kanpu* went up for a meeting, production descended to the former level. The *kanpu* went down the shafts again; production rose again. "But three days later when the *kanpu* came up, production went down again."

Thus, in spite of the Party's repeated efforts, the quality of industrial products, from matches to machine tools, has been on a sharp downward curve ever since 1958. Cracking rubber shoes, exploding vacuum bottles, ephemeral batteries, matchbox flints that did not ignite the match, rice mixed with grit, flour mixed with dirt, all came under serious considerations by the august Party. The famed Paoting No. 2 Machine Tool Plant turned out

14.62 percent waste products in the first quarter of 1959. In April alone 740 items manufactured were useless, including more than 100 steel rollers and 15 diesel engines. During the first five months of 1960 the Shanghai Machine Factory turned out 23.65 percent waste products. Of the paper made by a factory in Peking, 61.81 percent could not be used. An agricultural machine factory in Nanning built a pneumatic hammer. Soon afterward it refused to function. The workers nicknamed it "the Melancholy Hammer" and after repeated, fruitless repairs, put it aside. A locomotive factory in Chengchow had to hold weekly "quality analysis meetings" in 1961 to find out why its steel wheels had cracks and bubbleholes, and a textile mill in Tientsin held similar weekly meetings to study why fibers repeatedly snapped on the spindles.

The industrial situation was summed up by Shanghai's Party mouthpiece *Liberation*: "There are enterprises which produce machine parts that do not fit together, or throw into production new products not yet tested. . . . There are enterprises which produce the right articles but do not care about the cost"; and the *Liberation Daily*: "Some factories appear to have increased production on the surface. But because of an increase in waste and defective products, actual production has decreased."

By 1960 agricultural setbacks and industrial mismanagement resulted in a near breakdown of the economy. For lack of cotton, textile mills cut down their daily operation to four hours. Food-processing plants had to suspend operation for seven months. A cement factory in North China, with 40 percent of its 6,000 workers sick, curtailed its operation to a few days a month, grinding hay and dried grass roots for "substitute food." In that year almost no major construction, including railroad building, was carried out, except that of a military nature. This industrial paralysis still existed in late 1962, when the Hsinhua News Agency deplored the inferior pig iron from Wuhan Iron and Steel Works as a result of persistent insecurity in the workers' psychology, and their "lack of cooperation" with the *kanpu*.

China was and still is a predominantly agricultural country with an embryonic industry. Its most acute problem was and still is food vs. population; any government practicing any economic policy cannot escape this fact. The sensible way to modernize the economy is first to feed the people adequately, next to modernize agriculture, and then to build up industry. Rapid industrialization is possible only if enough external capital comes in the form of aid and loans, and is used cautiously to help and not upset the existing rural economy. Up to 1957 Peking did receive some aid from Soviet Russia. But instead of using it to import adequate agricultural machines and produce chemical fertilizer and insecticide, it lavished the money on giant steel mills, machine-tool plants, huge dams, strategic railroads that were economically unprofitable, and massive military installations for external aggression and internal suppression. Agriculture was brutally exploited for industrialization.

Things were still under control through 1957, although danger signals were already unmistakable. However, the devastating blow to the Chinese economy was struck in 1958 when the Theory of Imbalance was adopted. This theory, favoring selective breakthroughs in certain economic sectors and letting other sectors catch up to achieve a new, higher balance, fell flat on its face during the Great Leap. The basic fallacy stemmed from Mao's use of human beings as growth capital. The normal way of industrialization is to increase labor efficiency by improving production means. Instead, Mao used the labor-intensive method—human-sea method in production—under the most primitive and brutal conditions, thereby going in the opposite direction of genuine industrialization. In effect, the more people were thrown into the fray to substitute for capital and equipment, the less the labor efficiency; the more efforts made, the greater the dislocations. Even the emergency remedial measures taken since 1961, such as sending city residents to the farms, are operated in the typical style of the Theory of Imbalance.

In his economic route to the Instant Paradise, Mao not only copied Stalin but accentuated all the latter's weaknesses and errors. Soviet Russia has barely squeaked through after more than forty years of effort and sacrifice. Its agricultural productivity is still way below that of the Western nations and Japan; and it is increasingly veering toward the incentive system disdained by all loyal Communists. Communist China started on a quite different base from that of Soviet Russia. Its problems of overpopulation, infant industry, limited mineral resources, and a lack of arable land were not Russian problems. But areas with similar problems have industrialized or are industrializing successfully: Japan, Taiwan, and Hong Kong. These areas today have the highest standards of living in the Far East. But their path to modernization has been through free enterprise, not through the Communist methods, for which so much has been claimed yet so little proved.

VIII

THE BAMBOO
H-BOMB

TODAY, THE CHINESE ARE BACKWARD IN SCIENCE AND technology. This has not always been so. They are responsible for many major scientific inventions and discoveries. The compass is said to have been invented in China in the twenty-seventh century B.C. in the form of a chariot with a south-pointing device. Around the end of the first century they invented paper, which was introduced to Europe more than 1,000 years later. They printed books 700 years before Gutenberg. Early in the fifteenth century when Europeans were still using crude earthen vessels, the Chinese fashioned marvelous, translucent Ming porcelain. They invented the escapement device, which made the mechanical clock possible, 600 years before the West did. In the thirteenth century, they defended Kaifeng with the world's first rockets. They drilled artesian wells, used coal, natural gas, and mineral medicines long before the Europeans.

The Chinese excelled in astronomy. They made a celestial sphere forty-nine centuries ago, built a great observatory forty-six centuries ago, and recorded the 2446 B.C. conjunction of Mercury, Venus, Mars, Jupiter, and Saturn. *Shu Chin* (*Book of History*) records that two Chinese astronomers were punished for failing to predict an eclipse of the sun in the twenty-second century B.C. The obliquity of the ecliptic was determined with amazing accuracy in China about 1100 B.C. The Chinese circuit of heaven probably preceded the Greek Metonic cycle. Liu Hsin's planetary cycles antedated the famed Ptolemaic system, and Shih Shen's star catalog was two centuries earlier than that of the Greek astronomer Hipparchus. The Chinese observations of supernovae in the Milky Way are well-known. Their records of 372 comets between 611 B.C and 1621 A.D. were far superior and more accurate than those of the Europeans. They enabled Halley's Comet to be traced back to 240 B.C. and probably to 467 B.C.

The most monumental construction of human skill is the 1,700-mile Great Wall—the only man-made structure that would be visible to the naked eye from the moon. Built in the third century B.C., it is equivalent to a barrier eight feet high and three feet thick girdling the earth. Like a granite dragon, it undulates across desolate deserts and mile-high mountains from the Yellow Sea to the edge of Tibet. The Great Wall rises to a height of from 20 to 30 feet, with a well-paved highway on top wide enough for six horsemen riding abreast. Its 20,000 defense towers and 10,000 signal towers used a smoke-signal network that was the fastest communication system known to men before the telegraph.

From the first century B.C. for more than fifteen hundred years, the Chinese were among the foremost in mathematics, astronomy, medicine, architecture, and construction engineering. The Europeans caught up with them in science and technology during the fifteenth and sixteenth centuries, surpassed them by the seventeenth century, and have left them far behind since the Industrial Revolution.

Political turmoil and overpopulation are only partial explanations for China's stagnation in this area. More fundamental are the fallacious but once extremely useful Chinese cosmic theory of *Yin* and *Yang* and their philosophical outlook. These two combine to create the spirit of *mamafufu*, a term known to every old China-hand that is akin to the Frenchman's *comme ci, comme ça,* but with a much broader philosophical basis. It is a strange mixture of puckish irreverence for mathematical exactitude, a disdain for slavish meticulousness, a reluctance to assert one's rights to the letter, and a Taoist-inspired rebellion against stuffed-shirt Confucianism.

The *mamafufu* spirit is a solvent that makes human relations pleasant and genial, but is also a curse to Chinese science and technology. It is the reason why the Chinese, great craftsmen that they are, cannot turn out industrial goods of uniform quality. Standardization and precision production are alien to the traditional Chinese culture. The scientific achievements of ancient and medieval China were mainly due to individual talents and empirical experience, and not to systematized disciplines developed through logical deduction and abstract reasoning. Chinese native intelligence can be proficient in modern science only when it adopts Western methodology and insulates itself from the *mamafufu* spirit. Examples of this are Lee Tsung-dao and Yang Chenning, the brilliant young scientists who won the 1957 Nobel Prize in Physics for exploding the Parity Law—a sacred cornerstone of modern nuclear physics. Lee and Yang are both products of China's traditional culture who are doing advance research in the United States.

In pre-Communist China and now in Taiwan, even though science is not generally much understood and never sufficiently exploited, both the people and regimes have a healthy respect for it. Things are quite different under the Chinese Communists, who know the importance of science and technology but promote them with political dynamics mixed with traditional mysticism. It is against this frame of reference that one should examine Peking's dabbling in the atomic bomb, electronics, computers, automation, test-tube babies, and other applied sciences. In that land today, application has little to do with research, or attitude with capabilities, or pseudo-science with science.

It was at the beginning of the Great Leap that science was coupled with mythology in a Party-sponsored shotgun wedding. Under the slogan of "more, faster, better, cheaper," the Communists repeated thousands of times that the forces of nature yield before man's subjective fervor. The Party mouthpiece *Red Flag* labeled Western science and book knowledge "a pile of garbage." The *People's Daily* called them "superstitions." The Hupeh Party mouthpiece *Ideological Front* even claimed that if the Party doled out enough ideological persuasion and instructions, no task was impossible and the laws of nature themselves could be canceled. Scientists, engineers, statisticians—useless conservatives who "superstitiously believe in books and in European and American scientific achievements"—were ridiculed, discarded, and exiled to the farms. Army man Marshal Nieh Jung-chen became the supreme boss in science, and workers and farmers were put in high positions in the Academy of Sciences. The science guerillas had taken over.

The results were spectacular and instant. Established within a few months in 1958 were 1,000 iron and steel works, 17,000 coal mines, 4,300 power stations, 400 oil refineries, 1,000 synthetic oil plants, 30,000 cement factories, and "innumerable" machine, chemical, and light industrial factories. In all China "no less than 5 million technical innovations" were devised. Agronomy was blessed by 3,000 experiments, 400 inventions, and 248 volumes on applied techniques. Theoretical science was enriched by 34 volumes of work totaling 9.3 million words, and a planned 13 volumes on isotopes, ultrasonics and stimulant agencies. Students in 222 colleges invented 56,000 tools, with 1,500 up to international advanced standards. Freshmen in the Northwest University compiled textbooks on higher algebra, analytical geometry and theoretical physics. This in spite of the students calling it "foul play" and a professor being "stunned and unable to utter a word." A cowherd, who was an illiterate two years before, became an advanced researcher in the Peking Veterinary Institute. In that year, 72 percent of oil explorations were fruitful. Women workers in a machine factory in Shanghai drew up blue-prints for 10 kinds of new machines in one night, and built them in three days. Some 400,000 geologists were trained in record time. In a single province, 400,000 mathematical workers were "handing mathematics to the masses." Many blind people regained their sight through Marxism. When coal instead of coke was used in the backyard furnaces, the *People's Daily* said it meant that "the technical practices applied all over the world have become obsolete." The masses chanted an Annie Oakley-style Leap slogan: "Whatever others do, I can do better. Whatever they can't do, I'm going to try." It was Paul Bunyan incarnate, and Walter Mitty gone berserk.

Among the popular technical innovations were deep plowing and close sowing in farming. Instead of plowing 5 inches deep and planting rice sprouts 6 inches apart as normally done, the Party ordered plowing up to 2 feet deep and planting 1 to 2 inches apart. To prevent the plants from collapsing, suffocating and rotting, in some areas they were supported by bamboo racks, with hordes of peasants, day and night, fanning the fields with reed mats and paddling water to and fro. Some ingenious *kanpu* got medals by having several acres of crop replanted on one acre, and then beating gongs and drums to announce a record crop. The greatest innovator in agriculture was a South China *kanpu*, who had twelve times the normal amount of seed sown in an acre, then erected a layer of boards atop the field, put several feet of soil on the boards, and sowed more seeds upstairs. For air and light beneath the boards, he strung light bulbs and requisitioned electric fans to blow at the crop. He drafted 6,000 peasants, students, and shopkeepers for the job. Result: no harvest.

In 1961 a great innovation—a detachable precision lathe—was noisily exhibited in Peking. This lathe was invented in a Harbin factory proud of its "four withouts"—without large building, without large lathe, without large crane and without engineer. Over the opposition of engineers who called the lathe "difficult, impossible, unreasonable," the Party ordered its production. The *kanpu* in a village near Tientsin kept fishermen from fishing during the season to make a giant net 35 by 26,000 feet, weighing 36,300 pounds. Costing 14,132 man-days, the net was so clumsy that by the time it was hauled up most of the fish had escaped. The result: seven trips by 72 trawlers netted a grand total of 2,265 pounds of fish.

As 75 percent of China's local transportation still depends on primitive means, innovations were needed there too. Among them:

four horses drawing a train of eight carts, railless trains powered by old boilers, boats powered by old automobile engines pulling several crafts, and buses and trucks using coal gas carried in big balloons and refilled every six miles. In earlier years full loading on the railroads was accomplished by "inserting long pieces of cargo in spaces between round pieces," so that apples, ginger, fresh peas shared togetherness with insecticide. During the Leap this technique advanced to: "letting passengers occupy spare cargo spaces, and loading cargo into spaces between passengers."

Other innovations included making ball-bearings with village wooden machines, curing patients with the drugless "spirit of revolutionary optimism," curing mental patients with labor ("the revolutionary way of liberating the insane"), making drunken castrated roosters hatch eggs, beating live pigs with sticks to test if they were stuffed with sand, and "demanding feathers from live ducks."

Quick tricks were indispensable in this shortcut to the scientific millennium. In 1956 Peking drafted a twelve-year plan in science to train 10,500 advanced scientists and tackle 582 problems, so that by the end of the plan, science would be elevated to "international advanced standards." Two years after the plan began, science chief Nieh, judging from results, announced that the plan would be accomplished five years ahead of time, as, in fact, "certain parts of the plan have already been completed." In the same vein, within a couple of weeks cures were found for high blood pressure, ulcers, and diabetes. Schistosomiasis (a lingering disease) was cured in three days. After five months of spare-time training, 32 "low-grade medical workers" in a hospital were set loose to perform major stomach, intestinal, gynecological and obstetric surgery.

Inhabited since time immemorial, China is a paradise for archeologists. But the ancestral Chinese of the halcyon past never dreamed that their bones and messages to posterity would be scrambled up by their frenetic descendants. This happened when Maoist adrenalin was injected into painstaking archeology.

Ancient tombs and archeological sites have been discovered almost daily during the past one and a half decades because of extensive construction work. By the end of 1956 a total of 165 ancient cultural sites, 27,187 tombs and 362,026 archeological items were unearthed. Statistically, it was an immense harvest. Archeologically it was a tragedy.

Many priceless artifacts were stolen or destroyed, while others were unearthed with the typical swiftness of a shock-troop harvest. Things went on almost completely without control during the pre-Leap years. In the Yangtze Valley, ten Six-Kingdoms (220–587 A.D.) tombs and twenty Ming tombs were wiped out in dike repairs. A similar group of tombs near Nanchang disappeared during highway construction. In Kiangsu, Han tombs at ten construction sites were destroyed. Near Changsha, 958 Warring-States and West-Han (403 B.C.–25 A.D.) tombs were scrambled up. In Shantung, 1,000 ancient tombs were torn apart and the bricks used to build walls of wells. A 20-acre neolithic site with valuable objects in six feet of ashy soil was dug out as a fishpond. The soil, bones, and smashed artifacts were sold to peasants as fertilizer at the rate of 80 cartfuls daily.

Peasants and bureaucrats vied with each other at the treasure-hunts. Jade bracelets were carried away by basketfuls. Han pottery was ground in the mortar. Sung and Ming books were cut for paper pulp. Neolithic bones and paleolithic fossils were pulverized as fertilizer, or sold as "dragon bones" for medicine. Tang and Han funeral steles became part of manure tanks. Old funeral mounds were turned into kilns or razed for farmland. Iron spears and swords unearthed became children's toys. Even historic monuments above-ground were not left unscathed. In Chekiang, three Sung pagodas were pulled down as "superstitious objects" and their bricks used for construction. So far, no one has given an eye to the Great Wall, which has plenty of bricks.

Year after year in every province, despite Peking's repeated orders, the indiscriminate looting and vandalism have continued because illiterate Party goons have been taught to spit at anything old, and because of Peking's own policy of instant construction. Thus, 140 tombs of various vintages were unearthed from an ancient city near Loyang, in the area where Chinese civilization originated. Excavations had to be done day and night and artifacts scooped up rapidly because a large brick factory refused to delay its construction. At the Sanmen Gorge Dam, 78 neolithic sites were found. But the reservoir cannot wait. So only 0.7 percent of the diggings can be completed before water covers the sites.

Some 500 archeologists were trained in 1956, and another 341 during the Leap years. These men often make gross errors in deciphering inscriptions on ancient bronzes and pottery, and even in reading archeological magazines. But they have one virtue: speed. They link archeology with Marxism and pledge that their work will not delay construction. A small group of them in Honan wrote their reports on the spot, classifying and appraising objects from 2,800 tombs in five months.

While short-course graduates practiced instant archeology, genuine archeologists were sent to the farms to collect fertilizer and re-examine their wicked minds. The Party criticized them as wanting science only for science's sake, and writing too detailed and specialized reports. It said: "Archeology must be political, and sites and specimens must be studied in the light of Marxism," and "We are . . . against that superficial and exaggerated care in excavation which might impede production and construction." But the archeologists had their own opinions. One said: "The search for antiques is treated as a game. The reports are unmethodical and confused. The periods of sites are assumed." Another said: "The Party has only destroyed culture and not protected it." Such conditions, of course, cannot be gathered from the 1954 Peking Exhibit of Cultural Objects Unearthed by Construction Workers, and the neolithic museum near Sian, built in 1958, that impressed ignorant peasants and foreign visitors with the grandeur of ancient Cathay.

The Great Leap was mixed with another metaphor: "Walking

on two legs," which means modern and primitive methods must be used side by side. Along with indigenous steel, indigenous cement, indigenous ball-bearings, there were indigenous precision machine lathes, made of cast iron, wrought iron, cement, or wood. The Tsaidam oil fields had indigenous pipes, indigenous tanks and even indigenous drill-heads—1,000 of them.

Chinese meteorologists formerly used Western methods. In 1952 they switched to Russian methods. In 1958 they were ordered to incorporate indigenous methods. Youths trained for a few weeks were sent to local weather posts to supplement regular weather reports with peasant weather lore and "indigenous living meteorological instruments"—89 kinds of animals and plants sensitive to weather change. Thus, if leeches stay at the bottom of the jar, water-snails float on the surface, or gunpowder is not damp, it will be fine weather. One writer in the *Science Journal*, pointing out the undesirable results in previous rain-making experiments, suggested indigenous methods. The suggestion was probably facetious, as the only indigenous rain-making known in China is burning incense and kowtowing to the Dragon God.

The Chinese used to be quite advanced in medicine. Ergot for uterine disorders, and ephedrine for asthma and hay fever have been used in the West only recently, yet they have been used by Chinese herbalists for 5,000 years. Acupuncture, the painless piercing of long needles into neuralgic points along twelve pairs of invisible parallel meridians in the human body to cure many diseases, has also been practiced in China for many thousand years. Today it is earnestly studied by medical scientists in Japan, Germany and France who have found minute points of electrical activity at the exact spots mapped by the Chinese. In the ninth century, Chinese surgeons were performing good operations for harelip. On the whole, Chinese traditional medicine is a conglomeration of amazing cures, inscrutable theories, and pure superstitions. If someday systematic, scientific research is done, many old drugs may be rediscovered. After all, modern Western medicine grew out of medieval European medicine, which was not

superior to Chinese traditional medicine. The real task is to win-
now veracity from mysticism.

Instead of doing this, Mao Tse-tung, who believes in traditional
medicine above all, forced modern doctors to "walk on two legs"
by using old methods side by side with modern ones, and accused
all critics as political deviationists. Among the widely publicized
"indigenous treatments" were swallowing live tadpoles as a con-
traceptive, and inserting willow twigs into the body for messy
compound fractures. The *People's Daily* claimed indigenous cures
for color-blindness, polio, and cancer. The situation was summed
up by a professor of the Peking Medical College: "The Ministry
of Public Health has dragged [modern] pharmaceuticals back to
the eighteenth century."

In 1958, Yuhsien county in Shansi built in 24 days a mile of
indigenous railroad with cast iron from backyard furnaces. Immediately the propaganda machine went into action and the fad
spread to all the provinces. By 1960 7,000 miles of homemade
railroads were built for local transportation and to link up with
major lines. This "profound technical innovation" was said to
furnish "instant transportation and instant production." Rails were
made of cast iron and wrought iron melted in old oil drums and
hammered out by indigenous workers. There were wooden rails,
too. Along these novel railroads chugged indigenous locomotives
made of converted trucks and old boilers. Some had "man-push"
trains.

Although it was admitted that many rails were crooked, rough,
or full of blowholes, that the rate of waste was 80 percent, and
that the top speed of trains was only 15 miles per hour, the Party
decreed that it should be a long-term project because the cost was
less than one-fifth of the regular railroads. They "should be built
abundantly, quickly, and soon." The favorite methods were "groping, saving, substituting," "seeking treasures everywhere," and
"getting materials from Three Heaps"—coal heap, junk heap, and
garbage heap.

The indigenous railroads came after some nationwide campaigns in railroad transportation had backfired. Earlier, three campaigns had been pushed: full-loading, over-draughting, and daily 500-kilometer (311 miles) runs. Full-loading involved problems like how to load more in a 30-ton freight-car which could only hold 7 tons of hay. The problem in over-draughting was to overcome inertia at starting and momentum at stopping when a locomotive with a 1400-ton normal haulage was used to pull 7,000 to 10,000 tons. The solutions included dumping sand on the rails for traction and dashing up slopes. The daily 500-kilometer run was a national contest in squeezing mileage out of locomotives. The top prize was won by a senile locomotive logging 756 miles a day, though its normal daily mileage was only 155.

As most locomotives are vintage models of Mikado and Consolidation types, these campaigns resulted in awesome accident statistics. In one month in the Shanghai area alone 164 accidents were recorded. And the Chinese Reds had some real red faces when they discovered that the 100,000-kilometer and 190,000-kilometer safety run records of Labor Model Li Jung-loh and his famed *Mao Tse-tung Locomotive* were pure fraud.

To conserve materials, bus drivers were told to emulate a man in Canton who saved fuel by always coasting downhill. Truckers were ordered to get 106,000 miles out of every tire, and 16 miles out of every gallon of gasoline, as was done by Chungking truck driver Chang Lien-shen. Chang, explained the *People's Daily*, achieved this by trying always to use the cruising speed and never the brakes, and by stopping every 20 miles to cool off the tires and pick pebbles out of the treads.

In 1956 these transportation campaigns resulted in a traffic jam that lasted six months and covered virtually the entire populated part of China, from Harbin to Canton, from Shanghai to Lanchow. At eight railroad stations around Peking 4,700 freight cars were simultaneously waiting for unloading. Goods stacked in the stations overflowed onto the fields along the tracks, blocking the view of rail signals. It was the same in Tientsin, Tsinan, Taiyuan, Wuhan, Shanghai, and Canton. A similar jam took place along the

Yangtze River, with goods stranded in warehouses and on docks for four months in the main ports of Wuhan, Shanghai, Chungking, and Ichang. In Shanghai some 140,000 tons of shipping were held up as freighters waited two weeks to unload. At one time, lighters had to be used as warehouses.

Tens of thousands of tons of steel, machinery, and chemicals heading for Szechwan were stuck in Wuhan, where 30,000 tons of grain from Szechwan were also held up, rotting. Chungking's 12,000 tons of iron and steel products could not reach the nation's mines and factories, while several thousand tons of ore and pig iron sent to its mills were grounded at Ichang. Cotton in Paochi was damaged by insects when 59,000 insecticide sprayers could not get through. Six teams of coal prospectors in Southwest China stopped working when needed equipment did not arrive. For one month Kansu was without any drugs. During the latter half of 1956, a total of 2.7 million tons of goods were held up in Central and North China alone. As goods had priority over human beings, travellers were stranded all over China, with many selling their baggage to pay hotel bills. The situation was slowly and finally put under control when the haulage contests and races were abandoned. Commodity congestion in cities like Wuhan was alleviated by an emergency mass campaign, commandeering all available horse-carts, tricycles, hand-carts and human carriers.

Besides the deliberate over-exploitation of equipment and the disregard of safety measures, repairs were treated as an unnecessary evil until things broke down completely. This practice spread even to the most modern plants during the three Leap years, and repair work, when done, was slow. In 1956 Peking admitted that 31 percent of its truck were not working, with 25 percent regularly in repair shops, which usually took one to two months per job. During half of that year 142 of 321 ships under repair were delayed by dockyards. In 1960, 30 percent of the tractors and 20 percent of the irrigation equipment were in disrepair. When drought struck Shensi, half of the province's pumps were out of action.

A sudden nationwide repair campaign was launched in January, 1961. The *People's Daily* cautioned the *kanpu* that hurtling speed and discarding safety measures had caused many accidents, and that they should not ignore precision and timing in operating complicated modern equipment. Thus, in 2½ months 70 percent of neglected repairs were done on the furnaces and mills of eighteen major iron and steel plants. A furnace in the Chungking Steel Works did not give sufficient heat for two years, and everybody said it was due to the inferior coal. During the repair movement, exiled engineers were recalled who found the real trouble—leaking pipes. The repair campaign brought only a slight improvement, as during the 1961 spring sowing, 20 percent of the tractors were still out of action. One reason was that machine parts were worn out. Some tractors had been used for 15,000 hours without checking or overhaul.

Some equipment abuses were purely due to ignorance. In the factories managed by the First Ministry of the Machine-Building Industry, a total of 6,000 equipment accidents occurred in half a year, damaging 5,100 machines and idling 132,000 machine-hours. A mechanized coal mine in Shansi with only 70 cutting machines and extractors had 8,000 accidents in one year. The First Machine Factory in Tsitsihar was built with Russian aid and completely equipped with modern machines, but "soon after installation, 83.5 percent of the machines were damaged." The mechanized Tatung mine needed 50 percent more miners than non-mechanized mines of the same size. The reason given: stand-by miners must be used when the machines broke down, which was often. Peking once also admitted that 71.3 percent of the country's railroad supplies, including electric motors, were stored in open air.

Claiming that fish can live in all kinds of water—fresh, running, stagnant, and even factory tank water for cooling engines—the Ministry of Aquatic Products boasted that by 1962 Communist China would be top in world fisheries. So a craze for fishponds was touched off. In Honan, after the people were made to scoop up 300 million fish eggs from the rivers, the target of 5 million fish was instantly changed to 10 million. Dropping 300,000 fingerlings into the Shinsanling Reservoir near Peking, the Party predicted that a year hence the fish would be two pounds apiece and the nation would be 600,000 pounds richer in fresh fish production. A public-health campaign began in 1956 to eliminate the "four pests"—flies, mosquitoes, rats, and sparrows. To fulfill quotas of the kill, people handed in dried turnip tips as rat tails, children scooped larvae from cesspools and washed them in basins, and hawkers peddled dead flies and mosquitoes in the street. Restaurants in Canton demanded that customers swat a certain number of flies before they could be served. The waiters counted the dead flies on customers' tables, then brought out bowls and chopsticks without washing their hands.

In construction work, a favorite practice was "production and planning progressing side by side." The luxurious New Peking Hotel which has impressed many foreign visitors was badly planned. Steel bars used in the construction were so closely spaced that crushed stone in the concrete could not be poured through. The forty rooms in the Western Suburbs Hostel in that city were so designed that there was no place for a single bed. Finally the horizontal heating pipes were relocated vertically to make room for beds. A Peking opera theatre was built in the hostel, but there was no doorway big enough for stage props, so a huge hole was knocked out in a wall and stage props moved through the dining hall. During the construction of a handsome government dormitory, eleven doors had to be filled up and reinforcing pillars added to buttress the heavy horizontal steel beams, which were originally supported by flimsy brick columns. Most of the 5,000 units of housing built for Anshan workers collapsed after a heavy rain.

Changchun's automobile factory, Peking's pride and joy, was also planned and constructed simultaneously. Work on each part started as individual blueprints arrived. Workers were alternately waiting for materials or thrown in as shock-troops. The confusion was classic. In four months 256 accidents occurred.

The plant's water mains had to be shifted 14 times and its high voltage wires 28 times before things became final. Another major plant, the Harbin Electrical Machine Factory, was started without a budget or a contract. There was no over-all plan during its three years of construction. After completion it was found that the insulator plant was downwind of the boiler rooms—an undesirable position. So 32,280 square feet of warehouse space, 3,280 feet of drains, 9,840 feet of heating pipes and 1,093 yards of light railroad were torn up and rebuilt. The plan for a construction job in Kwangtung was drawn up in three days, and altered repeatedly by engineers—and workers. When it was 80 percent complete the whole thing collapsed. On the blueprints of a major mine shaft in Fushun, individual measurements did not add up to the total.

Sometimes elaborate construction was built for a nonexistent need. Party water conservancy bosses in Shensi learned from hearsay that some years ago there was a big flood in Nanshan. After 2.6 million man-days, 3.3 million cubic yards of earthwork, 18,000 tons of cement and 105,000 cubic yards of granite, a giant drainage canal elaborately paved with granite and concrete was built. It covered 248 acres and had 45 bridges. During the worst flood season there was only three inches of water in the canal. Other times it was bone dry. Pedestrians preferred to walk across the canal bed instead of the bridges.

Fettered by the *mamafufu* spirit, propelled by political libido, and guided by the star of pseudo-science, the end products of science and technology in Communist China are worthy of Ripley. The press repeatedly complained of funny-face mirrors, rock-like toothpaste, locks that refused to lock or open, alarm clocks that daily deviated 3 hours in time and 1 hour in alarm, slide rules that gave $3 \times 3 = 9.1$, drawing compasses with shifting radiuses, and children's T-shirts with collars for a one-year-old, waists for a two-year-old and long enough for a three-year-old. Another continuous complaint is the exploding vacuum bottle, which is a necessity in fuel-frugal Chinese households. Year after year countless vacuum bottles exploded when hot water was poured in. The Chinese, with a ready sense of humor, nick-named them "time bombs." One government office bought 13 of them and 12 exploded. The thirteenth never did because nobody dared to use it. The *People's Daily* in 1961 gave a citation to the Gold Coin brand of vacuum bottle because it did not explode.

In a single consignment of sulfuric acid bottles sent out by a state glass factory in Hunan, 3,414 bottles cracked when acid was poured in. Water-wheels sent to drought-stricken areas had valve leaves half an inch bigger than the encasement. Cement cracked upon drying and did not resist freezing, but it was "good enough for water conservancy works." There were mosquitoes in paraffin and flies in liver extract ampoules. The People's Health Publications House turned out a translated Russian medical book. It was accompanied by a 22-page errata supplement containing 321 corrections for the 336-page book. The Yumen oil field one year found 300 and another year 800 drill-heads made by the modern Shanghai Petroleum Machine Parts Factory useless. Five of the deepest oil wells in China, all over 9,800 feet, were drilled in the Koramai oil field, but "they were drilled blindly." Only one yielded some experimental oil; the other four had to be sealed up. New generators and transformers sent out by the Hsiangtang Electric Machinery Factory in Hunan were regularly followed by repairmen. Of all the millions of wells dug in China for irrigation, only 40 percent are good; 50 percent must be re-dug, 10 percent are useless. In 1961, the Loyang Tractor Plant repeatedly had to reject the faulty steel material sent from Anshan, shocking the Anshan technicians into frenzied remodeling of their rolling mills. But even with good steel, this tractor plant turns out bad tractors. Its best, the 54-horsepower *East Red*, has no automatic oil-flow regulation, and its air-filter does not filter air.

A new truck from China's best automobile factory in Chang-chun was used by a Shantung iron mine. When it reached a gentle slope the wheels started to spin and the steering wheel would not respond. "Shaking its head and wagging its tail," as the *People's Daily* described it, the truck went up and slid back, and "this went on for two full hours." Locomotive manufacture is still in an experimental stage. Most of the new products are from the Dairen Locomotive Factory, whose technical level can be gathered from a *Shensi Daily* account in 1960 about several trains trying to crawl up a winding slope on the Sian-Tungkwan Railroad. "Even if a locomotive is new and is pulling only a few cars, it would not listen to command." There were also spinning wheels, violent shakings, and slidings back and forth. "The engineer must stop the train by immediately dumping sand on the rails. If the sand does not help, he must resolutely return to the station, or the train would be de-railed." These new locomotives have a high depreciation rate. When the best locomotive on the Chinchow Railroad, *No. 22 Red Flag*, was inspected, many defects were discovered. The best locomotive on another railroad was found with 173 unsound spots. So the workers started a campaign of "great dissection, great inspection, great diagnosis, great bath, great cure," thus improving 135 sick locomotives in use.

Railroads are beset with serious problems. The important Mukden-Shanhaikwan Railroad was inspected in 1960 and found with "25,000 big and small problems." The building of the 424-mile Chengtu-Paochi Railroad was rushed through in four years. Great propaganda was followed by 2,000 great landslides. Trains can go only at 6.2 miles an hour. Another year was spent in rebuilding. Similarly, a year was required to rebuild the new Tientsin-Lanchow Railroad. The new railroad between Peking and Moscow, a second link through Mongolia, is 620 miles shorter than the old line through Manchuria. But "since the trains on this new line cannot run fast, for the time being it takes one day longer" to go to Moscow on the shorter line.

Possessing an estimated 90,000 trucks, and with little oil available, Peking has no great plans for a nationwide highway network. Practically all the "all-weather highways" are dirt roads, with an average speed for trucks of 11 miles per hour. In a few provinces with better roads the average speed is 25 miles. Some 80 percent of goods moved by road depend on the 5 million

animal carts and 10 million man-driven carts, most of which are
without rubber tires and ball-bearings. Local highways, even new
ones, have "only the embryonic shape of a road without the level-
ing process. When it rains . . . one cannot go an inch. Even on fine
days . . . it is more efficient to carry goods on one's shoulders."

In spite of these harsh realities, the Maoists dream their scientific dreams. In 1958, they wanted to build a meteorological network by 1963 "better than the U.S.A." It was to have a high-
atmosphere station every 124 miles, a weather station every 62
miles, a climatology station every 31 miles and a rain-gauge station every 12 miles. Each commune was to have its detailed
individual soil maps, temperature maps, rainfall maps, maps of
soil temperature, soil humidity, underground-water tables—to be
made by unskilled, sometimes illiterate, *kanpu*. There was to be a
separate meteorological network exclusively serving pig breeding,
to research "what the pigs want, what they are afraid of." The
Chinese Academy of Medical Sciences in 1958 issued a planned
target—a cancer cure in five years. At the 1960 Congress it was
claimed that scientists and miners were trying to invent completely automatic mining, "without man, without lift-truck, and
without pit-props." Even the U. S.-returned rocket expert Chien
Hsieh-shen was forced to make a magical claim, that with enough
sunlight and water, it is possible to produce a million pounds of
rice per acre—a figure 320 times the average U. S. yield.

The Maoists are trying to obliterate the difference between
empirical sciences like physics and chemistry and formal sciences
like logic and mathematics. To them all sciences are empirical.
"We cannot inherit the system invented by the bourgeoisie. . . .
We must establish our own system of science which should be one
of advanced scientific knowledge with Mao Tse-tung Thoughts
as its guidance . . . depicting creations of the masses and easily
to be mastered by the masses." Even Western mathematics is
tainted with slave, feudal, and capitalistic class-marks "which
have poisoned many mathematicians who misunderstood mathematics . . . like Einstein."

One example of Maoist mathematics is the application of linear programming, which means finding where a linear function of several variables gets a maximum value. When the Maoists apply this advance technique to their primitive transportation, it turned out to be: "In circular transportation, more than half of cargo carriers should be loaded. In linear transportation similar commodities should not flow to and from the same place"—a bit of horse sense which every Chinese coolie used to apply.

The top prize for wild plans must be given to the one for "shifting southern waters northward." This plan, different from the irrigation-canal network mentioned earlier, was started in 1958, much talked about in 1959, and seldom heard of since. A plan was devised by the Academy of Sciences and other water conservancy organs to build twelve giant canals to carry water from South to North China. Two of the four main canals were probably the most ambitious construction ever planned—and actually believed in—by any government anywhere. The first was to be a 1,049-mile canal starting from a high dam in Yushu (elevation 14,000 feet) in Chinghai and joining the Yellow River at Kweiteh. On the way the canal was to capture water from five major rivers and many small ones, and cut across the 19,352-foot Bayan Kara and the 20,008-foot Amne Machin Mountains. Its capacity was to be ten times that of the Grand Canal. The second was to be a 4,225-mile canal starting from Likiang (elevation 8,100 feet), Yunnan, to draw water from the upper Yangtze, and ending at the Yellow River near Tingsi, Kansu. With a capacity thirty times that of the Grand Canal, this mammoth ditch would have linked nine big rivers, skirted the Szechwan Basin (elevation 1,673 feet) and cut across five immense mountain ranges with elevations from 8,200 to 25,256 feet.

Work allegedly started on the first canal in 1958. But Peking has not yet told the world's engineers how it will hand-dig a canal on the Tibetan plateau in a region of rarefied air and perpetual snow, across two of the world's highest mountain ranges. Nor has it revealed how to make the water in the second canal flow upward from Yunnan to Sikang, and again from Szechwan to Kansu. It is conceivable that had the Great Leap continued, Peking would have announced a technical innovation using the energy of downhill water to pump the river uphill, or the indigenous method of a bucket-brigade of the masses.

In the pseudo-science wilderness of Communist China, there are a small group of genuine, competent scientists, including some very brilliant men educated in the West. Among them are: Chien Hsueh-shen, one of the world's leading experts in aerodynamics and jet propulsion, former professor of aeronautics at the Massachusetts Institute of Technology, chief of research analysis at the Jet Propulsion Laboratory of the California Institute of Technology, and chief of the rocket section of U. S. Scientific Commission; Chien San-chiang, winner of the physics award from the French Science Academy, and nuclear and radiation physicist at the Curie Institute; Hua Lo-keng, Cambridge- and Princeton-educated mathematical genius once commended by Einstein; Chao Chung-yao, U. S.-educated nuclear physicist; Wu Chung-hua, M.I.T.-educated specialist in gas propulsion and ternary current; and Ko Ting-sui, physicist from California Institute of Technology.

However, it is dubious how much these scientists can accomplish in the prevailing climate. Much was revealed during the 1957 free-speech period, when scientists openly accused the Party science bureaucrats of "forcibly treating ignorance as knowledge, impossibility as possibility. They create problems where there is no problem, and impose blind controls where there should be no control. As a result real scientists have withdrawn into themselves and become negatively pessimistic." Chien Hsueh-shen, who was warmly feted and praised upon his return in 1955 after twenty years in the United States, called the Party bureaucracy in the Academy of Sciences "a mass of darkness." He complained that Party interference with scientists resulted in much waste of their precious time, and that since his return he had never had any adequate opportunity to pursue his scientific research work. Li

Hsun, head of the Institute of Metals of the Academy, was even more frank. He said: "To put it in impolite words, the Communist Party does not understand science. . . . Isn't it a joke for people who understand little or nothing of science to lead a nation's scientific rseaearch?" Mathematician Hua Lo-keng made similar complaints. As a result, Chou En-lai was forced in the Congress to deny publicly the charges that the standard of scientific work under the Communists was lower than under the Nationalists, and that Party members controlling the scientists were amateurs. Eventually the scientists along with other intellectuals were slapped down and punished as "rightists," and the Party established the fact that "amateurs can and should lead experts." Chien Wei-chang, a prominent scientist, was forced to criticize his own deadly sins for suggesting a technical institute modeled after M.I.T.

The scientists certainly do not need the Communists, but the Communists need the scientists. When the Great Leap backfired, several leading scientists, including Chien Hsueh-shen, were wooed with Party membership. But even if Maoist totalitarianism could channel genuine scientific research, it suffocates the unexpected, spontaneous discoveries and inventions in theoretical science which are the touchstone of power and greatness of modern nations. Its practical application of science to forced industrialization has brought, and is still bringing, more damages than benefits. It is desirable for China to develop its indigenous science and technology with the aid of modern knowledge from abroad. But the "indigenous techniques" used are nothing but grotesque nonsense.

All this leads to the intriguing question of the atomic bomb. Ever since Vice-Premier Chen Yi said in May 1958 that Communist China would have nuclear weapons in the future, dozens of forecasts have been made about an imminent atomic test explosion by Peking. The forecasters included newspapermen, Indian Communists, an Ex-Korean spy, Japanese scientists, a British Nobel Peace Prize winner, an ex-premier of France, United

Nations delegates, a diplomat in Albania, American senators and intelligence experts, a former U. S. Air Force secretary, an anonymous U. S. disarmament official, and a Russian broadcasting station. Reports even persisted for a time that Peking would launch a satellite in 1959. The prevailing belief has been that Communist China will soon become a nuclear power.

The fact is that the prospect of Communist China's becoming a nuclear power is as inevitable eventually as it is unlikely in the near future. This, however, does not preclude the possibility that a test explosion may occur at any time.

Making an atomic bomb requires knowledge, experience, technology, engineering skill, raw materials, and economic potential. Today this knowledge is an open secret. Peking is not lacking in good nuclear physicists. Some experience has been supplied by Russian scientists and such renegade Western scientists as Joan Hinton, a U. S. physicist who worked on the Manhattan Project, and Italian-born Bruno Pontecorvo. It is engineering skill, raw materials and economic potential that are the crucial problems.

Few details are known about Peking's atomic program, but available reports show that besides a Russian-built 10-megawatt (10,000 kilowatts), heavy-water-type experimental reactor and a 25-million-electron-volt cyclotron in Peking, there are probably three more Chinese-built experimental reactors in Harbin, Sian, and Chungking, several betatrons and electrostatic accelerators, and a uranium ore-processing plant in Urumchi, Sinkiang.

China has very little uranium, most of which is in Sinkiang. Because of the inferior metallurgical facilities, the Urumchi-processed uranium must be further refined in Soviet Central Asia, and from there returned to China. For this service China must pay Soviet Russia with part of its uranium.

Isolating and purifying uranium-235 or plutonium, the fissionable materials for weapons use, is a most sophisticated and dangerous technique. It is also tedious and costly. It takes 25,000 kilowatt hours to yield a gram of plutonium. The Russian-built reactor is a primitive model mainly for experimental use, and not designed to produce fissionable materials in quantity. At full capacity it can produce an estimated 5 pounds of plutonium a year. Assuming that the three other reactors have the same capacity and efficiency, that they have been working at full capacity, and that the supply of refined uranium has been plentiful, the most generous estimate would be that a test explosion may occur within the next few years.

But these assumptions appear unlikely. According to Japanese intelligence reports, although it started to function on September 1958, the Peking reactor succeeded in isolating plutonium only in November 1960. It took the French nearly eight years after their first reactor became critical to explode a test device. In the summer of 1961, reports, some from the Russians, indicated that Mao Tse-tung was angry at the Russians for building an "unloaded" reactor which failed to yield fissionable material, and that Russian physicists had deserted the Peking reactor. Furthermore, it is dubious how much, if any, fissionable material the other three experimental reactors can produce. The huffy departure of the Russians also hints that Peking may be having problems in getting its uranium refined in Russia. All this boils down to the crucial question of how much fissionable material Communist China has or will have in the near future—by going it alone.

Even a test explosion does not mean that Communist China will have become a nuclear power. To say that a nation triggering a nuclear test explosion has automatically joined the nuclear powers is fallacious. To be a genuine nuclear power, a nation must achieve three successive breakthroughs: testing an atomic device, making and stockpiling deliverable nuclear bombs, and having the means of delivery. It is one thing to explode an atomic device the size of a Chinese junk, but another to miniaturize it into a transportable, compact bomb. Even if such bombs can be mass-produced, without adequate jet bombers or missiles they can only explode at home. As far as is known, Peking is not making a great effort to produce its own rockets, since expert Chien's talents have not been made use of. Communist China's rocketry is probably inferior to that of Israel and Egypt. The world is sure to hear a big noise once Peking sends up its first home-made rocket.

Undoubtedly Peking is trying hard to set off a baby atomic explosion. Its sole aim now is to achieve one-shot status, thereby vibrating seismographs and experts the world over, and then quietly slip back to its mundane problems in the rice paddies. Peking is realistic enough to know that it cannot become a nuclear power within this generation. This is amply supported by a survey of its statements on the subject made for domestic and foreign consumption. Before 1955 nothing was said about atomic weapons or warfare. Then Peking considered nuclear development out of its reach, was ignorant of the power of nuclear warfare, and uninterested even in its research. In January 1955, an atoms-for-peace pact was signed with Soviet Russia. Within three weeks at least fifteen editorials and articles appeared in Peking's three leading newspapers, attacking the United States for its atomic warmongering and praising Soviet Russia for its peaceful use of the atom. This was followed by a nationwide campaign on the same theme. During the ensuing few years the Communists generally disparaged the power of atomic weapons. Chien San-chiang, now chief of the atomic program, said in 1955 that gas masks, wet handkerchiefs, shelters, mine shafts and trenches would protect most people from an atomic bomb half a mile away. Mao reportedly said in the spring of 1957 that China would never make atomic bombs, because it could never catch up with the United States.

In May 1958, when the reactor in Peking was nearing completion, Chen Yi changed the tune, telling German correspondents that Communist China would have nuclear weapons in the future. Commander of the Air Force Liu Ya-lou also wrote in the *Liberation Army Press* that China would have "the most up-to-date aircraft and atomic bombs in the not-distant future." At the dedication of the Peking reactor, science chief Nieh Jung-chen said: "We warn the United States that it cannot monopolize and corner nuclear weapons." In late 1960 Liu Shao-chi said in Moscow that

China would soon become a nuclear power. A year later Chen Yi told a foreign correspondent that "when China has nuclear arms, the question of war will be settled." In August 1962, he again said in Geneva that it was "a matter of time." Most of these statements were for consumption abroad, and all stated the obvious. Communist China will be a nuclear power *someday*. So will the Congo or Monaco or Pago Pago.

Domestic pronouncements seem to pin-point the real situation. The *China Youth Press* said in early 1959 that man rather than weapon would decide the outcome of wars, and the militia "has a strength far superior to any new weapon. This is a truth repeatedly proved by the protracted Chinese Revolutionary War." Marshal Lin Piao in late 1960 told an army conference that China's "spiritual atomic bomb," built of courage and ideological consciousness, "is far more superior and useful than the physical atomic bomb." Meantime the Hsinhua News Agency was telling the nation: "The human-sea tactics can defeat nuclear weapons."

Still—the human sea.

Can Communist China adequately and sufficiently refine uranium and isolate fissionable materials when it cannot produce good steel and pig iron? Can it be sure that its nuclear warheads would explode over enemy territory when its vacuum bottles are exploding all over its own country? Can it make jet bombers and missiles and satellites with the same artistic license it puts into village ball-bearings, indigenous lathes, man-push trains on wooden railroads, double-deck rice paddies, clocks that gallop and trucks that refuse to run?

The answers are no—not in the foreseeable future. The unforeseeable future depends not only on a drastic economic recovery but also on a complete change of Peking's mystical outlook on science and technology. If no such change is made, and if another Great Leap takes place some day, it should not be surprising to hear of a bamboo H-bomb—made of indigenous plutonium and deuterium-tritium and the Thoughts of Mao Tse-tung.

IX HOME, CONFUCIUS, AND CHASTE WIDOWS

THE WORLD'S MOST MONOLITHIC SOCIAL SYSTEM, CON-
sidered in strength, scope and duration, is probably the Chinese
family institution. It is a unique system practiced by the world's
most populous nation for more than 2,400 years, covering every
phase of their private and public lives. It is omnipotent. And
ubiquitous. It is the anchor of traditional Chinese society. The
Chinese Communists have deliberately and systematically tried to
destroy it.

The family is the fundamental social unit in almost every society. But in China, through philosophical deliberations and historical accidents, it was sublimated into all human relations.
Politics, economics, religion and social activities became mere
extensions of the family. As early as 2,200 B.C., a Chinese leader
taught the people five basic human relationships. They were those
of king-subject, father-son, husband-wife, between brothers, and
between friends. But it was Confucius (551–479 B.C.) who elaborated and consolidated the family concept, which was to char-
acterize Chinese governments, channel Chinese economy, and
color Chinese psychology.

Confucius envisioned a perfect society in which every member
had a specific position, governed by innate morals and harmoni-
ously interrelated. The touchstone of these predominantly moral
relations was filial piety. This father-son relation when extended
to the king and his subjects resulted in the concept of obedience to
paternal authority, and when magnified to cover all mankind

became brotherly love. The Chinese family thrived under this basic idea and grew into a formidable institution which is responsible for China's many blessings and woes.

The typical traditional family was governed by a complex differentiation in generation, sex, and age. The father was the authoritarian but paternal head of the household; he chose the son's wife and profession and theoretically had the power of life and death over the son. Although his first duty was to obey his father, the son must observe equal filial piety to his mother. The proper relation between spouses was one of harmony and decorum. Brothers and sisters were ranked by age, though the ranking of sex among siblings preceded that of age. It was the tradition for married sons and their families to live in the same household with the parents. Such a typical "big family," usually consisting of three generations, was quite a phenomenon. It was a vast family bureaucracy, covering relations between the daughters-in-law and parents-in-law, between the wives of the sons, between the sons and their sisters-in-law, between the cousins, and among uncles and aunts and nephews and nieces. The situation became even merrier if the father had concubines who begot sons who raised their own crops of children. The traditional kinship included nine generations vertically, five grades horizontally, and covered twenty-nine categories of relatives, each with a pair of two-way titles and a distinct prescription for mourning.

Such a family though unwieldy in structure was diabolically cohesive. It moved about in Chinese society as a single unit, impregnable, unfissionable and unabashedly clannish. Although it shielded itself from strangers with figurative and literal walls, the family within itself generally practiced a natural communism. At meals the members ate not individual portions but from community dishes, which is still the custom today. There was little privacy within the family itself. Mail could be opened ethically by any family member. Knocking at another's door before entering was an unknown custom. It was bad manners for a couple to close their bedroom door except at night. Income and expenditure were often pooled, either partially or totally, so that widows, senile uncles, young morons, the crippled and even the lazy were all taken care of. A family shared the honor or disgrace of all its members.

This puissant togetherness produced many unique social phenomena. The traditional Chinese symbolically treated his ancestors as part of the living family. The ancestors were offered real food and wine at New Year and other festivals. They took part in all important family occasions like births, weddings and house-moving. At *Chingming*, the Festival of Tomb Sweeping, the whole family trekked to the family tombs to pay respects—rather gaily. When a Chinese died, his family, including even remote members of the clan, staged a noisy, colorful funeral complete with a banquet for all the mourners. The deceased was sent off to join the other ancestors with silk robes, a massive lacquered coffin and an elaborate tomb. Geomancy, the divination of the position of tombs and houses relative to the surrounding topography, was widely practiced to ensure family fortune and happiness.

The family consciousness links the murky incense smoke of the ancestral past to the animated wailing of bouncing baby boys. A son, or even better, many sons to continue the family and take care of the ancestors was considered the acme of bliss. For Confucius said: "Of the three unfilial sins, the greatest is having no descendant." Thus the most horrible punishment a man could receive in imperial China was not merely a death sentence, but the execution of his offspring and the obliteration of his ancestral graves. Sometimes families were formed even before the participants were born, as in the case of "belly-pointing marriages." Two expectant fathers who were good friends sometimes promised each other that if their babies turned out to be of opposite sexes, they would marry each other. A marriage was not a contract between two individuals but between two families.

So the traditional Chinese magnified his ego into an elaborate family which broke through the time barrier. It perpetuated itself by integrating the dead, the living and the unborn into an endless line that stretched beyond the womb and the tomb. This was his immortality. This was the bedrock on which all other superstructures were built. To preserve the family, Confucian tradition did everything possible to consolidate marriage. Divorces were frowned upon. The remarriage of widows was taboo. The family mind was so encompassing that even a man's mistress was integrated into the family as a concubine, who could never usurp the wife's title as long as the latter was living.

Although the Chinese thrived best among his clan, he had to have friends. The best of friends, however, became "brothers" or "sisters" through a blood vow. Chinese history and legends have many famous loyal friendships bound by this artificial family tie, the best known being the three brothers of the Peach Garden, epic heroes of *Tales of Three Kingdoms*, and the 108 swashbuckling Robin Hoods of *Water Margin* (*All Men Are Brothers*). In social intercourse with non-relatives, a Chinese still calls others "elder brother" or "elder sister" and himself "younger brother" or "younger sister."

The nation was construed as a big family. According to Confucian ideals, the people must obey the government like filial sons while the government must care for the people like a loving father. This paternal authoritarianism is of importance in appraising all forms of government in China, past or present. The emperor, however, was more of a father-image and high priest than an absolute monarch. The real government in traditional China was at the communal level. The agricultural mode of life rooted the people in their native places so that villages often consisted of clans. The village gentry, headed by village elders, performed many functions done in the West by the government. These invisible governments ruled by custom and tradition. They ran schools, built roads, irrigation systems and public granaries, meted out justice except in homicide, handled relief during famine, and took care of widows, orphans, and the aged who had no relatives. Ancestral shrines were community centers where worship, festivity, recreation, and arbitration of disputes took place.

The family mind also went into Chinese economic life. A family was not only a consumption unit but also a production unit, especially in rural China. Even artisans and craftsmen worked in the family. Employees in a shop or merchant's house lived and ate together like a family. To help traders who traveled far, native guilds were established in cities and towns, where a visitor could use his own guild as hotel, restaurant, bank, church, recreation center, and club. In South China non-marrying maidservants even today form sororities which provide mutual unemployment, sickness and old-age benefits.

In this manner traditional Chinese society entrenched itself and thrived for 2,400 years, from the days of Confucius to this century. It was essentially a society in which the family took the place of the government, the church, the factory, the bank, the public organization, and the Lonely Hearts Club. Then came the Opium War and a century of social turmoil. The Chinese reappraised their comfortable rut and found it inadequate. They discovered many evil outgrowths of the traditional family system. Filial piety sometimes became a tool of political and family tyrants. In-fighting was inevitable in the "big family," especially between the mother and the daughter-in-law, with the latter always coming out second best. Inequality between the sexes and the mania for sons resulted in concubinage, foot-binding, the drowning of girl infants by poor families, and the mummified tradition of erecting stone *pailou* (memorial arches) to honor chaste widows. Family solidarity grew into clannishness, which discouraged the enterprising and the adventurous, and encouraged the lazy and the spineless. Civic spirit was impossible to inspire. Geomancy, burials, funerals, weddings, and births became obsessions, sapped much time and money, and often caused families to go deeply into debt with lavish ceremonies to show they were filial to the dead or affectionate to the living. The worst was what happened to politics. Since the family was the smallest unit socially, economically and politically, when a man became a magistrate or viceroy, his first moral duty was to share the benefits with his family and to give good positions to his relatives. The traditional Chinese too often considered nepotism a legitimate means of traveling through politics on a family plan. Corruption was a natural and serious result. The Chinese conscience abhors doing harm to an individual, but it would not hesitate to do things at the expense of the collective man, for example, society or the nation, because the Chinese mind cannot encompass any society outside the family.

Thus, the big family, which was the core of traditional society, became the prime target of all social and political reformers of contemporary China. Imbued with Western concepts of individualism and the equality of sexes, the literati of modern China wrote profusely on the evils of the big family and traditional society. And Confucius, who glorified the family tie but was not responsible for its evil outgrowths, sometimes became a casualty of the richocheting epithets. These sentiments, prevalent and genuine among Chinese intellectuals and youth, found voice in the 1911 Revolution, in the Literary Renaissance of 1917, and in the May Fourth Movement of 1919. Along with the end of the imperial era in 1911 came a drastic social upheaval which was unbelievably radical for the time. Chinese men cut off their own queues, which were a Manchu custom imposed on the Chinese and had become the symbol of Chinese humiliation. Wailing diehards had their queues snipped off by scissors-happy youths in the streets. Footbinding, concubinage, opium-smoking, and the drowning of girl infants were condemned by the government and society. Young people glorified in the "freedom of marriage" and "freedom of love." Women entered business, the professions, politics and all social activities.

But the picture of modern Chinese society during the pre-Communist years was lopsided. On one hand, part of the enlightened society, mainly the intellectuals and urban people, had shattered many old traditions. In fact, in some respects they became even more socially unconventional and politically radical than contemporary Americans. On the other hand, life in rural China still stuck to the traditional ways. Centuries of habit could not be uprooted overnight. Most pre-Communist reformers, however, never meant to abolish entirely the old social framework, the traditional family concept, or Confucian teachings. They tried with slow and partial success to eliminate the excesses and abuses of an intrinsically good system. Confucius was still venerated for his philosophy and some of his moral concepts, although not for his political overtones. His idea of government by gentlemen, with officials guided by private conscience instead of public legislation, was considered unworkable and obsolete. This understandably critical attitude of the younger generations gave an opening to the Communists, who dislike the family system more for its cohesion than for its shortcomings.

The family anywhere is man's source of strength and courage, as well as his emotional harbor at times of natural disaster and personal misfortune. In China it was even more so. It was society itself. The Chinese Communists were acutely aware that their control of the people could never be effective unless the monolithic family system was destroyed, along with religion and conventional morals.

This they set out to do as soon as they came into power. The first step was land reform, which gave land to the peasants with the right hand and took it away with the left, but the real purpose of which was the liquidation of the rural gentry, which constituted China's real, effective government extended from the family. The second step was the new Marriage Law, which in practice made marriage more difficult and divorce fantastically easy. The third step was the elimination of religion, not by outright suppression but by perversion of various religious faiths into mere arms of Communism. The latest step was the commune system, which summarily put men, women, children, and the aged in segregated labor camps, destroyed ancestral graves, and reduced marital relations to brief, Party-rationed sex-breaks.

In conjunction with and in between these major steps, the Communists conducted countless "struggle meetings" or public accusations aimed at destroying filial piety, brotherly love, and friendship. Sons were forced to denounce fathers. Wives were pitted against husbands, brothers against sisters, employees against employers, friends against friends. In Communist China family members do not confide in each other, and friends avert their glances in streets.

To strike at the nucleus of the family, the Communists promulgated a deceptively "enlightened" Marriage Law in 1950, but it was implemented in a manner which revealed its unadmitted purpose. The main features of this law, such as the prohibition of child betrothal, concubinage, polygamy, and interference with widows' remarriage; the legal right of children to choose their own mates, the protection of illegitimate children, equal shares of inheritance for sons and daughters, and equal rights in divorce, were publicized as a bold, revolutionary liberation of the downtrodden people from the practices of a decadent society. It happens that all these points had already been initiated by the Nationalists in their Civil Code of 1931, and many Chinese had already availed themselves of these rights. Others, mainly the peasants, had failed to—because of their own conservative attitude.

In theory, under the Communist law, all applicants fulfilling the usual qualifications are allowed to marry. But in practice they cannot unless they get permission from the local government. Thus many marriages are forbidden because applicants come from different classes of a supposedly classless society, or are "attracted by each other's good looks and not labor productivity." All marriages involving Party members are strictly controlled by the Party.

Divorce is granted unconditionally and unilaterally, except to the husband of a pregnant wife and the spouse of a "revolutionary soldier." The law carefully enumerates the conjugal duties, including features like "labor production" and "joint struggle for the construction of a new society," but no mention is made of cohabitation and fidelity. An official of the Central Committee for the Implementation of the Marriage Law Movement declared at a broadcast: "It is prohibited to investigate or struggle against the unconventional sexual relations between men and women." The *Sian Masses Daily* put it more bluntly: "The People's Courts need not handle adultery. The exposure of adultery by a third party on any pretext, no matter from what motive, is strictly prohibited." Many judges who ruled against unfaithful husbands or wives caught in the act were denounced for their "suppression of the freedom of love."

Large numbers of Party activists were sent to the villages to "implement" the law. At accusation meetings peasant women were selected to "spit bitter water" by denouncing their husbands and in-laws. While some of the grievances were genuine, others were Party-manufactured and forced on the unwilling accusers. To show that they were liberated, traditional-minded, weeping widows were forced to remarry at mass ceremonies, the old ones to peasants and the young ones to Party members.

These measures resulted in social chaos which worried even the Communists. Official figures showed that the divorce rate shot up steeply: 186,000 cases in 1950, 409,000 in 1951, 398,000 in first half of 1952 (making the 1952 *pro rata* figure 796,000), and 1,170,000 in 1953. From 1954 on the number started to taper off but has since been hovering around the half-million figure. The ratio between divorce and marriage at one time hit 80 percent. A Tientsin paper estimated in 1953 that each year in four leading cities 2 million people, counting children and parents, were affected by divorce.

Jealousy, hatred and promiscuity generated by this policy resulted in many tragedies other than broken marriages. In Mukden 40 percent of the mental cases, which used to be rare in China, resulted from marital trouble. Many young women, mostly peasants, died as a result of their promiscuity. They committed suicide out of remorse, or were murdered by their husbands, in-laws, other women, or even traditional-minded Communist *kanpu*. The

Communist press carried numerous reports of peasant women being forced to marry Party members or raped by Communist officials to whom they went for marriage licenses. In 3 cities and 14 counties in Kwangtung, 1,024 murders and suicides took place in 20 months because of marital and sexual troubles. In Hsiangtan, Mao Tse-tung's home county in Hunan, 1,180 women killed themselves or were killed during a single month in 1950. Communist reports estimated that between 70,000 to 80,000 persons, mostly women, died each year because of these reasons.

The increase in illegitimate babies resulted in harmful abortions and infanticide. During one year in three counties in Kwangtung, 1,888 babies were drowned. In two years in a single special district in Kwangsi, 6,425 babies were killed out of shame. These and other statistics were reported by the Chinese Communists with increasing alarm until 1953, when all revealing reports suddenly stopped.

The break-up of the family released an immense female labor force for the Communists. There were only 700,000 women industrial workers in 1949. Ten years later there were 8 million. In 1952 only 30 percent of the peasant women worked in the fields. By 1958 over 90 percent were doing hard labor, of whom 73 million worked in water conservancy, 67 million in forestation and 13 million in experimental farming. By making menstruating and pregnant women pull plows, dig ditches, and haul stone, the average annual working days for women were doubled within two years. Many miscarriages resulted. The All-China Federation of Democratic Women reported that of the 120,703 coal miners in Manchuria, 74,885 were women. The importance of female labor may be gathered from a conference during the Great Leap when it was decided that all available women between sixteen and forty-five should be mobilized and graded into four classes, assigned physical tasks identical to men's to "foster competition," and encouraged to sever family ties.

The evils of traditional Chinese society can easily be, and have often been, exaggerated. From the modern point of view, this predominantly Confucian society was stultified, prissy, and feudalistic. But there were many desirable elements in that society that should not only be retained by the Chinese but are sorely needed in Western cultures. Old age was not a thing to be dreaded, but a time when one's care and affection were repaid by one's children. Invisible social insurance inherent in the family system took care of many people without the staggering costs and bureaucracy attendant in modern orphanage and old-age care. Very few people were entirely kinless or lonely, which is too frequent a curse in Western society.

Even some of the undesirable features in traditional Chinese society had built-in curbs. Confucian society was deliberately non-egalitarian, but it was not rigidly stratified like the feudalistic society in Europe. China has had no hereditary aristocracy for over 2,000 years, and has never had a caste system. Its traditional classes were scholars, farmers, artisans and tradesmen. The scholars were the most respected. They governed China for some twenty centuries. Next came the farmers, who were considered the nation's foundation. Artisans and tradesmen came next. They were small in number and mere offshoots of the old society, as craftsmanship and trade were considered vulgar necessities while learning and farming were noble pursuits. These classes were more fluid than they appeared, however. As the study of Chinese classics depends mainly on persevering self-education, scholars came from all other classes. Once a man was educated he automatically became a member of the scholar-gentry regardless of his financial status or origin. The *nouveaux riches* were not socially respected until the second or third generation when they acquired scholarship. The imperial examinations were open to all classes, so that the mandarin bureaucracy was constantly reinvigorated. When a mandarin retired he invariably returned to his fields and orchards as a gentleman farmer. Peasants were often engaged in crafts or trade as a sideline. Even a full-time artisan or trader usually had a tiny ancestral plot of his own.

The authoritarian feature of the Confucian concept was balanced by paternalism. Emphasis on inner morals in rulers and the ruled, though not always practiced, was nevertheless a strong curb. The fluid classes were made even less distinguishable by the family lines cutting across them. Kinsmen of all social strata mixed freely at religious and clan functions. Marriages between different classes were not infrequent, although almost all were girls from humbler families marrying into families of higher standing.

Confucius stratified his society by differentiations in generation, in sex, and in age, but such a stratification was deceptive. Status in generation and age, though not in sex, changed for each person through life, so that nobody was at the receiving end permanently—except the women. There are, however, some popular fallacies about the status of women in traditional China. Confucius put the woman below the man, but he tempered this with the status of generation and age, and mellowed it with harmony between the spouses. The Chinese woman was far more influential than Western sociological legends would have us believe, since she received filial obeisance. Even before her husband she was not necessarily a picture of submissiveness.

Concubinage stemmed from the traditional, but not Confucian, double standard. Its respectable aim of strengthening the patrilineal line was too often a disguise for erotic motives. It was definitely a social illness. Like all social illnesses it was more a symptom than a cause. Western cultures have still not found an adequate remedy for marital infidelity. Whether a wife with a concubine in tow is unhappier than a divorcee, and whether a concubine is unhappier than a mistress, are questions for the philosopher to ponder rather than the moralist to judge.

Outside the family the woman had little formal status. But since society *was* the family, few bothered about it. Many important political transactions, however, were effected via the "apron-string relation," or the *sub rosa* network of wives, aunts and mothers. Look into Chinese history and one finds behind every throne a delicate female hand. Far more great dynasties were toppled in

China by the cherry mouths and almond eyes of fragile Chinese women than ever dreamed of by the militant feminists of the West. The august Ming Dynasty, for instance, was vanquished by the Manchus because of a beautiful woman. For many thousands of years Chinese women excelled in painting and even more in poetry. During the last imperial dynasty nearly 1,000 woman poets were published. The woman in traditional China was intensely feminine, and probably because of this she was not so helpless as she seemed.

Under the Communists, Chinese women were emancipated from the family and gained "complete equality." But they were emancipated from the family to become chattels of the state. They gained equality in hard labor. Fathers no longer arrange or forbid marriages. The state has taken over the prerogative. During the high tide of the communes, many people in China no longer had homes—humble and even ramshackle homes, but nevertheless homes. In their place were 3.6 million public dining halls, 5 million infant depots and nurseries, laundries and sewing centers, run along the grotesque lines of an insect society, until the communes broke down.

Instead of the old virtues, the Chinese Communists preach the New Morality. Filial piety is feudalistic and decadent. It should be substituted with unquestioned obedience and loyalty to the people, which means the state, which means the Party. Friendship based on mutual respect yields no benefit to the proletarian cause. Maternal love is not biological nor instinctive, but stems from the selfish desire for old-age support and private ownership. Marriage is not a private relation but a public matter. The first responsibility of a married couple is not to each other but to production—not of babies but in labor. Romantic love is bourgeois, egoistic, and degenerates into personal happiness. Proletarian love yields to the revolutionary spirit and is based on lofty Communist morality. These public sermons have not defined sex, but during the early Yenan days the Communists used the term "one cup of water" to describe their concept of sex. Engaging in sexual relations was just like drinking a cup of water, no more and no less. Many escapees testified that male and female labor conscripts at work sites were required to perform fornication duty by drawing lots, unless both parties wanted to call it off. In Communist China, the term "lover" is used to label without distinction one's sweetheart, spouse, or sexual partner.

Pa Jen, a prominent Communist writer and Peking's first ambassador to Indonesia, was purged because he wrote that the search for love, the attachment to maternal love, the joy of life, the hatred of death, the craving for a happy life, the admiration of high mettle and gallantry were "all things common to mankind." The moral arbiters in Peking sternly corrected him: "There is fundamentally no such thing as sentiment common to mankind, nor as common human nature. . . . There is no such thing as 'human love.'"

X LITERATURE
OF THE ILLITERATE

DURING THE 1958 GREAT LEAP, A TALENT EXPLOSION TOOK place in China that put the cultural brilliance of the Tang Dynasty to shame. It was the Chinese Communists who ignited the fuse. Within a few months 1,500 writers and artists in Shantung turned out 700,000 words and 5,000 works of art. A primary school in Manchuria completed one semester's arithmetic in four weeks. In Shanghai 2,500 plays were authored. A poet, who was an illiterate only two months ago, composed 4,000 poems in 20 days. Suddenly, the Party discovered 200 million poets in China.

This instant culture of the Instant Paradise gushed out not only from inspired amateurs but also from professionals. Lao She (or Lau Shaw), author of *Rickshaw Boy,* was appointed a cultural foreman to assign production quotas to leading writers and artists. The editor of the magazine *People's Literature* was ordered to write within one year ten plays and short stories for children; the editor of *Poetry Periodical,* ten short stories and twenty poems; and several hundred other novelists, playwrights, and poets, quotas of ten or more literary works. As a Shanghai newspaper said ecstatically: "Wherever the Party Committees put their hands to literature, production increases."

After all, China was the most civilized nation at some point of the world's history. Even though over half of its population is illiterate, it is the most literarily-inclined country whose adoration for scholars once bordered on mania. Culture, China's richest heritage, is not found in museums, galleries or expensive opera houses. Through a virtual osmosis, art and literature are closely woven into the texture of Chinese life. They are found not only in esoteric writings and paintings, but also in the operatic arias hummed by laborers, in the classical New Year couplets on village huts, in the exquisite embroidery and lacy paper-cuts made by peasant women, in the elegant jade, ivory, bronzes, and ceramics made by lowly craftsmen, and in the magnificent palaces, temples, pagodas, and rock gardens dotting the Chinese landscape. It is remarkable for any nation that the conversation of illiterates is sprinkled with sages' sayings, their behavior steeped with Confucian philosophy, and statesmen, warlords, and bandits compose poetry.

Rich nuances and terseness make the Chinese language the most suggestive and epigrammatic. These peculiarities also make it inadequate in logical and scientific exposition, but give it finesse in evoking moods, depicting nature, and leaving ideas unspoken but impinging on the reader's consciousness. This is especially so with classical Chinese in which every word is carefully weighed for its euphony and overtones in meaning. Classical prose, however, mainly affords a vehicle for philosophical and ethical concepts, and the pleasure of *belles-lettres*. It is in fiction, written in the vernacular, that Chinese prose excels in the portrayal of life. Until the recent past, fiction was not considered cultivated. Hence novels were generally written in the lively nonclassical language and their themes were less punctilious. As a result fiction was truer to life and yielded some of China's greatest novels during the past several hundred years. Among them are: *Dream of Red Chamber,* a sensual romance; *Water Margin* (or *All Men Are Brothers*), an adventure of valiant outlaws; *Tales of Three Kingdoms,* a historic saga; and *Golden Vase Plum,* an erotic novel.

The highest achievement in Chinese literature is in classical poetry. Unlike the Westerners, the Chinese love poetry and are not ashamed of it. All Chinese scholars and many Chinese politicians write poems. For a long period the composing of classical poems was a requisite of the imperial examinations at which state officials were selected. In the old days when a warlord won a battle, when a politician retired, when a bandit faced the execution squad, or when a jilted lover committed suicide, he would often write a poem. From official edicts, astrologers' horoscopes to schoolboys' *billets-doux*, from judges' verdicts to herb doctors' prescriptions—all were often written in classical verse.

Chinese poetry reached its zenith during the Tang Dynasty, the era of such great poets like Li Po, Tu Fu, Po Chu-yi, and Wang Wei, whose works are revered to this day. Dainty and lyrical, Chinese poetry usually sings of secret longings, unrequited love, the beauty of nature, and the futility of fame and wealth. It reveals the vagabond in the outwardly Confucian Chinese and is strongly influenced by Taoist romanticism as is Chinese painting, which is inseparable from Chinese poetry. The themes, the moods, and even the impressionistic techniques are similar in Chinese poetry and painting. Most paintings are embellished with verses. Many famous poets were also good painters.

Although early Chinese painting was influenced by the Persians and Greco-Indian Buddhists, during the Tang Dynasty Chinese philosophical and poetic trends entered painting and a great school emerged. Completely oblivious of the human body and only occasionally interested in still objects, painters from the Tang Dynasty on, concentrated on *shan-shui* (mountain and water) or landscapes.

In a Chinese painting, the colors are simple and tones subdued. It spurns perspective and physical likeness, as two-dimensional presentation of perspective is a concept of the logical mind and physical likeness is the interpretation of the naked eye. It appeals directly to emotion by conveying an impression of reality through mood, atmosphere, and rhythm, while keeping the physical essence from disintegrating into geometrical gyrations. A bamboo does not look exactly like a bamboo, yet the viewer knows it is a bamboo. The Chinese painter takes long walks by mountains and rivers. He takes no notes, makes no sketches and memorizes no details. He only absorbs impressions. The breaking away from physical form and delineation, which modern Western painters are still trying to do, was delightfully accomplished by Chinese painters 1,000 years ago.

Merging into and inseparable from painting is calligraphy, which, done with the same sensitive, responsive brush, is considered even a higher art than painting. It is considered pure art, as it dispenses even with the material form, but concentrates on abstract composition and rhythm. As in painting, brush strokes in calligraphy vary widely but empty spaces are supremely important. Nothing delights a cultivated Chinese more than the suspended momentum, the subtle rhythm, the powerful suppleness and the eloquence of blank spaces in fine painting and calligraphy. Jade, bronze, ceramics and embroidery, much treasured by Western connoisseurs, are considered by the Chinese as crafts or lower forms of art, much inferior to painting and calligraphy.

The May Fourth literary revolution marked a tumultuous change in Chinese culture. From then to the Communist takeover in 1949, there was a period of creative ferment marked by widespread, and sometimes wild, experimentations. The greatest change was in literature, when Hu Shih and Chen Tu-hsiu unfurled the banner of *pai hua* (the vernacular) and of a new Western-oriented literary consciousness. A tremendous volume of Western literary and philosophical writing from more than twenty countries was translated and avidly read. Turning their back upon Confucius, Chinese intellectuals looked to Aristotle, Schopenhauer, Nietzsche, Voltaire, Kant, and Hegel. Due to the social messages in their writings, Dickens, Turgeniev, Sinclair, and Gorky became as popular as Hugo, Zola and Tolstoy. Innate romanticism and newly acquired Western individualism caused Chinese youth to gravitate toward Rousseau, Thoreau, Emerson, Byron, Shelley, and Keats. Art students imitated Matisse and Cézanne. Musicians played Beethoven, Schubert, and Chopin. Sad-eyed young men suffered the sorrows of Werther. The more fiery ones went through the conflicts of Dostoyevsky's Ivan Karamazov. Girls rebelled against the traditional family in the fashion of Ibsen's Nora Helmer. Many young women either imitated or lived vicariously the episodes of Anna Karenina, Madame Bovary, and Lady Windermere.

This upheaval was sometimes zany but always kaleidoscopic and pregnant with possibilities. It revitalized the Chinese culture and meanwhile produced many social and cultural incongruities. Education was appreciably promoted by the government, individual reformers, and American missionaries, who founded many fine modern institutions of learning. Literacy was pushed, but ineffectively, because private educators were short of funds and the government was preoccupied. The time-consuming study of the written language touched off various unsuccessful attempts at Romanization of the characters.

Due to the craze for anything Western, folk art remained with the *hoi polloi* and did not interest the intellectuals. While the Chinese opera continued to thrive, and ballad-singing and drum songs were enjoyed by the peasants, Chinese music and singing in purer forms virtually died. In their place came Western popular and concert music, and a new version of popular Chinese songs whose effect, however, was minimal. Chinese cinema seldom rose above the third-rate level because of its cheap imitation of Hollywood. Chinese painting and classical poetry were still appreciated, but they merely survived and were not revived.

In literature, the classics were progressively pushed into the esoteric realm by the thriving of *pai hua*, in which form most novels, short stories, and plays were written, virtually always with social messages. *Pai-hua* poetry became the vogue in the Twenties. It is usually in *vers libre*, combining romanticism with imagism, both of which are innate with the Chinese. A new crop of writers came into being. Besides Hu Shih and Chen Tu-hsiu, there were Hsu Tse-mou, leader of the new poetry, Lin Yutang, humorist and philosopher, Lao She, novelist, and many others.

The writers who directly influenced Chinese politics were the leftist writers of the proletarian literati. Among them were Lu Hsun, biting satirist who became the official Communist literary idol after his death; Mao Tun, novelist on social injustice and class strife; Kuo Mo-jo, trumpet-tongued rebel; Ting Ling, unconventional woman writer; and Pa Chin, novelist critical of the traditional family. These writers were the voice of the angry intellectuals during the pre-Communist era, and were greatly responsible for winning many other intellectuals over to the Communists.

When the Communists came into power in 1949, a confused but fertile cultural era ended, and another one began. The Chinese Communist attitude toward culture was laid down by Mao Tsetung in 1940 in his *New Democracy*. Labeling China's traditional and later Western-influenced culture as imperialist and semifeudal, he said: "This reactionary culture serves the imperialists and the feudal class, and must be swept away. . . . The new culture and the reactionary culture are locked in a struggle in which one must die so that the other may live." In 1942 Mao added a prescription for the New Culture: "Proletarian art and literature are part of the entire cause of the proletarian revolution . . . the Party's artistic and literary activity occupies a definite and assigned position in the Party's total revolutionary work and is subordinated to the prescribed revolutionary task." Mao's artistic and literary criticism has been a dogma ever since.

To achieve these aims, the Communists promoted literacy, tried to abolish Chinese writing, metamorphosed education, burned books, rewrote history, re-interpreted old literature, prodded writers to write and purged many for doing so.

To cut off the dastardly old culture, within the first three years of their reign the Communists burned 600,000 books and 3,000 sets of book mats in the city of Shanghai alone. These were books in publishing houses and libraries and did not include privately owned books destroyed by frightened individuals. *The Commercial Press,* pre-Communist China's leading publisher for half a century, had 15,000 titles in 1949. By 1952, over 14,000 had gone up in smoke. The next biggest publisher *Chung Hua* had its titles reduced from 13,000 to 2,000. Some 95 percent of the books on literature, geography, and history and 97 percent of those on social sciences were burned. So were all the books of the three next biggest publishers. Many books of fiction and poetry were destroyed for propagating "bourgeois sentimentalism."

In education the Communists have done a titanic task—statistically. They took over 227 institutions of higher learning from the Nationalists. During the Great Leap 5,483 "institutions of higher learning" were turning out Complete Communists. Statistics for secondary, primary and literacy education were equally impressive. In one month Chekiang province established 6,500 high schools, and in six days a county in Kiangsi established 300 primary schools. These figures certainly indicate that a tremendous number of people were being "educated."

But a more important point is the quality of that education. The so-called "red-expert" universities (ideology first, technology second), the spare-time universities, and the normal schools are actually erratic evening classes taught by a strange breed of teachers. In 1958 in the Kiangsi hills, 102 red-expert colleges appeared overnight with an enrollment of 55,000. At the start, it was proudly claimed, there were no buildings, no money, no textbooks and no teachers. But the masses created everything. Hillbilly *kanpu*, demobilized soldiers, carpenters, and poultry farmers served as teachers. The students immediately built classrooms, supported the schools by their own labor, and created their own texts to teach themselves.

Conditions in genuine universities and schools are better. But the students must labor, which is second only to political indoctrination. In big cities college students spend about a quarter to half, and high-school students about five-eighths of their time at labor. In 1960, 120,000 students in Peking, and 200,000 in Mukden worked as farmers and construction workers. In smaller cities and towns the students are virtual free-labor brigades at the beck and call of any town government, people's bank, textile cooperative, or postal office to farm, dig canals, demolish city walls, take census, fight epidemics, or catch flies. Although these practices have been going on since 1958, the Communists officially decreed in 1960 that all college and high-school students must "consolidate study with labor, and go to factories, mines, construction projects and farms to eat, live and labor with the masses." Professors and students who cried plaintively "Treat students like students" were condemned as rightists. Conditions improved somewhat in 1961, but the following year more students were sent to the farms because of the worsened food situation.

After several thousand years of evolution, the Chinese language has become messy, esoteric, illogical, beautiful, exquisitely refined, infuriatingly inexact, and a titanic headache to Sinologists. It has only one written script, but its pronunciation falls into many dialects. The great difference between classical and vernacular Chinese further complicates the problem. With the adoption of *pai hua*, a movement for a common spoken language, Peking Mandarin, which coincides with *pai hua*, was pushed in the late 1910's. By now some three-fourths of the Chinese can speak or understand this common language. A phonetic-symbol system was promulgated by the government in 1918 and later pushed by the Nationalists. But it did not solve the fundamental problems arising from the characteristics of the Chinese script. Some missionaries and Chinese scholars tried Romanization but these attempts never went beyond the academic level because of insoluble problems and strong opposition.

The Chinese Communists, however, with Russian assistance, have favored Romanization from the beginning. Mao once said that China's old culture was "rotten and should be completely destroyed." In order to do this, "our written language must be reformed." In 1956 Peking officially announced the adoption of a set of Roman alphabets to replace the Chinese script. Opposition from Chinese intellectuals both inside and outside the country was strong, because the critics realized that this would result in a complete cutting off of the cultural heritage. Chinese script evolved from pictures and its monosyllabic ideographs have vast numbers of homonyms. Peking Mandarin has only 470 syllabic sounds representing tens of thousands of characters or words. A medium-size dictionary has 110 characters all written differently and all have different meanings, but all pronounced *li*. Sometimes, a single word is pronounced differently for different meanings. Furthermore, the Chinese language has no parts of speech. The use of each word is solely determined by its position in a sentence. If the language is Romanized, some 70–90 percent of existing Chinese words will have to be discarded because of the homonym problem. Thus all classics and much vernacular writing of the past could not be translated into the impoverished new language. Even in this skeletal form it is often unintelligible. All these built-in hitches, however, did not discourage Peking, which thundered in 1957: "The phonetic reform is a necessity for the masses, and the Party will not yield to the sentimental feelings of 5 million intellectuals."

But by 1959, the language reformers retreated in the face of a Romanized Babel. One major reason was that Romanization presupposes the disappearance of dialects, which would take a couple of generations to achieve. Even Mandarin is pronounced by most people with local accents. For example, Mao Tse-tung speaks Mandarin with a turgid Hunan tone, Chou En-lai with a heavy Shaohsing twang, Chu Teh with a peppery Szechwan accent. Their common language sounds as common as those of a Cockney, a Brooklynite and a Texan. When talking they manage to understand each other. When reading the standard Romanization, which requires reading aloud to be understood, probably none of them can decipher half the text. If phoneticized according to their individual pronunciations, the versions become different languages. By now the Communists still propose to replace the Chinese script with Roman alphabets "eventually," but in reality they have conceded that the alphabets would co-exist with the old characters indefinitely. Most probably the alphabets will gradually and silently disappear in a few years. Technically, it would be easier for the Chinese to switch to English or French or Russian than to this artificial half-measure. Languages are born of the living people, not of zealous politicians or linguistic engineers.

More difficult than burning books, abolishing the script, and obliterating liberal education is the eradication of so-called bourgeois idealism, not only in political scholars, but in the leftist literati and even in some of the most loyal Communist writers. Since the Communists came into power, several hundred literary purges, including a dozen major ones involving many thousands of intellectuals, have been officially recorded. One of the best-known cases was about the *Dream of Red Chamber*.

This eighteenth-century novel, read by every literate Chinese, is a poetic romance about Cha Pao-yu, a brilliant, neurotic young scion of a mandarin family that lives in a resplendent villa. Enjoying the gaiety and pampering of many attractive female cousins and maid-servants, Pao-yu is in love with a delicate, melancholy cousin. When she dies of consumption and heartbreak after Pao-yu marries another cousin as arranged by his parents, his torment causes him to forsake everything and become a monk. The novel is allegorical, panoramic, has a touch of Taoist mysticism and is considered by many as the best artistic fiction in Chinese literature. During the past century or so, many Chinese scholars tried to interpret the *Dream* as an allegory depicting real people and situations. There is even a special study, called *Redology*, devoted solely to the research into this novel. Eventually Hu Shih, "Father of the Chinese Renaissance," after exhaustive research into the background of the author, concluded that the novel was mainly autobiographical. This judgment has been generally accepted by contemporary Chinese scholars.

In 1954, Yu Ping-po, a respected poet, professor at four leading universities and Europe-returned scholar who had devoted 30 years to *Redology*, and whose conclusion agreed with that of Hu Shih, published a critical article on the novel, reiterating his past opinion that its prime function was "to induce the reader to affirm the reality of life, to stimulate him in his striving for love and happiness." This brought upon Yu the wrath of the Party, which finds in all literature, ancient or modern, Eastern or Western, only Marxist heroes and reactionary villains. Two completely un-known Party literary hacks claimed that the novel was a piece of socialist realism, and that the hero and heroine were rebels against the feudalist family, bureaucracy and landlords. For six months, every publication, every school and every cultural or-ganization in Communist China was ordered to criticize Yu's de-cadent point of view. After several tens of thousands of sympo-siums, several millions of words of damnation and repeated confessions by Yu, the purge developed into an anti-Hu Shih campaign. Many intellectuals were punished with corrective labor. Hu Shih's son was forced to denounce his own father, who was in the United States. Hu, known to less dogmatic Chinese as a champion of democracy and liberalism, was labeled a "war crimi-nal" because of his evidential method of thinking and investiga-tion, and because he had been influenced by John Dewey.

There were many other similar purges. In 1951, *The Life of Wu Hsun,* a movie based on the true story of a nineteenth-century beggar who gave his money to build a school for the poor, was receiving praise from all Communists. Then a button was pushed by the *People's Daily,* and the movie was denounced as glorify-ing a slave of a feudalist society. Everybody who had praised the film had to eat crow.

Throughout 1955, heavy artillery fire was concentrated on an old philosopher, thinker and educator, Liang Shu-ming, who in-sisted that China's problem was not one of class struggle, but one of cultural and racial self-salvation through education and a com-promise of things East and West. Liang, however, never really capitulated. His "confessions" were full of veiled, eloquent de-fiance.

Then there was Wu Tsu-kang, well-known director of stage and screen, and author of twenty plays. He was punished for pointing out that since the Communists came to power, very few new talents had appeared in the theatre, cinema, and dance, and for revealing that the secret police constantly watched the actors in a Peking theatre.

Many purges were aimed even at established leftist and Party writers. The biggest was against Hu Feng, Lu Hsun's favorite disciple and for twenty years a member of the Party. Hu had the audacity to call Mao's Yenan forum talk on literature a "totem," to condemn the Party and police control of literature as "knives hanging over literary writers," and to say that the fine literary progress made since the May Fourth revolution was suffocating under rigid Party tenets. After a prolonged, nation-wide campaign, Hu was denounced as a counterrevolutionary and went insane in prison.

Other Party faithfuls purged included Feng Hsueh-feng, editor of the *Literary Gazette*, for saying that Soviet Russian literature was inferior to old Russian literature; Chang Chin-yi, vice-president of Shanghai writer's association and noted leftist writer, for writing to a student: "You will have peace if you look upon darkness as light and disgrace as honor"; and Ho Chi-fang, writer and leading denouncer of Hu Feng, for saying that the Party had made a serious mistake in destroying traditional Chinese culture. Another literary idol toppled from the Communist pedestal was Ting Ling, for several decades admired by leftist writers. She was punished for revolting against excessive Party control and for her advice to young students on "One Book-ism"—"once you have written a book, nobody can ever slap you down." Although she was a Communist for twenty-five years, and the winner of a Stalin prize, she was repeatedly humiliated and has been doing menial labor.

A literary work may be praised today and denounced tomorrow. Writers, artists, and dramatists simply ceased producing anything in order to save their own skin. By 1956 Communist China had become a cultural desert. In the early Fifties it was easy for a writer to plot his story with dark villains of Kuomintang bureaucrats and greedy landlords, culminating with the inevitable happy ending of "Liberation." After repeating themselves for a number of years this theme no longer had any real meaning. The old targets for satire or condemnation had disappeared and the use of any new target would be a sign of counter-revolution. Thus formerly prolific writers like Mao Tun, Pa Chin, Shen Tsung-wen, Hsieh Ping-hsin and Yeh Chao-chun have not written any novels for over a decade. Kuo Mo-jo, Lao She, Tsao Yu and Tien Han, who did write a little, produced works far inferior to their pre-Communist writings. Some twenty major works in fiction were done during this period, but mostly obsequious eulogies of the new regime by new authors. Much of the highly praised writings are memoirs of the revolution by old *kanpu.*

While Chinese history is being re-written, philosophy poses no problem. Moscow-returned young scholars can easily use Marx and Zhdanov to explain everything in the universe. Poetry is a barren field. The ban on traditional drama was lifted in 1956 when the public turned their back on revolutionary plays, but 100 of the 360 old dramas were altered in theme. Peking has made some 400 movies, generally with good acting, mediocre technique and fulsome themes. Music is the only area where some real progress has been made through Russian influence. Research into ancient Chinese music resulted in the discovery of some lost classical music. In painting, the favorite is of course the Russian school—a sort of nineteenth-century photographic naturalism most fitting for poster and magazine ads.

Due to their persistent popularity, some well-known old novels are republished, but with extensive deletions and revisions. The best-known anthology, *Three Hundred Tang Poems,* was reissued with two-thirds of the best poems of China's greatest poets replaced by second-rate verses.

In 1959 a poem praising the new regime was published in *People's Literature.* It said in part:

> In the vast spaces of the universe,
> The life of man is but a meteor gleam;
> In the endless river of time,
> It is but an infinitesimal ripple . . .
> Yet in comparison with thee,
> The world of man is inglorious.

The author, Kuo Hsiao-chuan, was castigated by Party critics for such "old-fashioned, trite, pessimistic, Taoist and Christian" thoughts. An art critic, commenting on an exhibition of Chinese painting, deplored that among the paintings only 28 percent were about agricultural and 10 percent about industrial production. Another critic rejected Mi Fei's style of painting rain as unrealistic. Mi Fei, a Sung Dynasty scholar-painter, is one of the greatest Chinese painters of all times.

Other works are highly praised, like these lines by poetess Fan Ling-ju:

> A rainbow brush touches the universe,
> The universe blossoms in splendor;
> Who may this painter be?
> The great and mighty Mao Tse-tung.

Another example of proletarian literature is a story for children, in which seven children form a labor corps and for three months move six million pieces of stone for construction. In spite of the forty-below temperature that caused their shoes to freeze on their feet and the skin of their palms to peel off on the freezing rocks, the children work day and night, even when others rest.

To the unenlightened intellectuals who called this proletarian literature "a mass of vulgarity," a Party culturist offered a bristling but somewhat babbled retort: "It is now impossible for the masses not to write. Of course, capitalists cannot understand this. But what is so ridiculous about it?"

What is so ridiculous about every poem singing of the great and mighty Mao Tse-tung? Or paintings of tractors, steel bridges and dams embellishing the traditional misty landscape? Or barrack-shaped cultural palaces? Or men hugging men foxtrotting at dance parties? Or the turning of cultured illiterates into uncultured literates? These questions are answered by the ghosts of the elegant past that still hover over changed China, laughing into the night at the hick mandarins aping the new barbarians across the steppes.

PART THREE

THE MACABRE PILGRIMAGE

XI SOFT SELL
AND STRANGLEHOLD

ONE OF THE MOST DEVASTATING CHINESE PSYCHOLOGICAL
gimmicks is known as "red face—white face." In traditional opera
the hero's face is painted red and the villain's white. The tactic is
to show the victim alternately the hero's and villain's face—reason-
ableness and intransigence, persuasion and force, the smile and the
snarl. It is a concept not entirely alien to the West, where the
spider's invitation to the fly is a crude version. But it took the
Chinese Communists to refine this innocuous trick into elegant
barbarism.

The two faces may be used by the same person at different
times, or by two accomplices at the same time, or the same person
at the same moment to different victims. Thus the trick has great
variety in degree, sequence and frequency. It can often trap an
unwary person, or lure a determined one into giving ground.
Twenty years ago Mao Tse-tung described it in his turgid Marxist
manner: "The United Front and the armed struggle are the two
chief weapons for defeating the enemy. The United Front is . . .
for carrying on the armed struggle. And the Party organization
is the heroic fighter who wields the two weapons . . . to storm
and shatter the positions of the enemy." In other words, the
United Front isolates the hard-core enemy temporarily as the sole
target, and mesmerizes all other potential enemies, onlookers and
busybodies into neutrals and duped allies. Mao has used this two-
edged weapon well. His *ta ta, tan tan; tan tan, ta ta* is a military
version of "red face—white face."

He used the red face—white face trick successfully on the Nationalists by alternating periods of cooperation, alliance, and fighting. He used it on the Chinese people successfully—until recently. Before and immediately after the Communists came into power, he promised land to peasants, protection of private enterprise to businessmen and industrialists, a coalition government to non-Communist politicians, freedom and democracy to intellectuals, and an Instant Paradise to all.

But when the Communists had consolidated their power in 1950, Mao began a series of perpetual "movements." The Land Reform liquidated 10 million "landlords and rich farmers." The collectivization and communes enslaved 500 million peasants. Two counterrevolutionary suppression campaigns in 1951 and 1955 eliminated all overt opponents at that time. The Three-Anti Movement and numerous rectification movements eliminated opposition in the Party and the government. The Five-Anti Movement liquidated the industrial and commercial class. Intellectuals were suppressed with the Ideological Reform, the Anti-Rightist Movement, the Anti-Ancient-Love-Modern Movement, the Surrender-Your-Heart-to-the-Party Movement and numerous literary purges. Within the first three years, 350 Catholic priests were executed, 1,250 imprisoned, and some 200,000 Moslems killed or imprisoned. Most Taoist priests were executed as counterrevolutionaries. Tens of thousands of women died in the New Marriage Law movement. Then came the Great Leap and the communes. The control, the stranglehold, seemed complete.

These mass movements, each involving at least tens of millions and often the entire population, are effectively implemented by a horrendous control network. The Chinese Communist Party is controlled by its Central Committee's Politburo, whose Standing Committee is the supreme authority. For soft sell abroad, Peking has domesticated eight captive non-Communist "democratic parties" which are represented in the People's Congress and the Chinese People's Political Consultative Conference, both sounding boards of the Party.

Outside the government and the Party, the population is controlled in every facet of its life by "people's organizations." Among them is the Communist Youth League (China's Komsomol), the reservoir of Party recruits with 25 million youth, ranging in age from fourteen to twenty-five, in 1 million cells distributed among factories, mines, farms, schools, armed forces, shops, and communes. The reservoir for League recruits is the Young Pioneers, with 50 million children, aged from eight to fourteen, indoctrinated with the Code of Five Loves: for state, people, labor, science and public property—but not for parents or friends. The All-China Federation of Youth takes care of non-Party youth organizations. Some 18 million industrial workers belong to 160,000 unions under the All-China Federation of Trade Unions, whose functions are production increase and political indoctrination, but not wage increase or strike. Women come under the All-China Federation of Women. Writers and artists come under the All-China Federation of Literary and Art Circles. And there are similar associations controlling religious sects, students returned from abroad, overseas Chinese, domestic servants, etc.

Most of these mass organizations are run by the United Front Work Department of the Party Central Committee. In addition, key positions are held by Communist Party members and the memberships spotted with people whose Party affiliation is secret. These organizations indoctrinate their members, push mass movements, conduct discussions, and hold criticism and struggle meetings. Their members "help" nonmembers toe the Party line at places of work, play, and residence. Members of the Youth League and Pioneers, being potential Party members, act as activists in all movements, and form "supervisory garrisons" in factories and on farms.

These are appendages of the Party and government. Within the government, the main control apparatus consists of the army; the militia; the People's Court, which besides regular courts conducts temporary People's Tribunals (kangaroo courts); the People's Procuratorate, a suprajudicial watchdog which inspects law-enforcement and can "suggest" that the courts revise verdicts; and the Ministry of Public Security, which is a behemoth police organ taking care of political, economic, and military security, and corrective labor by means of special public security force, regular police, household police, secret police, and labor-camp guards. Although this ministry on the surface takes orders from the State Council, its important decisions are made by the Party Central Committee's Social Affairs Department, which is the real authority for espionage and secret-police work. Both in function and personnel, the Social Affairs Department penetrates all levels of the Ministry of Public Security and all security units of the People's Liberation Army. The number of plainclothes agents in the secret police alone is estimated at 1.8 million, distributed among 28 provincial, 2,000 county and 26,000 commune units.

Within this network, all public and private organizations in Communist China are under the rigid control of the Party, whose members openly fill the key posts and secretly act as plants in the rank and file. On top of this are millions of *kanpu*, ranging from high Party members to the lowest non-Party workers, who implement Party policies, fix tax rates, decide production targets, approve marriages and divorces, purge dissidents, conduct meetings, and make up radio-listening and newspaper-reading teams. Travel regulations restrict traveling between provinces, sometimes between towns. Except a few national newspapers, all provincial and local papers are forbidden in other areas, so that the population of one area is kept from knowing what is happening elsewhere.

This bird's-eye view of the network should be supplemented with some worm's-eye views. Inside the Army, the political reliability of every soldier is secretly classified as "activist, intermediate, or backward." Every squad is divided into "mutual-aid units" consisting of three to five members: a leader who is a Party member, an activist or League member, and a backward element. Each unit drills, labors, eats, sleeps, and is indoctrinated collectively, with the backward element constantly flanked by the others. They are even accompanied to the toilet "for friendship's sake." Twice a week the unit holds a meeting of self- and mutual-criticism, plus regular thought-appraisal meetings. Every three days the squad submits a political report to the platoon, which reports once a week to the company. While political laggards are checked by the Party members, the latter can also be checked by any non-Party member. During times of combat any Party member may shoot a higher officer if he is suspected of wavering. Each regiment has a secret security unit, which puts three plants in each company, or one in each platoon. These members pose as privates, who do not even appear progressive, but they hold in their hands the fate of all enlisted men and officers.

When a new soldier enlists he is generously given leave to call on his friends and relatives, who are later required to tell everything they know about the soldier, so that any lie about his past experience and background is easily detected. The troops stage frequent "challenges" against each other in combat and labor production. During combat forced marches, a couple of laggards are usually executed as saboteurs of morale and their bodies left on the highway. The units behind might then be told that the soldiers were killed by the enemy because they did not march fast enough. In the dreaded human-sea tactic, either civilians armed with grenades or the soldiers themselves are driven forward. As each soldier and each unit are constantly checking on each other, everybody has only one direction to go—forward. This was the reason why Communist soldiers fought like "fanatics" in the Korean War, and yet more than 14,000 of the 21,000 POW's refused to return.

The control of the general population is just as tight. In cities and towns household police are ubiquitous and constitute a special section in every police bureau, with small street units taking care of ten to fifteen households. The household police check minutely on census, births, deaths, travels, overnight guests, marriages, divorces. They have complete dossiers on each and every household, each and every individual. They must know an individual's source of income, education, class category, family background up to three generations, personal history from the age of eight, his friends, his relatives in and outside China, his mode of living. Such information is gathered from census material, individual "chats," and reports wrung from unwilling neighbors and friends.

The household policeman may drop in anytime for a friendly chat with the sheep of this fold. Each time he makes a report afterwards. Such visits always start with inconsequential small talk. Sometimes the visit is limited to this seemingly pointless talk. At other times, say, after the resident is visited by someone whose face is unfamiliar in the neighborhood, the policeman drops in the next day—all smiles, all courtesy. He starts with the weather, then asks what dishes you folks had last night, and are you busy these days. When the resident feels he can no longer stand the suspense, the policeman asks him—again casually—about his family history and personal experiences, all of which are already in the police files. Then he asks what the resident's attitude toward the People's Government is, and his opinion about counterrevolutionaries and what should be done about them and their accomplices. Meanwhile, his casual glances take in the condition of the room, the movements and expressions of family members.

If the resident is suspected of something, or his statements do not check, he will have a string of smiling, polite, casual visitors dropping in for chats. They are not the regular household policemen but activists from the Party, League, unions, and other mass organizations. And this goes on until the resident is cleared or arrested. The police have infinite patience, infinite finesse. And in addition to the household police, reports from children in kindergartens, servants' discussion groups, neighborhood meetings all end up into the steadily growing dossiers.

In the rural area, such control is much easier in the form of peasant work teams. The mobile fishermen are required to attend periodical meetings and their families kept on land when the trawlers are at sea. The fishermen are formed into units of five to fifteen boats each, with mutual guarantees against defection, and with one to five secret policemen planted in each unit.

The propaganda organs are organized as tightly as the army. For example, the head office of the Hsinhua News Agency in Peking has a staff of several hundred persons classified into 30 grades. It has three intra-office publications: a daily newsletter available to all the staff, a daily reference sheet on news from foreign news agencies accessible to the upper fifteen grades, and a top secret pamphlet seen only by department heads. All correspondents upon assignment are given guidance on the "gravity points" of a story, its "writing angle," and a set of prepared questions for any interview. Proofreaders have an important position. They are all Party members divided into three grades. Those of the top grade have the authority to change copy but are severely punished for typographical errors.

The network of control extends to the remotest corners of the nation. Peking's policy on national minorities in China appears to be a liberal one, granting autonomy and self-determination. In reality it is internal colonization. It has trained among China's 100 national minorities, totaling 35.3 million people, some 500,000 Party members, 900,000 Youth League members and 480,000 *kanpu* who are, however, not trusted as they are understandably on the side of their own people. The system of autonomous areas appears unnecessarily complicated and confusing, but it, too, has its purpose. Peking has been systematically zoning areas of Han Chinese (as distinguished from minority Chinese) into the autonomous areas. For example, originally the Inner Mongolian Autonomous Region had 800,000 Mongolians and 1.5 million Han Chinese. In 1954–1955 Suiyuan province and part of Jehol were incorporated into the region, thus the percentage of Mongolian population in the region was decreased from 35 to 11.

A single minority is often cut up into separate autonomous areas. For example, the Tibetans live in Tibet and many other areas in the Northwest. Peking established ten separate autonomous areas, all for the Tibetans. The Ninghsia Hui (Chinese Moslem) Autonomous Region has 1 million Han Chinese and only 600,000 Hui, but the region excludes the 500,000 Hui in the adjacent Kansu province.

Within a chopped-up minority area Peking sometimes inserts a different minority—the Imperial Chinese tactic of "using barbarians to check barbarians." Within the Sinkiang Uighurs Autonomous Region, for example, Peking created five autonomous special districts and six autonomous counties for six other tribes. There is a Hui autonomous county inside a Mongolian autonomous special district, which is inside the Sinkiang Uighurs Autonomous Region. In addition, severe restrictions are imposed on the minorities. In 1959, about 2 million nomads in the Northwest were forced to become farmers.

The rigidity of the control network is only equaled by the variety of the tactics used to make it work. One is the trick of creating a nation of volunteers. During the Korean War, countless rallies were held and activists harangued the crowds on "the patriotic duty of aiding Korea and resisting America." They invariably terminated their speeches by volunteering to reduce wages, contribute money, or "support the rear" in Manchuria, adding that anyone against these measures would be unpatriotic. Then the audience was asked: "Anyone opposed to these patriotic gestures please raise his hand." Nobody did. So the group had "unanimously volunteered." Not everyone who thus volunteered was selected, but the Party could pick whomever it wanted. And the activists were never selected, because they were needed to activate other meetings.

As soon as the Communists came into power they announced that they would magnanimously forgive and forget all those who had opposed them or associated with the Nationalists. They were promised immunity but required to register for the record's sake. During the first year a few did but most were afraid to. The Communists were unobtrusively investigating all this, but because of the large number of people involved many remained undetected. Then a number of people with innocuous former Nationalist affiliations who failed to register were severely punished, while some with significant anti-Communist or pro-Nationalist activities who *had* registered were forgiven, praised or even rewarded. These cases were widely publicized. The implications were unmistakable: if one did not register he would be discovered and punished; if he did, he would have nothing to fear. Thus hundreds of thousands who had had the most casual connections with the Nationalist regime soon flocked to register.

When the registration was completed, at dawn on a spring day in 1951, soldiers, policemen and security men in Shanghai suddenly seized everyone on the list and other potential resistants as "counterrevolutionaries." For two days and two nights, the terror-stricken city saw tens of thousands livid-faced men and women arrested, tied with ropes, and carried in trucks slowly cruising the streets with sirens screaming. For weeks Shanghai had the atmosphere of a macabre carnival, with music and dancing accompanying the executions. The erstwhile greyhound-racing Candidrome daily echoed with "unanimous roars" of: "Kill! Kill! Kill!" as batches of prisoners were brought up. This First Counterrevolutionary Suppression Movement liquidated 150,000 people in Shanghai alone. Similar terror arrests were carried out in all other cities.

Peking does not censor letters with blue pencils or scissors as in other Communist countries. All letters of suspects and some letters of the general public are read, however, without any deletions or seizure even though "incorrect political ideas" are found. They are re-sealed and forwarded to the recipients without any telltale mark even though copies of significant passages are filed away. When a person is picked for condemnation or when a mass movement starts, he is asked veiled questions about things mentioned in the erring letter, but never told in the beginning that his letter has been read. During the Five-Anti Movement many were accused of incorrect ideas or activities. When they refused to confess, they were shown copies of letters they mailed abroad as early as three years before. Such incidents were publicized, creating the impression that whatever one did or said, the Party knew, even though it did not take immediate action.

Peking seldom executes nationally known people, even though

they may be publicly humiliated, forced to confess, and sent to labor camps. And only a small percentage of the vast number of those killed are publicly executed. These public executions are staged according to the needs of the moment, usually with much fanfare and with students, factory workers, and members of mass organizations required to attend and write their "impressions." Most are secretly executed, or simply rot in prison. A political prisoner, who refuses to give in despite brain-washing or physical torture, is often told that he will be executed. He is taken with another prisoner to a secret execution ground, where the other prisoner is shot before his eyes. Guns are then aimed at him as if to shoot, but at the last moment the execution is called off, and the prisoner taken back to his cell for a sumptuous meal, where in many cases the shock causes him to give in. According to the *People's Daily*, once accused, a prisoner must be "presumed to be guilty. . . . Giving the accused the benefit of doubt is a bourgeois weakness." It condemned Chia Chen, a Supreme People's Court judge, and several of his colleagues, for standing up for the independence of the judiciary: "The People's Government, under the direction of the Chinese Communist Party, has the power to supervise and lead all state organs, including the court."

All these control and terror tactics enabled the Chinese Communists to rule the 600 million Chinese as no other regime has done in history. The ultimate terror weapon, however, is "reform through labor," or slave labor.

Forced labor has been used extensively since 1952 after tremendous numbers of men were arrested as counterrevolutionaries. It was initially patterned after Siberian labor camps but through the years has grown more elaborate and extensive. Forced labor covers "reform through labor" or corrective or punitive labor, applied to ordinary criminals and political prisoners; and permanent and seasonal conscripted labor, applied to semiskilled workers, calamity victims, the unemployed, peasants, minority tribes, troops, and in recent years intellectuals, students, and civil servants. Types of work cover virtually every phase of physical labor but organizationally may be roughly divided as follows: prison workshops and full-size penal factories where most of the inmates are ordinary criminals, short-term political prisoners, children under twelve and old people over fifty; construction sites in densely populated provinces, where work is done mainly by conscripted laborers; state farms and similar labor camps, mainly peopled with serious political prisoners; construction of highways, railways, corvées, in remote border areas, mainly done by the vast number of political prisoners plus calamity victims.

By any standard, both punitive and conscripted labor in Communist China are forms of slave labor. How important slave labor is to Peking was admitted by the Minister of Public Security in 1954, when he said that it "not only helps to develop the country's various constructive enterprises, but also saves the nation a great deal of expense and constitutes a definite source of wealth for it."

Conscripted laborers are all "volunteers" who get "paid" with meals but must supply their own bedquilts and wash basins, and sometimes simple implements like shovels and crowbars. They are organized into military units, and they work by emulation drives and quota guarantees. Their work sites are usually surrounded by mile-deep security zones policed by troops.

Life of these conscripted laborers may be gleaned from press stories extolling their "heroism." Shanghai's *Liberation Daily* said 3 million peasants at the famous Huai River project had to sleep in tents in freezing weather, with two sharing a cotton quilt. Tools were so short that many used bare hands to shovel snow for hours. Hankow's *Yangtze Daily* described how 600,000 working on the Ching River project waded knee-deep in Tungting Lake for twenty-four hours, carrying their bedding and tools. At the work site they had no tents so they slept in the open. Sparks burned the faces and eyes of maskless soldering workers but they kept on. In closing a cofferdam, workers used their bodies to block the current, staying in the water for eight days and seven nights, "getting one meal every three days." Dredging a swamp full of trapas, the peasants used their naked backs to bulldoze the ooze and thorny plants. Of the 600 on this job, all were injured, 150 got gangrene, and 150 sickened from swallowing swamp water. In one month 100,000 on the Ching River project got sick or were injured.

Chungking's *Hsinhua Daily* praised the construction workers of the Chengtu-Chungking Railroad who labored "without distinction of day and night," and "many slept 30 hours in 18 days." Many fainted from dynamite smoke in digging a 2,600-foot tunnel near Chengtu, as it had no ventilation facility and only oil lamps. But many more stormed into the tunnel "so that they were often injured or killed by flying rocks."

Sian's *Masses Daily* wrote about the construction of Tienshui-Lanchow Railroad in the Northwest badlands, where water is strongly alkaline. Workers had to drink this laxative water disguised with salt and pepper. All got sick. When snow fell it became "the most cherished thing," but there was no time to melt it. So "while working they stuffed snow into their mouths to soothe their parched throats, while continuously shaking their limbs to keep warm." Building a wooden bridge across a deep chasm in thirty-degree-below weather which froze the ground solid for three feet deep, workers lay in ditches holding piles driven by others. Three days produced fifty corpses. Swept by icy winds, more than a hundred workers hurtled to their death in six days while climbing scaffolds on soaring cliffs.

Hsinhua News Agency said workers on the Sikang-Tibet Highway slept on a layer of twigs atop snow, and labored in 25-degree-below weather at an altitude of 17,400 feet, where mere walking makes one gasp. "The civilian workers could eat one meal a day at most." Within two months 3,500 of 8,000 perished. But by then the second batch of 25,000 laborers had arrived.

Such is the situation of conscript labor; that of punitive labor is much worse. Both groups of workers get two hours of indoctrination daily; but political prisoners must work 14-18 hours as against conscript laborers' 10-14 hours. These lowliest slave laborers get five minutes for a meal, three minutes for the toilet, must sleep facing the guards, keep absolute silence all the time except at indoctrination, when they must talk. If they cannot fulfill work quotas their meagre rations are cut. To squeeze everything out of a prisoner, he is first sentenced to death, then the sentence is suspended for a couple of years, pending the result of his labor. Many worked themselves to death trying to avoid execution. Those who inform against others have their sentences reduced.

A survivor of the Sunkiang Collective Farm, a slave camp in Manchuria, said the 3,000 inmates were each allotted a piece of virgin land, frozen solid half of the year, to be farmed with primitive implements. In two years 900 died. The *kanpu* always used high-sounding, almost loving words on everyone. Those who died were praised as "heroes on the battlefront of production." In one of the rare, successful revolts, 160 inmates and 15 guards escaped. A survivor among the 1 million slave laborers in Sinkiang reported that all political prisoners were tattooed on the left arm with a black star. The monthly mortality rate was 10 percent, but the supply of recruits seemed inexhaustible. Another survivor, who had worked for five years in a chain-gang in the Northwest, in spring 1951 marched for two months with 300,000 others for 840 miles from Sian to the Yumen oil field. The journey resulted in 10,000 dead, 30,000 sick and 70,000 too weak to work.

The *Hsinhua Daily* once reported a scene in the Sunkiang Collective Farm: "When the *kanpu* announced: 'This will be your work as long as you live,' some hanged themselves, others dashed into the electrified barbed wire."

Communist China has labor camps in more than 2,000 cities and towns, but the bulk of slave laborers are in huge invisible camps like construction sites. These areas range from frozen Kiamusze near Siberia to the malarial swamps of Hainan Island, from the alluvial Huai delta to the sky-high plateaus of Tibet. Huge groups are moved by forced migration to prevent escape and revolt. The Communists have moved Han Chinese to the hills, mountain aborigines to the plains, Sinkiang Uighurs and Chinghai Huis to Manchuria, Manchurians to Hainan Island, Cantonese to North

China, and central China peasants to Kansu. Thus each group became a minority, helpless, linguistically incommunicative, easily spotted; it is difficult to escape and almost impossible to revolt.

Perhaps no one will ever know exactly how many Chinese have been put to slave labor, or how many have perished from it and from executions. In 1956 a U.S. Government report estimated a total of 20 million slave laborers in China by the end of 1953. In 1955 an official report submitted by the United Nations Secretary-General and the Director of the International Labor Organization to the 21st session of the United Nations Economic and Social Council quoted the number 25 million, including 1.5 million sent abroad. In 1956 the I.L.O. Committee on Forced Labor in its report said that although it was unable to assess the total number of slave laborers in Communist China, it was convinced "that forced labor exists on a very large scale, and the number of persons involved represents a considerable proportion of the total population." In 1960 Chinese Nationalist and independent sources estimated that 30 million were killed and 90 million were at forced labor.

Estimates vary, especially due to the inclusion or exclusion of permanent conscripted labor. Punitive and conscript labor are difficult to distinguish as the two groups are often found on a single construction project. The term "killed" may or may not include those executed. The number of people who died of slave labor is several times that of those executed, as can be gathered from the working style reported by the official press and survivors. In this respect some enlightening statistics were given by a Party delegate attending a public health conference in Shanghai in the winter of 1960–61.

According to Chinese reports not confirmed by the Communist press, this delegate reported that during the Communist decade, 42 million people died of epidemics such as cholera, malaria and meningitis, 24 million were crippled and maimed and 31 million died of accidents and physical exhaustion while working. Of the 31 million killed by work, nearly 8 million died of accidents and exhaustion at the backyard furnaces, 4.8 million on machine and transportation work, 4.2 million on highway, railroad, and bridge construction, 5.4 million on corvée work, 3.9 million on other construction work, and 4.8 million collapsed in the fields. Of these deaths, 42 percent or 13 million took place within the first 18 months of the Great Leap.

In building the Instant Paradise, a total of 24 million people were crippled, and 73 million were killed by overwork, accidents, exposure and disease. At this point statisticians might throw up their hands, and sophists argue their heads off. But the simple, elemental truth is that Communist China is committing the biggest auto-genocide in human history. In such a network of terror, the individual is naked, helpless and absolutely enslaved by the diabolical state. Everyone in Communist China has to barter his body and soul for a precarious, momentary survival. Any revolt or even overt discontent seems unthinkable. Yet men's yearning for freedom is paradoxically heightened by oppression, for freedom looks the sweetest to those who have completely lost it. The Chinese people are proving it by doing the unthinkable.

XII

THE HUNDRED FLOWERS
AND THE FRENETIC GARDENER

IT WAS BY THE IDYLLIC WEST LAKE IN HANGCHOW, A picturesque resort visited for centuries by poets, painters, high monks, gourmets, and honeymooners. No place in China is as richly endowed with history, legend, and romance as the West Lake, which delights many with its misty hills, pavilion-dotted islets, monasteries, pagodas, weeping willows, lotus blossoms, and delicate green tea. The time was April 25, 1957. Engaged in pleasant chitchat at the airport were Communist China's Premier Chou En-lai, Deputy Chairman Sharaf R. Rashidov of the USSR Supreme Soviet, and Soviet Ambassador to Peking Pavel F. Yudin. They were waiting for the arrival of USSR Chief of State Kliment Y. Voroshilov.

Chou offered to be a guide for the Russian guests, and Rashidov remarked that leading comrades seldom had time to see places.

Chou said: "Yes, one should visit various places often, because staying all the time in Peking will generate bureaucratism. Peking's high city walls are liable to separate the leadership from the masses."

Rashidov quipped: "High city walls have their advantages. They can confine bureaucratism."

Chou laughed and replied: "They have another advantage: if the masses oppose bureaucratism the city walls can act as a shield. But this is no insurance. City walls can be breached. Nearly forty years ago our students in Peking stormed through the city walls to oppose the bureaucrats and warlords of that time."* He pointed to the two children who came to offer bouquets, saying: "If we don't change our bureaucratism, they will breach the city walls eventually." Then Chou told the children: "If there still is bureaucratism in our leadership ten years from now, you should oppose it."

The youth of China took up Chou's invitation, not ten years but a couple of weeks later. Chou did not realize that the May Fourth Movement he mentioned was soon to be re-enacted with equal violence and more significance. In May 1957, again in Peking, another troubled young generation of China rose to defy the bureaucrats. They breached the high walls of modern totalitarianism, but were eventually subdued by all the might of a police state. The youth of China together with other intellectuals in the summer of 1957 wrote another page in history, over which their countrymen will sing and weep in the years to come.

The Chinese Communists at first had a couple of years of honeymoon with the intellectuals and students, who were generally critical of the Nationalists and wishfully hoping that the change would be for the better. After their initial consolidation of power, the Communists in 1952 began to crack down on the intellectuals with a complete shake-up of the educational system, an "ideological remolding" (brainwashing) of all students and teachers, and a series of purges among artists and writers. By 1956 the intellectuals were totally disenchanted and restive. In that year shortages in food and daily necessities appeared when peasants joined the cooperatives. In some schools students were fed wheat bran for three months and they had to use text sheets as toilet paper. Bad food caused students of Szechwan University to beat up the school's Party officials and burn down the dining hall. Thirty of the rioters were sent to a labor camp. Some 100 primary school students were sent from Hangchow to Taiyuan for construction work. As originally they were told they were to work

---

* This was the May Fourth Movement of 1919.

in a chemical plant, the teenagers held a meeting and told the Party: "We have been cheated." Repeated purges had eliminated most middle-aged teachers, so that university professors were either older than fifty or younger than twenty. At one time 4,000 professors were kept away from their jobs by punitive labor. With Party bureaucrats running the schools, professors of hydraulic engineering were teaching reinforced concrete construction, and those of Western literature were teaching Chinese literature.

The simmering discontent of youth received additional fuel in early 1957 when suppressed news of the Hungarian Revolution seeped into China. That spring the voice of youth began to be heard. College students in Shanghai and Peking refused to attend indoctrination classes. High- and primary-school students all over China asked questions about "external and internal events of last year," about Hungary, Poland, and Soviet Russia that the teachers "dared not answer." In March, teachers and students in Canton's South China Normal College held debates on Hungary, condemning Soviet Russia. Some participants were arrested. Although the incident was not reported in the press, news soon spread to schools in other cities. Some 800 students of the Communist *Kanpu* School near Peking held an anti-hunger strike. The entire group was sent to a labor camp in Manchuria. Students of Tsinghua University and the Technical School of Geology in Peking also struck, demanding from the Party "peaceful coexistence and mutual non-interference." Students in a high school in Paoting rioted; 240 of them were punished with forced labor. Even the once dedicated Communist Youth League had changed. Most of the 22 million members slackened in discipline and lived in safe mediocrity. Many said: "Politics is useless." Others "want freedom."

In face of this ominous ground swell, Mao changed his tactics. Political indoctrination in schools ceased to be compulsory. Immediately these classes were deserted. Some formerly forbidden subjects were allowed. An old professor resumed his course on Western philosophy. His first lecture on Bertrand Russell was packed with students, who also eagerly attended resuscitated classes in Chinese classics.

It was learned much later that in 1956 and early 1957, a clique in the Chinese Communist Party headed by Mao fought against powerful opposition to this liberalization. Mao was not for genuine democratization, but for a gimmick, a temporary and controlled opening of safety valves to release the pent-up emotions of the intellectuals. Early in 1956 Chou tried to appease the intellectuals with a soothing speech. In May Mao aired his poetic description of "Let a hundred flowers bloom; let a hundred schools contend." Intellectuals and members of captive "democratic parties" were invited to criticize the government. But living under a totalitarian regime, the Chinese knew too well to accept the invitation. On February 27, 1957, Mao lectured about his Hundred Flowers for four hours at the Supreme State Conference. At subsequent official meetings everybody praised Mao's humility but nobody criticized the government. Their attitude was expressed by the chief librarian of Futan University, who said: "Today I may speak as I will, but after some time, after a year or two, will not a written record of my words be brought up against me?" and by another professor who said: "If I say everything now, will it all go unpunished forever?"

Chinese prudence was at work, and the flowers refused to bloom. For several months through speeches, meetings, and the press, Mao applied hothouse heat to the bashful buds, promising immunity and finally staging artificial criticism meetings and publicizing the remarks. The blossoms, coming out shyly and sparsely at first, soon grew in profusion.

And—suddenly it was spring. Blossoms on campuses were started by the students of Peita (Peking University), which spearheaded the memorable May Fourth Movement in 1919. In May 1957, in the liberalizing atmosphere of the Hundred Flowers, the students of this university remembered poignantly what their predecessors did thirty-eight years ago. One evening they held a "Freedom Forum" at which nineteen students jumped on the stage to address the meeting. Shouts of "Continue the May Fourth tradition!" and "Raise the May Fourth torch!" soon filled the air. Two students of Chinese literature recited a poem they composed, *The Time Has Come!* It starts: "The time has come to demand freedom from the Communists . . ." It was a tumultuous evening of applause, tears and shouts. It was youth on fire.

Soon wall newspapers appeared on the campus, announcing a "Democratic Wall" on which all might express their opinions. An article said: "Marxism is outmoded. . . . The proletarian dictatorship is a resurrection and variation of monarchism, an absolute feudalistic concept, a political system to fool the people." It labeled the Communist Party "a party of new aristocrats," the *People's Daily* "a Great Wall blockading truth," and the official Hsinhua News Agency "a machine manufacturing poison." It demanded free and democratic education. The writer of this article was Tan Tien-yung, physics senior and a member of the Communist Youth League. He and others also organized The Hundred Flowers Society, which was joined by 6,000 of the 7,000-odd Peita students. Printers in the university press drove out Party overseers and printed the students' speeches and a pamphlet titled *Democratic Relay Baton*, which were mailed to thousands of schools all over China. It started a prairie fire.

Demonstrations broke out in twenty-three other institutions of higher learning in Peking. Students of the Petroleum College staged an anti-hunger strike. Those in the Russian Language College put up anti-Communist posters. A student of the Peking Medical College wrote a "Death-Defying Song" and bombed the home of the college's Party commissar. The People's University, cradle of young Marxists and a strictly Russian institute on Chinese soil, also held a demonstration, led by twenty-one-year-old Lin Hsi-ling, law senior co-ed, veteran of the People's Liberation Army, and pillar of the Youth League. Lin gave numerous speeches and publicly denounced the Communists, classifying them as "confused, decadent, and mummified," and declaring: "We need action, and we must rely on an uprising of the masses."

She became the heroine of Peking's collegians. A young engineer in the same university said: "The intellectuals . . . do not have as much peace of mind as they did under Japanese occupation or under Kuomintang rule."

The Peita students sent two delegations to Peking's Tsinghua University and Tientsin's Nankai University. Although the delegation leaders were arrested by the secret police, the wave kept on. In Tsinghua 8,000 students shouted: "Proletarian dictatorship is out-moded!" and "Long live democracy!" In Nankai, after a mass meeting, a poster appeared at the main entrance: "Annihilate the Communists!"

In Nanking, students of Nanking University staged an open forum, declaring: "People are stifled; scholars are frustrated. The young and old are full of sorrows." A professor called upon the Communist to "liberate the people for the second time." They wrecked the *Hsinhua Daily* when it refused to print news of the meeting, and captured several policemen sent to quell the riot. They threatened a mass revolt and "to do it with guns."

In Wuhan, 1,000 students of Wuhan University paraded in the streets, distributing their *Torch Press* to applauding pedestrians. They destroyed the files in the school's secret service office, tried to seize the college broadcasting station, saying: "The Wuhan University is worse than a Fascist jail," and "Down with Fascists!" The most violent, however, turned out to be teenagers. Some eight hundred students of the Hanyang First Middle (High) School demanded the Communist Party's withdrawal from the school, demonstrated in the streets, beat up Communist officials, tied up the magistrate, and used knives, javelins and clubs to battle six hundred Communist musclemen. These youngsters, who grew up under Communism, shouted "Welcome back the Kuomintang" and attempted to attack Hanyang's power plant, jails, and ammunition depots.

In Chengtu, a co-ed of Szechwan University gave a lecture titled "Mao Tse-tung, the False Marxist; the Communist Party, Crafty, Ruthless Exploiters." That two-hour lecture was attended by ten thousand teachers and students from various schools in the city, plus civil servants, railroad workers, and peasants. Some two hundred students of the Chengtu Normal School wrecked a police station, beat up a Party union boss, and said: "The Communists are skilled only in organizing riots, disturbances, and in repressing the people, but are incompetent at running schools."

In Port Arthur and Dairen in Manchuria, striking students of the Engineering College were joined by other students, peasants, dockyard and steel-mill workers. Excited people roamed the streets "shouting and looking for trouble."

In Shanghai, students of the Futan University demanded Mao's resignation. Those in the East China Water Conservancy College declared: "We are slaves in the new society." Those of East China Normal College held secret meetings "attempting to create a second Hungarian Incident."

In Canton, students of South China Normal College condemned Soviet Russia, labeled the Chinese Communists a "devil's bloc," and demanded justice for a purged professor who had committed suicide. Students of South China Engineering College used loud-speakers to tell soldiers that military expenditures should be used for education.

On Hainan Island, 2,000 students demonstrated in Wenchang. The magistrate fled. Their efforts to contact other cities on the islands were foiled when telephone lines were cut. In Sining, high-school students declared: "The revolutionary fervor of the peasants has reached the saturation point. They will rise all over the country if they have weapons and leaders," and tried to organize "a peasant army with intellectual leadership." In Kwei-lin, students of Kwangsi Normal College said: "The Communist society is worse than the feudal society," and "There will be riots and uprisings in China." In Nanchang, students of the Liuchuan Normal School, who averaged nineteen years old and were all under twenty-three, planned to win over the army for a "Little Hungary." They said: "The gun is less powerful than the pen.

The gun can kill a man but not change his ideals." They expected "a mere call would make the peasants rise." Similar disturbances by students took place in Lanchow, Kunming, Foochow, Tsingtao, Tsinan, Soochow, Wusih, Chinkiang. For two months, the youth of China in every part of the nation except Tibet and Sinkiang exploded into violent defiance and enjoyed delirious freedom of speech.

Meanwhile, the more mature non-Communist intellectuals, writers, artists, professors, and high government officials took up the invitation to bloom and spoke their secret minds. Economist Wu Pan-nung said Party members in his Economic Research Institute used Marxism as Buddhist monks chanting liturgy. The aim of their research was "to become seraphic monks." Deputy Director Yen Hsi-chun of the National Bureau of Surveying and Cartography said Party members ran scientific organs and colleges as if leading an army. Professor Yang Shih-chan of Central-South Finance and Economics College said: "The number of intellectuals who killed themselves during past purges by jumping out of windows or into rivers, taking poison, slashing throats, and hanging cannot be counted with the hair on one's head." Lecturer Wang Te-chou of the People's University said: "It is all right to put up machine-guns when riots occur. But the trouble is that the machine-guns can be turned around." Minister of Food Chang Nai-chi said state enterprises were less efficient than private enterprises, and Communist bureaucratism was more dangerous than capitalism. Huang Shao-hung, member of the Congress Standing Committee, complained that there were no criminal and civil law codes, no police regulations, and inmates in labor camps were kept there indefinitely.

The critics attacked the USSR. Gen. Lung Yun, vice-chairman of the National Defense Council, complained that Russia looted factories in Manchuria after the war, that China had to bear all the expenses of the Korean War, and that Russian loans were of short duration and high interest. They attacked the Chinese Communist Party. Professor Ku Chih-chung of Peking Normal University said: "No matter how bad was the Kuomintang, it never made its members a political aristocracy." Chu An-ping, editor-in-chief of *Kuang Ming Daily*, satirized the concept of "The Party—the universe." He said people were criticizing the "little monks," but none had done it to the "old monks." Then he proceeded to criticize old monks Mao and Chou.

The most devastating criticism of the Party was from Lecturer Ko Pei-chi of the People's University: "Some say the standard of living has been raised. Whose standard of living? That of the Party members and *kanpu*. . . . You Communists say to yourselves, 'We are the state.' . . . If you act wrongly the masses can overthrow you. To kill Communists and overthrow you is not unpatriotic, because the Communist Party is not serving the people. Even if the Communist Party should perish, China will not. . . . The masses want to overthrow the Communist Party and kill the Communists. If you do not reform, and continue to degenerate, this will be inevitable."

They even attacked the fundamentals of Marxism. Professor Lei Hai-chung of Nankai University said the Communists were still satisfied with the conditions perceived by Marx and Engels sixty years ago. Yung Tse-cheng, member of Tientsin Federation of Commerce and Industry, said: "Marxism-Leninism transplanted to China does not work." Minister of Communications Chang Po-chun said Marxism was outdated.

These critics soon infected the intellectuals inside the Communist Party itself, touching off the spectacle of many members, most of them with from ten to twenty or more years of Party-age, openly attacking their own Party. Hsu Liang-ying of the Chinese Academy of Sciences said the Communists should inherit from Western revolutions "things like freedom, equality, universal love, and individualism." Jen Chien-chiao, Party cultural boss of Shantung, said the Communist Party was "without a shred of democracy" and "even worse than the Kuomintang." Liu Pin-yen, author and editor of *China Youth Press*, called Communist *kanpu* "stupid, old-fashioned, uncultured, uninspired, decadent, cowardly" who "only know how to play poker and read children's books, are uninterested in literature and culture, and spiritually empty." He added: "Human rights have been trodden down; human dignity has been humiliated." Wang Jo-wang, editor-in-chief of *Literary Monthly* and a twenty-year Party member, said the Communist rule had made "black and white, right and wrong undistinguishable, so that evil air rises and benevolent air falls." Lo Pin of the Department of Propaganda in Kansu, called Marxist indoctrination "spiritual slavery."

Mao was directly attacked by Yen Wen-chieh, a section chief in the Ministry of Foreign Trade. He criticized Mao's theoretical writings: "As if a single essay could solve all the problems and theories of the world; as if there is no other knowledge beside it." Li Te-chi, member of the Academy of Sciences, opposed people shouting all the time "Chairman Mao ten thousand years." He suggested turning Peking's Chungshan Park into London's Hyde Park. Liu Sha-ho, editor of a poetry magazine in Szechwan, said: "I long to go to a capitalist country to lead a poor but free life." Lu Chien, poetry editor of *People's Literature*, called for "another revolution" and "another May Fourth." Huang Chiu-yun, editor of *Literary Study*, said that countless talented writers in China "are unwilling to whitewash reality against their conscience, and unable to portray life realistically. They cannot bear to shut their eyes to the people's suffering, but are forced to keep silent about the things that shock their conscience." Yen Yi-tsai, secret policeman in the Ministry of Chemical Industry, praised the United States, pointed out that peasant opposition was mounting, foresaw a nation-wide uprising, and requested his withdrawal from the Communist Party.

The revolt of the intellectuals began to affect the peasants. In Canton, street-hawkers beat up Party *kanpu* in broad daylight. In Honan 90,000 peasants staged 320 riots in July. Within three months after the start of the Hundred Flowers, the official press reported at least 27 anti-Communist rebel organizations in 11 provinces. The *People's Daily* expressed its apprehension with a mixed metaphor: "The little typhoon of flower-blooming has blown from the cities to the villages."

Mao Tse-tung, hitherto undisputed master over 600 million silent, servile, frightened Chinese, suddenly found himself, his regime, his party and his cherished dogmas publicly and violently attacked by ten thousand voices—the *vox populi*. The realization, that such spontaneous impeachment could take place in a country where even freedom of silence was denied, not only stunned Mao himself but acted as a traumatic shock to the entire population. Before, everybody hid his thoughts and feelings. Now, everybody knew that the next fellow thought and felt just as he did.

Instead of the fragrant flowers he worked so hard to cultivate, Mao had coaxed out thousands of monster cacti with millions of barbs. It was the most disastrous gardening ever practiced. The frenetic gardener had to act immediately. As Party propaganda chief Lu Ting-yi said, the critics "hope very much to have a Hungarian Incident in China. They intended to seize control of the intellectuals, industrialists, and businessmen, then the entire nation. They hope that the students will touch off a nation-wide chaos, so that they can pick up the debris." In the second week of June, giant Party shears began to clip. Rioting students were subdued by troops, secret police, and Party goons, and their leaders condemned to slave labor or execution. Meanwhile, the alleged text of Mao's February 27 speech at the Supreme State Conference was made public on June 18. It turned out to be an extensively doctored and cut version of the actual speech, as it was originally heard and at times quoted by 1,800 high government and Party officials. In the original speech Mao admitted the liquidation of 800,000 persons up to the end of 1953, condemned the disposal of counterrevolutionaries by means of a normal curve (15 percent death, 25 percent forced labor and 60 percent police surveillance) and promised complete immunity to the critics in the Hundred Flowers campaign. These and other significant points were deleted from the published text, which is believed to have been cut from the original 40,000 to 25,000 words.

This was followed by an "anti-rightist" purge, conducted all over China, with students and teachers forced to denounce each other. All classes were suspended. In their place came endless purge meetings at which everyone was required to write a twenty-page confession, covering his thoughts from the age of seven and informing on "suspects." At the end everyone had to sign a pledge not to oppose the Party, not to attend unauthorized meetings and not to talk to the rightists. Everytime a political prisoner was publicly executed, students and teachers had to go, watch and write notes about their impressions.

After prolonged denunciations, three cabinet ministers and two members of the National Defense Council were kicked out; fifty-four members were expelled from the Congress; twenty-one suspended from the National Committee of the Chinese People's Political Consultative Conference; and over fifty top provincial officials were fired. In Peking University, a batch of eighty-five professors were put to work carrying nightsoil and gathering cotton. In People's University, 38 percent of the faculty was exiled to camps in Hopei and Manchuria, and the whole group of journalism seniors were sent to camps in the Northwest. Some four hundred members of the Communist writer's association got hard labor. In the head office of Hsinhua News Agency in Peking, citadel of Red propaganda, thirty staff members were arrested, five correspondents and a group of college student trainees were missing, and the deputy director was "struggled" to death. In 1957 and 1958, more than 1 million intellectuals were forced to scrub lavatories, pull carts, feed pigs, plant crops, carry rock, or work as miners. Many committed suicide. In a single municipal district in Peking, 2,000 persons suffered nervous breakdown.

Thus ended the Hundred Flowers—a brief, blissful interlude of delicious freedom and devastating truth. Communist China could never be the same again, in the eyes of the Chinese people and of the Communists themselves. For the first time the people publicly expressed in unmistakable terms their contempt and hatred for the regime. The brutal repression, while averting an imminent revolution, only strengthened the convictions people had voiced. But even at the height of the purge a few chose to be openly defiant, to "leave a fragrance for ten thousand generations," as the Chinese saying goes. A student in Peking University while being purged wrote on the wall newspaper: "If winter comes, can spring be far behind?" and boldly signed his name. Lan Yu, editor-in-chief of the People's Publishing House, and nineteen-year Party member, shouted at his purgers: "You can chop off my head, but you cannot suppress democracy!" Tsinghua professor Hsu Chang-pen argued eloquently with his denouncers: "You don't know how to influence the people, but you want to restrict them. If you cannot say anything new, why don't you let somebody else speak out and tell the truth?" Prof. Peng Chao-yuan of Peking Engineering College, who returned to China from California Institute of Technology in 1955, "confessed": "I regret that I returned to China too soon." Professor Chang Ming-tao of Tsinghua confessed: "Ostensibly I like the Communist Party, but my heart has moved farther away from the Party every day."

Although Ma Yin-chu, then president of Peking University and an authority on economics and population, was quiet during the blooming period, he rose defiantly to wage an "essay war" against more than two hundred Communist hack writers during the anti-rightist purge. Ma, seventy-five-year-old U.S.-returned scholar and critic of the Kuomintang, refused to alter his ideas on economics and population, saying: "One must uphold truth, at the risk of his personal advantage and his own precious life. . . . I will fight with my single spear on my lone horse until I die fighting. I will not surrender to those critics who use force but not truth."

Many leading scholars of Communist China have now become experts in Marxism—without being seduced by it. Since the Hundred Flowers, some defiant ones have been using Marxist terminology and quotations to debate publicly with semi-educated Party hacks. They were ready to be martyrs. But the Communists were afraid to kill them. Chu Kuang-chien, China's foremost authority on aesthetics and a follower of Croce, repeatedly used clever Marxist arguments and Chinese *double-entendre*. Professor Feng Yu-lan, a noted philosopher, said he had confessed 136 times between 1949 and 1958. In 1960 he was still confessing: "I am completely under the influence of my thoughts. Having gone through a number of reforms I am slightly improved. But recently the failing reappeared in its original form."

After a year's suffering and humiliation under forced labor, survivors of the 1 million intellectuals were recalled. During that year Peking created economic chaos by the Great Leap and the communes, and in 1959 they again tried to woo the intellectuals. But talks of another Hundred Flowers fell on deaf ears. In spring of 1960 many "Meetings of Immortals" were conducted. This poetic Chinese term was used to flatter the intellectuals, to whom the Party explained its new tack, hoping for aid and advice from the only group of people that could reconstruct the nation.

It is an acute irony that Chinese intellectuals, many of whom had placed high hopes on the Communists, should within only a few years turn to active loathing of the new regime. The Hundred Flowers have proved this beyond any doubt. In China's long history, intellectuals have always played a significant part. Historically, the attitude of each regime toward the intellectuals went through the phases of utilization, suspicion and suppression. That of the intellectuals toward each regime: illusion, discontent, and rebellion. The speed of this cycle generally determined a dynasty's lifespan. Almost invariably during the last days of a regime the rulers have tried to suppress the intellectuals.

Following the anti-rightist purge, Chinese intellectuals became, in the words of *People's Daily*, "dead silent, pessimistic and listless." The Communists complained that many teachers evaded expressing their opinions when discussing political and academic topics. When asked by Communists about any opinion, they answered with a soft question: "What do *you* think?" Taoism was back at work. This negative attitude is more complex than it sounds. It began before the Hundred Flowers and grew more intense after the purge. While some chose open defiance, the majority found escapes.

By the end of 1957, Peking discovered with a shock that in more than twenty provinces, youngsters were humming and singing, not the new Communist songs, but old Chinese and Western hit songs. Such "yellow music" was so popular that even many *kanpu* and Youth League members became inveterate addicts. Equally popular was "yellow literature." Young people turned away from Communist literature to popular *wu hsia* tales about valiant outlaws who assassinate bad bureaucrats and help the poor. Civil servants in Peking and other cities were found in the office indulging in pornography inserted in Marxist books. The *Literary Gazette* reported that in some government bureaus the Communist *kanpu* even formed "defense alliances" for mutual lending and an early warning system.

Most of the escapists, however, found something nobler. The perturbed *People's Daily* called it: "Three One-ism—one solitary lamp, one cup of tea, one volume of classics." College and high school students, abetted by their teachers, were rediscovering China's ancient classics—something the youth of modern China had been so ready to disown before. Youth, actively loathing the present but frustrated by totalitarian repression, listened to the echoes from other centuries, found mellow wisdom and timeless ideals in an incredibly beautiful world. The patient virtues and longing for serenity and solitude of the ancients, once ignored and ridiculed by young China, suddenly became a spiritual refuge from the ugliness around them, giving them solace, secret courage, and hope. The ancient roots came to life in spite of—or rather because of—the ferocious changes forced upon them. This is yet another Chinese paradox.

Classics became popular in 1956, and were openly defended by students and teachers during the Hundred Flowers. During the Anti-Rightist purge and the subsequent Anti-Ancient-Love-Modern purge, classics were the forbidden fruit ecstatically savored in quiet classrooms and at private moments. A survey by Shanghai's *Wen Huai Pao* revealed that Chinese classics had become a silent craze, while "people's literature" and Russian novels were spurned. The *People's Daily* complained that in Peking University the students were absorbed in Confucius' *Book of Odes*, and "laughed at our worker's, farmer's and soldier's literature." *Literary Gazette* reported that professors indulged in scholarly analysis and encouraged students to "read books with doors closed," adding: "What is more astonishing is that the students like it." A professor in Amoy University said at his lecture: "Today after the land reform and collectivization, I have lost the little plot of land to which I could have retired to lead a hermit's life. The only thing I can do is to chant, in the middle of the night, the ancient poems." Students of that university were fascinated by classics and their conversation was full of classical terms and allusions. Conditions were the same all over China. During the Anti-Ancient campaign, students in Yunnan slipped out of the meetings to fish and contemplate; those in Tientsin "all day long showed a sad countenance, sobbing and envying the hermit life of the old poet Tao Yuan-ming."* As the *Teacher's Daily* explained: "The less they like present conditions, the more they love the classics. The more they love the classics, the less they like present life." Classical sayings like: "Man lives in this world; life is death, death is life" became very popular. Many students spent their free moments wandering by rivers and lakes, lying in the shade, and reading the verses of Tang poets Li Po and Wang Wei.

Even some modern Chinese novels which hitherto had indirectly helped the Communist revolution became a devious escape. The most significant case was Pa Chin's *Home*, as extensively reported by the magazine *Book Reading*. This novel enthralled an entire young Chinese generation when it was first published in 1931. Its theme is the conflict between the old and the new, a perennial personal problem faced by every young Chinese during this century. On one side are tradition, Confucian morals, and the

---

* Famous poet and essayist of the fourth century.

big family; on the other, young love and the dream of personal freedom. The principal characters are three brothers and a sister in a traditional family. The hero is Chueh-hui, a fiery-eyed youth—sensitive, passionate, untamed, ready to fight for his own happiness—who leaves his home in disgust when the maidservant he loves commits suicide after she is betrothed to someone else.

Pa Chin, now a captive author, has been paying lip-obedience to the Communists but has not written anything for more than a decade. In 1958, *Home* was re-published in Communist China along with Pa Chin's collected works. Inexplicably it returned to thrill another young generation—brought up under Communism. Peking was perplexed. All the evils of the traditional family and old society had disappeared, yet youth was fascinated. Why?

Book Reading asked its readers the reason, and the response surged in. One student wrote: "My family was a big family too. Oh, those New Year reunions of all brothers and sisters! How we enjoyed those wonderful moments!" Another wrote: "Pa Chin's influence was great, is still immense, and may grow." One reader reported the reactions of his classmates after reading the novel: "Some talked of freedom, of going 'Pa Chin's way,' of the beauty of friendship. Some wanted to create a 'new revolution.'" A group of students wrote that their "only regret is that Pa Chin does not write anymore."

Those who professed to criticize Pa Chin's influence betrayed more than they ostensibly wrote. They made such remarks: "Youth grown up in this society are happy, but after reading Pa Chin they become pessimistic"; "It is easy to see that a great many of the young, after reading Pa Chin, turn to pessimism. . . . They dream of the pleasures of the big-family life of the past"; "This may explain why many comrades, even thirty to forty years of age, after criticizing Pa Chin, slowly fall back again under his pessimistic influence"; "Pa Chin's books advocate the capitalistic life, individualism, love, freedom. Today for youth they are dangerous."

A loyal Communist emphasized with concern that the bewitched youth included many children "reared by the Revolution, whose parents have suffered and often died for the Revolution, who themselves are the hopes of the Revolution." Instead of heroically holding up the torch of the Revolution, "they like to read *Home*, and to imitate Chueh-hsin (Chueh-hui's elder brother), playing his flute on rainy days. They weep. They look at the moon and sigh." He asked: "Far more than all they learn and understand in their political study, what is it that penetrates and moves the heart of these young people, and really troubles them?"

That subversive something he was looking for cannot be found in his Communist philosophy. He has to look elsewhere. He has to penetrate youth itself—incorruptible, rebellious youth. The writings from Confucius to Pa Chin have had other messages for other eras, but they are giving new messages to the youth of China, who seize them for their private world. For each generation must discover the truth anew. Each generation must suffer its own disillusionments and create its own new dreams.

XIII

ROUND TRIP
TO THE POINT-OF-NO-RETURN

IN THE SUMMER OF 1958 COMMUNIST CHINA STARTED mankind's most colossal, awesome experiment with human lives— the commune system. It horrified the world with its systematic brutality, and stunned Communists elsewhere with its boldness. For Mao Tse-tung was staking the lives of his Party, his regime and, perhaps in the final analysis, world Communism itself, in history's biggest crap game. Mao declared at the outset that it had to be a problem of "who will vanquish whom."

The year of 1957 was not a happy one for Mao. Since the accelerated collectivization of 1955, peasant resistance had been growing. Then his garden of the Hundred Flowers got out of hand, forcing him to repress further the intellectuals he tried to appease. In November that year Mao attended the fortieth anniversary of the October Revolution in Moscow, where he had hoped to get increased Russian aid. The mission appeared a failure. Mao returned in silent disgust to Peking, where he launched the violent Great Leap by shifting emphasis from state-owned heavy industry to local indigenous enterprises, and driving the peasants to farm and produce steel with primitive methods.

In order to deploy manpower, conserve raw materials and food, and tighten control, the commune system was announced on August 29, 1958. In spite of strong opposition within the Party, Mao believed the communes would bring many advantages. That year's fantastic "bumper harvest," which eventually was admitted to be false, lured him into thinking that even with the tightest control, the peasants would acquiesce if they were adequately fed. The communes could fully exploit the nation's labor in farming, industrialization, and construction, control the population in thought and action, create a 100-million-men militia, and crack the hardest Chinese nut—the family system. Thus the communes, "the most beautiful flower of Marxism," came into being.

The communes were meant to be self-supporting and self-contained agricultural-industrial-military units each consisting of 10,000 to 40,000 people. Each commune would have 16 departments administering agriculture, industry, water conservancy, defense, science and culture. The inmates would be organized into military units from squads to regiments. All men and women from fourteen to forty would belong to the militia, from forty-one to fifty to the reserves. When a baby was one month old, he would be taken by the state and put in the commune nursery; at three, the kindergarten; and at seven, the grade school. There would be no more families. Husbands and wives would work, eat, and live separately with their own sexes in public dining halls and dormitories, and get a sex-break once a week in assigned rooms for an assigned length of time. The aged would live in "Happy Homes." Each commune was to have its own schools, universities, hospitals, dining halls, libraries, laundries, sewing teams, cultural centers, and broadcasting stations. Everyone would wake up, eat, go to the toilet, work, rest, exercise, drill, get indoctrinated, and go to sleep by the sound of a bugle, in military formation. In such a life no one would need to worry, for by the "fifteen guarantees," the state guaranteed to take a person from his mother's womb, raise, feed, clothe, indoctrinate, work him throughout his life, and when he dies, deep-bury him beneath the rice paddies so that his body chemicals would enrich the fatherland in a final gesture of loyalty.

Within three and a half months, 122 million peasant households, or 99 percent of China's peasant population, were organized into 26,000 communes. They would become an Orwellian utopia, the Instant Paradise envisioned by Mao Tse-tung, mystic, political genius and cave-dweller from Yenan. This was the image transmitted to an apprehensive world. Had Mao succeeded in the gamble, he could conquer the earth, and perhaps other planets, with this new species of insect-men. But he did not.

Things did not turn out exactly as planned. As soon as the commune system was announced, there was a run on banks, restaurants, and shops. People spent whatever cash they possessed to get whatever goods were available, and consumed them. Peasants all over China, often joined by village *kanpu*, slaughtered their livestock and poultry and feasted for days, and hoarded immense amounts of grain for their own use. Conditions were similar in the cities. People went to restaurants and ate themselves sick. Others who had two quilts sewed them into one. One man equipped his six-year-old son with a wardrobe that would last until the boy was sixty years old. Another converted his bank account into a coffin for himself. The next day when he heard that coffins would also be nationalized, he sold the coffin for cash and spent it. This grotesque nation-wide consumer spree dealt an initial blow to Mao's fond dream.

The communes were not as efficient and tightly organized as they sounded. In most places the peasants, after attending a meeting, instantly found themselves members of communes. Houses in a handful of communes were torn down and rebuilt into public buildings. But as this practice was too expensive, name plates hung up on temples, ancestral shrines, and bamboo shacks transformed them into dining halls and "Happy Homes." Most dining halls were in open fields under a tree, where crouching peasants gulped down the goo ladled out from public kitchens. Kitchen *kanpu*, wallowing in so much food and authority, wasted tremendous amounts of grain and fuel, and "practiced corruption and favoritism." "Hospitals" had no doctors, no nurses, and few drugs. Peasants injured at work often could not get even tincture of iodine or mercurochrome. In the Happy Homes, old people slept on straw and ate two meals of porridge. In the nurseries wailing babies were fed thin porridge by sub-teenagers or senile old women. A mother, whose baby lost six pounds after two months in a nursery, cried: "My baby is an orphan before I'm dead!" Military training consisted of marching to work and to meals with the *kanpu* shouting, "One, two; one, two." Each commune had a few dozen rifles discarded by the People's Army, jealously guarded by trusted *kanpu*. The peasants carried wooden rifles and sticks. All this would have been delightful idiocy had it not been accompanied by a driving ruthlessness. People were forced to get up at 4 A.M. when the bugle sounded, and were forced to work for as much as twelve to seventeen hours a day, plus frequent "night battles" during which they "refused to eat until our job was done." They marched for ten or twenty miles to dig for coal and minerals in the hills. They slept alfresco, singing: "The sky is our mosquito-net, the rocks are our pillows." During the first few months the communes issued "wages and bonuses." The system worked so well that some peasants, after having the cost of "free meals" deducted from their wages, found themselves owing the government money after a month's hard labor. The Hsinhua News Agency reported that on receiving their wages "some of the peasants were moved to tears." It did not elaborate on the exact cause of such emotional outbursts.

Food in the communes actually was increased—for the first month. Then it was slashed by one-third. Meals were divided into categories: the Labor Table, for able-bodied peasants doing heaviest work; the Semi-Labor Table, for women and youth; the Non-Labor Table, for old people and women on maternity leave; and the Special Table, for official visitors. The Labor Table served mainly miscellaneous cereals, sweet potatoes, some rice and vegetables. The Non-Labor Table served gruel made from wild plants, turnip leaves, and ground corncob cores. The Special Table served chicken, pork, and fish. Evidently as early as 1958, before the famine became serious, selective starvation was practiced. People from seven to seventy were exhorted by such slogans: "Two eat the rice of one; one does the work of two."

Women, having been completely emancipated from their housework and babies, competed with men in "challenges" in hard labor. Grade schools organized children into "little farms" and "little factories." Grandfathers and grandmothers in Happy Homes marched in brigades with poetic, historic names, spending their days collecting manure and watering fields, and their evenings darning clothes for others. To comfort the dead, some communes had re-usable public coffins, with sliding bottoms to drop the bodies into "graves"—pits dug in rice fields. In some South China communes burials were more practical. The bodies were put in a pool of chemical solution to make instant fertilizer. Bones from ancestral graves were dug up and also used for fertilizer.

Passive resistance, including sabotage, increased with the suffering of the peasants. Meanwhile, village *kanpu*, bewildered by their own ignorance but harassed by Party pressure to be experts in everything, fouled up the entire rural economy. Short rations and peasant resentment decreased rather than increased production. Manpower was squandered and misused so that four months after the normal harvest time, the *People's Daily* was calling for a "shock assault" to harvest grain. Meat, vegetables, poultry, and most daily necessities virtually disappeared. The transportation system became chaotic, so did accounting in the communes. Higher officials sent to inspect communes found themselves helpless about the mess.

On December 10, three and a half months after the Peitaiho Resolution announced the communes, a second resolution in Wuhan ordered an initial retreat in the face of unspeakable confusion and misery. This retreat slightly relaxed the control on private ownership, family relations, and dining hall participation. Daily work should no longer exceed twelve hours "under normal conditions," and the hours of shock-troop production "should not exceed two days and two nights at one stretch." Peasants were given five to eight hours of sleep.

In November 1960, emphasis was completely shifted to production brigades. This was an actual return to the cooperatives, which were now called communes. But the cumulative effects of natural disasters, bureaucratic bungling, and passive resistance were just beginning to be felt. Farm production slumped. Supplies for factories and construction projects fell to a trickle. People were physically exhausted. Malnutrition and epidemics were taking alarming tolls. In January 1961, the Party Central Committee decided on a complete reversal of tactics. Its communiqué, admitting that the agricultural setback had affected industry, ordered that capital construction and heavy industry be slowed down. Vast numbers of peasants put to work in industry and construction during the past three years were sent back. Students and numerous regular industrial workers in idle factories were sent to the farms. Many of the country's 5 million artisans, collectivized in 1955 and put to work on backyard furnaces and night-soil brigades in 1958, were sent back to resuscitate the handicraft industry. The Vice-Minister of Light Industry proposed the re-establishment of the traditional small markets, shops, stalls, and even roaming street-hawkers and repairers. In Shanghai alone some 10,000 housewives conscripted into the factories were sent home.

As most commune kitchens, dining halls, sewing centers and laundries disintegrated with the communes, now an emergency movement began to form "repair cooperatives" to patch up articles and houses after years of total neglect. Factories worked day and night making desperately needed cooking pots, water kettles, kitchen knives, and other household utensils, most of which were earlier thrown into the backyard furnaces. In Hunan 4.5 million such articles were made and 1.2 million repaired in four months. Production statistics were suppressed, except those for steel. The book *Ten Great Years*, issued in 1959 and full of boastful statistics, was banned in anticipation of a "revised edition" which has not appeared.

Party faithfuls were urged to cultivate "the spirit of investigation," and to "report, not hide, the truth." College students were now told, "The main task of higher education is study." All important courses were again given to "old professors." Chinese classics and Western literature were re-introduced to eager college classes, and praised as indispensable to literary writers. The official press went light on politics and Marxism, concentrated on classical literature, philosophy, and even nonpolitical jokes. The *People's Daily* criticized the hitherto highly praised collective cultural works: "Each painter has his own style and each writer has his own views. If there is a patchwork the result will not be good." It also said that a good educational foundation "absolutely could not be achieved by a single leap," but could only be achieved slowly, and quoted the ancient sage Hsuntzu: "Ceaseless small steps span a thousand miles; continuous piling of mud builds mountains." Comedies reappeared on the stage and over the air. Exit restrictions for unproductive people were relaxed for a while. More food was given to the population in 1962. This was not so much due to a slight improvement resulting from the cessation of many bunglings as to a fear of serious disturbances because of a food shortage.

In agriculture, the slogan of the moment became: "Learning tricks from the old farmer." Shanghai has always been hated by the Chinese Communists for its "imperialistic influences" and its wily, blasé residents. Although the city suffered mismanagement under the Communists and many of its skilled workers were sent to the hinterlands, it still retains some traditional technological superiority—a fortunate capitalistic residue. The new line has been: "Study Shanghai; catch up with Shanghai." Engineers, skilled workers and factory *kanpu* in Peking, Tientsin, Mukden, and Canton were sent on pilgrimages to Shanghai to "fetch sacred scrolls"—a poetic Buddhist expression meaning reverent learning.

The soft sell has again come to the fore.

The Party took great pains to explain to puzzled comrades that the change should not be regarded as a revival of hateful capitalism. That was essentially true, for it was a change of tactics rather than philosophy. The remedial measures adopted were merely a temporary retreat from overregimentation. The compulsion to regiment was still there; the old pattern was still the favorite.

During the Great Leap the favorite slogans were: "One day is equal to twenty years," and "catch up with England in fifteen years." Now they were: "The difficulties in our economy are temporary in our progress," and "We must struggle amid hardship forever." Intellectuals were urged to be "masters, not slaves of material things." They should concentrate on "spiritual joys." Peasants were given lengthy accounts of great famines in Imperial China, and persuaded: "By thinking of the past and the majority of the people, it is quite easy to see in the present misery the happiness of the people of our country." A comrade, who "spat blood like a fountain" but was healed by a letter from Mao Tse-tung, urged the disease-ridden population: "If we show weakness before our diseases, we cannot defeat them."

Among all these changes of tone, the strangest was Marshal Chen Yi's speech to Peking's college graduates in the summer of 1961. In the name of the Party Central Committee, Chen eased away from some of the Party's major ideological points. He said that past demands for more indoctrination of students was "unfair," that "if specialized studies are not esteemed, the science and culture of our country will be forever backward," that students who had said wrong things should not be discriminated against, that a youth should not be classed according to his family origin, that individualism is difficult to eliminate, and that a person's change of mind cannot be effected by force.

He added: "Speaking of myself, my own mind is very complex. It has Communist ideas, and the ideas of Confucius and Mencius; and also capitalist ideas. After taking part in the revolution for forty years, I still cannot say that I am 'thoroughly Red.' I can only say that my Communist ideas are dominant, but my ideas of Confucius, Mencius, and capitalism are possibly not yet completely chased away."

Marshal Chen, as a vice-premier and a member of the Politburo, was speaking for the Party rather than for himself. For he also wrote in a Kwangtung Party publication *Upper Current* an article entitled "We Have Been Too Stupid." In it he quoted

Mao Tse-tung's admission to the Party Central Committee: "We have been too stupid. Since 1958 we have suffered many setbacks. . . . The main reason is that we did not believe in the experts and did not listen to their words."

The Party Central Committee's official organ *Red Flag* in September 1962 made one of the most frank admissions when it implied that Peking's ambitious industrialization plans would be shelved indefinitely, that those who believed in quick industrialization were wrong. Soon after, the Central Committee announced a reshuffle of some top Communists as scapegoats for the economic failure, and acknowledged that popular resistance in the country was continuing.

The Instant Paradise seemed more distant than ever.

The tactical retreat and the beatification of misery, while meant to prevent a crisis from growing into a catastrophe, came as a severe face-losing repudiation of the Party's own ideological stand. Politically it was a virtual surrender—even though a temporary surrender—to the traditional ideas and basic human values which the Party had been trying so hard to liquidate. Can this return from the point-of-no-return save the day? Or will Mao's remark "who will vanquish whom" become his famous last words?

XIV

WHEN TAOISTS SHADOWBOX MAOISTS

Unbending rigor is the mate of death,
And yielding softness, company of life . . .
The strong and mighty topple from their place;
The soft and yielding rise above them all.

THIS PARADOX OF LAOTZU, FOUNDER OF TAOISM, IS THE
Chinese people's secret of survival. The basic concept of Taoism
is *wu wei* (do nothing). Its negativism toward the world of man
is enlivened by a childlike, joyous love of nature. This love per-
meates Chinese painting, poetry and yearning for the idyllic.
From the Taoist philosophy stem the Taoist religion and alchemy,
now both considered superstitions, and the useful antithetical
technique of wisdom through stupidity, action through inaction,
and strength through weakness.

This technique is often applied to physical things. The picturesque circular stone arch bridges found everywhere on the
Yangtze delta were built on the principle of resisting by yielding.
The area's spongy silt makes rigid foundations impossible, so the
Chinese developed this flexible stone arch which adapts itself to
the rise and fall of the silt and the weight of traffic. These bridges
look fragile and delicate, but have great hidden strength. More
than a thousand years ago, high Taoist monks in the sacred mountains of Szechwan developed a school of shadowboxing called
taichi. Based on concentration, breathing and curvilinear movements, the *taichi* looks like a dreamy ballet but is a deadly system
of self-defense utilizing the opponent's strength to fight the oppo-

nent. Centuries ago, it is believed, *taichi* was introduced into Japan where it became judo.

The Taoist technique is also applied to human relations. Dealing with an overwhelming force, it does not use an immovable barrier, but a formless, resilient, all-engulfing softness. This is the difference between a Maginot Line and guerilla warfare. To fight this softness is like stabbing silly-putty or slashing water. It cannot be broken because it yields; it always comes back because it is never broken. The Chinese are not oaks, but bamboos and willows.

The Chinese Communists, or Maoists, have discarded the traditional philosophies, but by both habit and design have retained the Taoist tactics to use along with naked force. They have used them successfully in foreign relations. They have used them with less success on the Chinese people, or the Taoists (in the nonreligious sense), who retreated into apparent submission, then came out to fight back with the same tactics. Peking did for a time crush the unyielding, monolithic Confucianism, but not Taoism, which is nowhere and everywhere.

For more than a decade the Taoists have been shadowboxing the Maoists. This other-worldly warfare can be divided roughly into three periods. From 1949 to 1956, the Maoists used their soft-hard tactics on selected population segments, which either acquiesced or defended themselves with positive negativism—faked enthusiasm, lip-obedience, pretended stupidity or mere escapism. The winner of the first round was the Maoists.

From 1956 to 1960, the people increasingly used subtle offensive tactics, such as lefthanded compliments, satire, arguments loaded with Marxist quotations, and invisible sabotage. They frequently forced the Communists to abandon their Taoist tactics and resort to naked force. The second round was a draw.

The third round, beginning around 1961, found the Maoists increasingly on the defensive and the Taoists increasingly using un-Taoist offensive tactics like orthodox sabotage, straight talk, riots, mass uprisings and revolutionary organizations. The winner of the third round was the Taoists, although whether the third round is the last round remains to be seen.

The simplest form of resistance is voting with one's feet. Escape from Communist China is not easy due to internal travel and exit restrictions and the immense geographical barriers at its borders. The two tiny enclaves of British Hong Kong and Portuguese Macao are the only practical exits for the bulk of the population. Within 14 years from 1949 to early 1963, an estimated 3.5 million Chinese were fugitives from their own country. Up to the beginning of the communes, most refugees came from four provinces; by late 1959, they had come from 16 provinces; by late 1960, from 22 provinces; by mid-1962, at the time of the tragically abortive Great Exodus at the Hong Kong border, refugees in the Free World were found from every province of China. These refugees included not only Nationalists, industrialists and merchants whom Peking wants to liquidate, but liberal politicians, Communist Party members, army officers, air force pilots, enlisted men, militiamen, policemen, secret servicemen, students, professors, writers, actors, musicians, painters, athletes, doctors, nurses, factory workers, farmers, fishermen, Catholic priests, Buddhist monks, nuns, lamas, housewives and children. Never in the history of China have so many home-loving, land-rooted Chinese so desperately wanted to escape from their own country.

Since not all can flee, the rest have to take it on the chin. After all, the stoical Chinese had survived countless wars, famines and changes of dynasties. But this time mere submission was not enough. For the reticent Chinese, no freedom of silence is far worse than no freedom of speech. The people who love most to be left alone found themselves flushed out of their acquiescent shells. Thus began the bizarre Oriental shadowboxing.

The Communists themselves are past-masters in elusive words and actions. They once banned translations of American scientific and technical magazines because "they contain poison." When the ban was lifted they said: "Science has no national boundaries." Mao himself loves to toss out a pithy saying pregnant with overtones. Judging the initial reactions, he would then define exactly what he meant. During the Hundred Flowers a Marxist theoretician suggested that free discussions be limited to certain areas, adding that the limits would be "infinitely wide for those within the People, and infinitely narrow for the Enemies." Mao also invited criticisms, promising immunity. When the blooming got out of hand Mao revised his policy speech. He said he had invited criticisms, yes, but only from the People. Then he defined the People as "those who support Communism." Those against it were classified as Enemies. To make things more elastic, Mao quoted a paradox from Laotzu: "Fortune depends on misfortune; misfortune hides in fortune."

Dealing with the slippery Maoists, the Taoists use even more elusive tactics. Prof. Feng Yu-lan, a renowned philosopher who emerged unscathed from countless brainwashings and confessions, used Marxist quotations and frequent "Chairman Mao says" to prove that the world's greatest mystic Laotzu was a materialist. One has to know the subtlety of the Chinese language as well as Marxist terminology to decipher from his esoteric essay that he meant the exact opposite of what he said. In the same vein Lu Kan-ju, former Vice President of Shantung University, wrote an essay "demanding" that Chinese poets of the 6th century "join labor reform."

It is fascinating to see how Maoists and Taoists have locked their elusive horns. The Communists liquidated private enterprise in Shanghai, initially by trying to force on it impossible quotas of government bonds. The capitalists were required to attend meetings lasting eight to ten hours, during which Communists in relays gave polite, persuasive, long-winded speeches day after day. This tactic was nicknamed by laconic Shanghailanders "fatigue bombardment." Soon the industrialists devised a counter-technique. They attended the meetings with ostentatious relish, bringing buns, vacuum bottles of tea, and toothbrushes. The unspoken message behind the camping paraphernalia so neutralized the fatigue bombardment that the Communists had to give it up.

Where else in the world could a sanguinary battle be fought with such sophistication?

Then the Communists confiscated private enterprise by means of "joint enterprise" under which the owners were paid salary and dividends and their experience utilized. Some owners retaliated by eagerly accepting government orders, then purposely let the workers waste the raw material. When ordered to stop it, they replied innocently: "Since the workers are the boss now, we cannot do anything about it." Eventually the Communists said that former factory owners must decide for themselves whether they wanted the dividends, which officially were available. That was a clever Taoist stroke, and the industrialists were stuck with it. They grumbled: "Cats naturally like fish. It would be simple if you just took away the fish. But letting us smell it and saying it's up to us, that is a real dilemma."

Such battles confuse even the devious Russians. In 1957 some philosophers from Communist China visited the China Problems Research Center in the U.S.S.R., and had an impossible time explaining to the Russian philosophers how capitalists could be liquidated without total physical annihilation. Leader Feng Ting of the Chinese group made a report after their return. With understandable ethnic pride he recounted with relish how the nebulous Chinese truth about shifting superstructures and the changing nature of antagonisms left the Russians bewildered, split and arguing among themselves.

Being Chinese themselves, the Maoists can usually understand what the Taoists really mean, and thus they often get hurt. In 1959 Shanghai's *Wen Huai Pao* was angry at people who implied that life under the Communists was worse than under the Nationalists. The paper complained that instead of saying it outright, the people said: "In the past we had no money and could only look at the things we wanted. Today we have money but cannot buy anything." Communist critics were incensed over some ostensibly loyal philosophers at Peking University, who slipped a tiny "perhaps" or "maybe" into their Marxist writings to "show opposition in a crooked, covert way." A young professor once explained to his class that the Taiping Rebellion of the 19th century failed because the rebel leaders had no culture and despised the old gentry. The Maoists instantly recognized themselves, roaring: "What this points to is quite clear!"

A lecturer on Marxism in the People's University was accused of being a counter-revolutionary because the Party found that he "carried out vicious insults against the Party and Comrade Mao Tse-tung, but his words are such that they sound like praises." Professor Chu Kuang-chien, a leading authority on aesthetics, is an eloquent Taoist past-master who uses Marxist terminology to confound the Maoists, who complained: "He likes to use ambiguous words and argue in an abstract way. Seen on the surface, what he says is reasonable, but in fact the ideas proposed are confusing." A famous storyteller in Nanking, "Dim-Eyed Kan," described a well-known episode from the popular novel *Water Margin* in which the hero Wu Sung kills a tiger by slamming it against a rock. He quoted Wu Sung as saying: "Ha, ha! I thought Emperor Cat was so tough. But he is no match for the rock." He was executed for that. The Communists realized that "cat" in Chinese is a homonym of "Mao," and "rock" is the "shek" in Chiang Kai-shek. An old farmer in Kwangtung was asked at a discussion meeting whether the Communists or Nationalists were better. He replied: "Of course the Communists are better. They give us two *liang* (Chinese ounce) of rice." He disappeared the next day. "Two *liang* of rice" in Cantonese slang means "very little." Captive liberal Chang Nai-chi, who was fired as Minister of Food in 1957 because of his criticisms during the Hundred Flowers, was later ordered to give a penitent speech. On the using of pig manure as fertilizer he quoted in his confession an official remark: "More pigs, more fertilizer; more fertilizer, more grain; more grain, more pigs and again more fertilizer and again more grain." Then he added his own praise: "This opens up a future infinitely beautiful." The Maoists were sure the praise was an insult, "although on the surface Chang Nai-chi appears to be . . . more optimistic than anybody else."

The Maoists realize that the farcical acquiescence and tongue-in-cheek eulogies from the public make them look silly—at least in Chinese eyes. One has to know the language to realize that the deadliest insults in Chinese are always couched in exquisitely polite words.

The reason why Peking's bureaucratic bungling has damaged its economy so heavily is mainly due to the invisible sabotage by peasants and workers. Subtle go-slow strikes, eating up of livestock, strewing grain in the fields during harvest, intentionally working the wrong way, over-doing things when an order is found senseless, these and many other tactics used by millions of unorganized, surreptitious individuals have produced a cumulative result that no amount of coercion can correct. As early as 1953 the *Hsinhua Daily* reported that factory workers purposely "disobey technical instructions . . . resist authority negatively." *People's Daily* in 1954 said workers deliberately did not follow proper working processes, designs and blueprints, "causing tremendous damage to our national economy." Secret police chief Lo Jui-ching in 1956 told the Congress that his agents were poorly equipped to deal with sly industrial sabotage such as falsified charts, altered laboratory data, forged blue-prints, and machine parts that had been tampered with. This happens even in munitions plants.

Orthodox forms of sabotage, such as forest arson, crippling work animals, smashing oil pipes, and setting fire to cotton mills, are numerous enough to fill a book even from Peking's own reports. Manchuria's *Northeast Daily* said: "Saboteurs are frequently found in electric plants and power stations in Anshan, Fushun, Changchun and Peipiao, using sand, iron slabs, etc." *People's Daily*, reporting on the serious sabotage on the Yangtze Bridge and the dike-repair during the 1955 Wuhan flood, warned: "as long as the counter-revolutionaries are not exterminated, our lives and happiness will not be completely secure." By mid-1955 the People's Court had dealt with 255,000 cases of economic sabotage. The number has increased since. In 1961 Radio Peking admitted a rash of railroad sabotage with explosives.

Mass uprisings and riots are hard to learn about. For example, in spring 1952, 20,000 Chinese peasants and minority Hui people in the Pingliang area in Kansu staged an armed uprising. They killed several thousand Communists and occupied four cities for nearly four months before being crushed by troops. This was mentioned briefly once in Sian's *Masses Daily*, a local paper, five months after the outbreak. Most large-scale mass uprisings took place in the sprawling hinterland provinces, where large numbers of poor peasants, conscripted workers and slave laborers strain the control network.

Besides the Tibet revolt, well-known because it took place next to India, several similar large-scale uprisings have occurred in Northwest China during the past decade. In each case the Chinese population and the minority tribes were united against the Communists. In Chinghai, an uprising in 1952 forced the Communists to send "peace envoys" 17 times; another in 1956 by 110,000 nomads resulted in the massacre of 800 Communists. In 1957, a revolt started by 1,000 Chinese Moslems grew to a force of 30,000; they carried banners and portraits of Mohammed, occupied 250 square miles of territory, killed 1,000 Communists, and fought several pitched battles against two Communist divisions and 200 armored cars. A large portion of the rebels finally retreated westward and evaporated into the deserts of Tsaidam Basin. In 1959, a similar armed rebellion, touched off by the nationalization of livestock, took place in an extensive area in Chinghai, Kansu and Szechwan.

In Sikang in 1956 the population in 20 counties, largely Tibetan, staged a massive revolt which finally developed into the 1959 uprising in Tibet. In Sinkiang in 1956, rebels in ten counties attacked Red troops, communication lines and labor camps. In 1959, when news of the Tibet revolt reached Sinkiang, a joint uprising by Chinese, Hui and Uighur slave laborers destroyed bridges, tunnels, trucks and mines. Many were massacred but a large number escaped into the wilderness. Because of this revolt, construction on the Lanchow-Urumchi Railroad was inordinately delayed. In the fall of 1961, a Hsinhua News Agency broadcast revealed a serious armed uprising in Fukien province opposite Taiwan, and appealed to the rebels to lay down their arms and accept the government's "generous amnesty."

In the coastal provinces, resistance is usually in the forms of spontaneous riots and secret political organizations. Peasant riots have been especially frequent since the communes. Numbering thousands each year, they range from fistic brawls, eating up sugar cane and grain on the spot, to bloody attacks like the one in Wuhua, Kwangtung, in April 1962. Led by a Colonel Chung, a Red Army veteran just released from slave labor, some 8,000 peasants in Wuhua attacked the militia and looted granaries. It was quelled after the troops shot down hundreds of rioters.

In May 1962, 5,000 coal miners in Lotaito, Kwangtung, rioted when they learned that 3,000 of them were to be sent to Chinghai. Led by 500 "suicide members," the miners fought a losing battle against two companies of security guards.

In June 1962, when Peking had to stop the face-losing exodus of refugees to Hong Kong, some 10,000 people rioted in Canton when refused train tickets to the border. Rushing to the scene, the mayor of Canton tried to pacify the crowd: "We are in a difficult period. You must control yourselves. Don't listen to people who incite you." But his jeep was overturned and the railroad station attacked. The riot was quelled by troops, and followed by a daily curfew in the city.

Peking is also worried about "counter-revolutionary organizations"—clandestine political and armed groups of peasants, workers, students and religious sects. Because these underground groups could be a serious threat to the regime's existence, they have been ruthlessly crushed.

Three such groups were active for several years in 17 counties in the 500-square-mile Peking-Tientsin-Paoting triangle. Their tentacles reached into mining, industrial, economic and construction departments of the government. They used coal shops as secret arms depots, and had a special team for cutting cable wires. Before they were uncovered, they raided government supply centers 54 times and buried alive 19 *kanpu*. Members of two other societies, disguised as jugglers, pedlars, fishermen and menders of cooking pots, sabotaged railroads, murdered *kanpu*, looted government depots 394 times in 60 cities along the Yangtze River, Lunghai Railroad, and Tai Lake.

Many counter-revolutionary organizations are semi-religious in nature. The most famous one is the *I Kuan Tao*, a vast secret society with millions of followers in every province in China proper. The name *I Kuan Tao* (One Pervading Way), comes from a Confucian quotation: "My Way is one unity pervading all things." It is predominantly a Taoist sect liberally incorporating Confucianism and Buddhism. Most members are illiterate, superstitious peasants and laborers. Like all grassroots semi-secret societies in Chinese history, the *I Kuan Tao* is a superstitious, sometimes criminal sect in normal times but becomes an underground political organ in times of turmoil. This sect originated in North China and was already active against the Japanese during World War II. After the Communists came into power it spread all the way to South China. The Communists liquidated tens of thousands of sect members in 1954, with the press full of detailed accounts for months. Since then it has gone underground. The magnitude of the organization may be gathered from the fact that in Northwest China alone there were 12,000 Taoist chiefs. In Chengtu, four Taoist chiefs were executed, among them a rickshaw puller and a cigarette pedlar. They conducted a training class for sabotage, penetrated into the government, and looted granaries. In Lanchi, Chekiang, the Taoists used an industrial chemical company, a stationery store, firewood and charcoal shops, and hillside caves as hideouts.

A similar organ, *Hui Tao Men* (Mass Way Society), according to Lo Jui-ching, won over a large number of peasants in 27 provinces. Among their activities were the destruction of several collective farms in Manchuria and the poisoning of 72 *kanpu* in Fukien. Another Taoist sect, the *Tou Mu Tan*, covered 16 counties in Hopei. The members plotted for a "Royalist Army," planned attacks on Communist governments, and exchanged death vows.

In a riot in Hsishui in 1952, 70 Taoists fought Communist troops with "swords, spears, or bare hands, chanting liturgy and drawing spells and incantations." When this organization was broken, the Communists found that 50–60 percent of the peasants in 50 towns investigated were members. A China Buddhist People's Alliance Army was uncovered in Anhwei. It recruited members through the clan system. Even non-relatives must first become "relatives" through a blood vow. Similar organizations in Hopei alone included the Big Sword Society, the Society of Confucian Virtue, the Red Lantern Society and the Red Spear Society. Some of them were resurrected from namesake societies 300 years ago when the peasants used underground tactics to resist the Manchu invaders.

Workers in the Penki Iron and Steel Company, in Liaoning, formed a China Civil Administration Party. Members included "outwardly progressive" technicians and members of the Communist Party for over five years. They had an elaborate party program, regulations, radio blueprints, chemicals and equipment for making high explosives and pen-size pistols. They repeatedly conducted test explosions in the hills and killed lone soldiers and policemen for their arms.

Organizations were formed by young students. The leaders of the Humanity and Democracy Alliance in Wuhan turned out to be five high-school students being trained as Communist *kanpu.* All the members were between 18 and 25 years old. Similar groups were discovered in Shanghai, Changsha and Sining. Chen Yu-sheng, a fourth-generation overseas Chinese from Indonesia, went to study in Changsha's Hunan Normal College. In 1959 he formed the Patriotic Students Federation "to help overthrow the Communist regime." In three months 300 of his schoolmates joined. By the end of the year the membership reached 2,317, including many students from other schools. Their attempts to contact nearby peasants in early 1960 were discovered. At a kangaroo court, 34 of the leaders were executed, and over 2,000 students sent to labor camps.

Slave labor does not seem to cure the subversiveness. One

group, whose discovery in 1957 shook the Communists considerably, was located in Chekiang and consisted of ex-slave laborers and family members of slave laborers. They infiltrated into power plants, colleges and schools and sent agents to Peking, Shanghai, Tientsin, Wuhan and Canton. They planned for an uprising in October but were arrested in August. Resistance groups are found even inside some labor camps. The most prominent one is the Committee of Persecuted Comrades, in the Chingho Collective Farm near Peking, the biggest labor camp in North China. Founded by nine political prisoners who made blood vows beside the graves of dead inmates, this group devised many ingenious ways of communicating with prisoners in other compounds. Their activities grew from sabotage to an abortive mass escape. Because of this, all labor camps with more than 10,000 prisoners were split into smaller ones, and a nation-wide investigation of "dangerous elements" in all camps resulted in several million prisoners being sent to the border areas.

A few examples show how underground resistance is carried out in a particular area or period. A delegate reported to the Congress in 1955 of his investigation of resistance in Szechwan's Wenkiang Special District. He said: "The sabotage of counter-revolutionaries are various in kind and numerous in number." From 16 towns and 28 villages inspected, he found much rumor-mongering, spread of discontent and sabotage. Peasants opened water gates and flooded the cotton fields, threw darnels in the rice field, crushed crops with stones. One night 70 pigs were poisoned. Assassinations: many murderers were never caught. Corruption: 171 party members in a single county were "bought over" by subversives. Arson: one village had eight fires in six weeks, with 200 houses burned, all set by a Taoist sect. The congressman ended his report: "What is more serious is that the enemy's sabotage and resistance are almost omnipresent." In early 1958, more than a dozen anti-Communist organizations were discovered at about the same time within the city of Swatow.

The *New Hunan Pao*, boasting of the achievements of the

militia in Hunan, Mao's home province, said in late 1959 that the Hunan militia in a decade put down 1,692 revolts and handled 19,584 sabotage cases. It was "day and night guarding all railroads, highways, bridges, canals, tunnels, granaries, factories, mines and reservoirs." During the first half of 1959, the Hunan militia was guarding 207,382 granaries, 2,340 factories and mines, 4,483 big reservoirs. In boasting about the achievement of the militia, this paper gave yet more evidence that Communist China is the most elaborately guarded nation of all times—against its own people.

Between 1950-1954 the Ministry of Public Security was expanded four times in size and ten times in personnel. Still the counter-revolutionaries came. Secret police chief Lo said in early 1958 that in less than a year he mobilized 750,000 *kanpu* and one million activists to conduct 328,000 investigations on 1,770,000 people. They discovered 3,000 counter-revolutionary organizations, 65,000 counter-revolutionaries, 9,000 suspected counter-revolutionaries, and 26,000 bad elements. Of these 5,000 were in the Communist Party, 3,000 in the Youth League, and 220 in top government organs. Lo commented: "It proves that our various fronts and almost all our organizations have been infiltrated by counter-revolutionaries. . . . Many have infiltrated into our inside organs; some have burrowed into our livers and intestines."

By the end of 1959, Peking reported a total of 8,323,680 cases of uprisings, sabotage and other forms of resistance. Of these 2,570,000 were organized cases. Early in 1961 a Party Central Committee communiqué admitted: "roughly 10 percent of the Chinese people are making use of the present difficulties through national disasters or shortcomings in operations of our work to push on sabotage activities," and "roughly 9 percent of public functionaries of the Party and government are bad elements."

In a nutshell, during an entire decade in Communist China, counter-revolutionaries were discovered at the rate of 2,253 daily or one every 38 seconds. By 1961, Peking was still battling 60 million saboteurs and 10 million "bad elements." In that year resistance activities included 146,852 granary raids, 94,532 arsons and 3,738 revolts, figures taken from the horse's mouth—a fantastic situation.

One reason for this phenomenon is that brutal suppression and defiant resistance feed on each other. Many were accused as counter-revolutionaries as scapegoats or for the slightest expression of discontent. A cargo boat shooting the rapids in West China overturned and the boatman was punished as a counter-revolutionary. A boy making aerated water according to an article in a popular science journal was injured by an exploding bottle. The author of the article was called a counter-revolutionary. These victims after punishment became real counter-revolutionaries. The Communists admitted that large numbers of youth had a "psychosis of vengeance" because their parents and relatives were persecuted. It is only natural that personal safety is secondary to people who are out for vendettas. At least three quarters of China's population have had close friends or relatives persecuted. The reservoir of resistance is inexhaustible. On this continued resistance despite severe punishment, Mao once said: "There are certain people who would rather die than change, and would prefer to keep their granite heads to meet God."

Many outsiders still cling to the impression that even though dissatisfaction may be widespread, there are still loyal segments of the population, such as industrial workers, Party members and the armed forces. This was true during the first few years. But now their mood has changed. As early as 1953, two types of security organs were formed specifically to deal with workers' resistance: the Comrade Trial Commissions to deal with go-slow tactics, and the mobile Special Courts to deal with industrial sabotage. Liu Shao-chi, an expert underground labor instigator during Nationalist days and now Chairman of the People's Republic, complained a couple of years ago: "The labor unions, instead of developing production, one-sidedly emphasize workers' livelihood and welfare. They put welfare first, in opposition to production." Chen Jung-wen, ex-publisher of Peking's *Daily*

Worker, was purged in 1958 because after a tour of factories he suggested less of a stranglehold on the de-natured unions, about which the workers were most bitter. The periodical *China Workers* reported that workers "wanted people's unions, and even free unions," and that at discussion meetings the workers boldly defended their former capitalist factory owners or showed deep sympathy for the peasants.

The prevalent attitude of intellectuals in the Party and the League was clearly shown at the time of the Hundred Flowers. Around that time Chief Prosecutor Tsui Tse-ping revealed that 40,000 persons in the Kirin provincial government were "politically and ideologically unreliable," and the situation was identical in other parts of Manchuria. In 1958 many *kanpu* were sent to the farms, some to the border areas. A number of them took part in an uprising in Chinghai. At a meeting of village *kanpu* in Shantung a year before the communes, several *kanpu* openly sided with the peasants. The *People's Daily* quoted their remarks: "The government is taking too much grain," "rations are not enough for the peasants," "80 percent of the peasants are discontented," "peasants' livelihood is worse than before the Liberation." The mouthpiece of the Communist Youth League, *China Youth Press,* revealed that its members "cannot hold firm to their standpoint, cannot distinguish between right and wrong, sympathize with rightist opinions. . . . Everywhere they are spreading ideas that are anti-Socialist, anti-Party and anti-People's Democratic Dictatorship." The Party and the League's political foundations started to loosen in late 1956. By now the process has reached the upper strata.

Communist China has an estimated 2.5 million standing military force, one million public security troops and police, and 20 million militiamen. Quantitatively this striking force is staggering. Qualitatively it is something else. Even if these forces were well-disciplined and loyal, their strength would be the strength of an occupation army. The fact is that the armed forces began to weaken in 1956. Next to Party members, the armed forces get the best treatment. Around the end of the Civil War, the discipline and morale of Communist soldiers were the finest in China's living memory. To this day many still have this image. The Red Army's fighting strength was still considerable during the Korean War, although this strength was exaggerated by several factors that were seldom noticed. The fierce human-sea tactics, unlike the Japanese kami-kazi, were due to the diabolical control system rather than to fanaticism. The outcome of the war would have been quite different were it not for the sanctuary created by political considerations. The fact that two-thirds of the POW's despite family ties chose to go to Taiwan showed the state of loyalty.

In 1954 the armed forces were reorganized from a guerilla to a regular army pattern. Next year the forces switched from the supply to the salary system. Formerly, officers and enlisted men both wore drab uniforms and lived frugally. The reorganization created a *nouveau riche* spirit in the officers and they began to live it up. A lieutenant's pay became three and a half times that of a primary school teacher's; a major's, more than a college professor's. Officers' wives flaunted their jewels and fur coats, so that the public said: "The People's Liberation Army has the thoughts of warlords."

What was worse was the growing discrepancy in the treatment of officers and enlisted men. The soft life of the officers created resentment among the enlisted men. By 1956–1957 the *Liberation Army Press* reported that the deterioration of army discipline had become "quite serious." In four months a single regiment near Peking registered 91 infractions of discipline, of them 16 were defying officers. It said: "In various military units one frequently sees unkempt appearance, flippant and listless actions. . . . What is more serious is that during drills officers act freely without taking care of their units. Company and platoon leaders do not personally lead their units, so that the processions become chaotic. Columns do not look like columns; lines do not look like lines." To remedy the situation, every year tens of thousands of officers above regimental rank were required to join their companies as enlisted men for a few months.

The nation's economic crisis began to hit the army by 1957. While officers still got rice or flour, the enlisted men got part of their food in miscellaneous cereals. To improve army food, soldiers were required to plant vegetables and keep pigs. Such labor activities kept on increasing so that by now the Red Army has become a big labor force, farming and building railroads, highways and dams. Families of technical soldiers used to accompany the garrison and receive special privileges. In 1958 they were sent to the communes. The resentment was so deep that during the shelling of Quemoy that year, artillery soldiers purposely missed important targets. It was one reason that the 575,000 shells fired in three months did little damage to Quemoy. In 1958 special privileges for families of all enlisted men were abolished, and they were organized into commune labor teams. By 1959 treatment of the army got worse. Soldiers' rations were cut one-third, and they were engaged in ceaseless political activities and labor chores. Veterans returning to their villages found their families living a hard life and they themselves pressed into labor corps. These veterans, numbering about ten million, out of resentment created many incidents in the villages. The *Liberation Army Press* said that some officers and enlisted men "yearn for or praise the democracy of the capitalist class, and are dissatisfied with or actively oppose the dictatorship of the proletariat. . . . Some oppose the Party leadership; some oppose all political activities; others oppose labor." A very alarming feature, according to this paper, was officers' and enlisted men's "sympathy for the peasants." Their suggestions were to "raise farm prices" and "slow down industrialization." Soldiers openly offered their opinions to the Party. "Peasants' life is too hard," they said, often specifically explaining, "I am speaking from the standpoint of the peasants." The security problem in the armed forces reached such a proportion that secret police chief Lo Jui-ching was appointed Chief of General Staff of the armed forces in September 1959. At the same time General Peng Te-huai, a hero of the Korean War who actively opposed the commune system, was replaced by General Lin Piao. Minister of National Defense Lin Piao put the whole situation in a nutshell not long ago when, after enumerating various "corrosive and disintegrating influences" in the armed forces, he said: "If our political and ideological work (in the armed forces) cannot be done well, all other tasks would be fruitless."

In spite of heavily increased indoctrination and Party control, military morale deteriorated further. Refugees reported that in 1961 soldiers in some barracks in Kiangsu refused to get out of their beds for morning drills as a protest against reduced rations, that part of the navy in Shanghai mutinied unsuccessfully, and that in 1962 a number of veteran Party members in the navy at Yulin and Hoihow, on Hainan Island, were discovered to be counter-revolutionaries.

The modernization of the armed forces also brought personnel and technical problems. Mutual contempt created serious friction between experienced, illiterate *kanpu* who cannot handle modern weapons, and young cadets who can but have no combat experience. What is worse, top commissar Hsiao Hua of the People's Liberation Army revealed at a military conference in 1960 that the modernized Red Army had met "insurmountable difficulties" in handling jets, radar, and eventually missiles and nuclear weapons. He lamented that those who could be trained to operate modern equipment are "politically most unreliable," intellectuals who are "quick to display faked enthusiasm, but actually they harbor a deep resentment against Communism." Illiterate recruits are more reliable, but "technically useless."

It would be naive to expect the Peking regime to topple directly by popular discontent. Uprisings, though numerous and at times sizable, have little chance of success in a vast country where any trouble spot can be promptly sealed off by troop deployments. Secret organizations so far have also been ineffective. On the surface a successful revolt seems hopeless. But this kind of resistance should not be underestimated, and may in the long run prove effective.

The Chinese people living under Communism for over a decade have learned the regime's strength as well as its vulnerable spots. Young students know how to argue with bureaucrats, using typical dialectical logic. Counter-revolutionaries—they should be in all fairness called revolutionaries—know how to organize underground cells even inside the Party and government. This significant trend has exploded the myth that any subversive move is hopeless in a police state.

Some of Peking's repressive measures are seeds of trouble. The Chinese peasants have been conservative and submissive mainly due to their attachment to their land, families and ancestral graves. These have been taken away or destroyed by the Communists. They have nothing else to lose except, as the Chinese saying goes, "a pair of pants and a belt." The primitive militia is a questionable asset in national defense. It may be a boomerang if Peking tries to throw it against a hostile population.

Chinese peasants have played a unique role in history. Several great dynasties have been toppled by peasant uprisings. Since 1957 millions of educated people have been exiled to rural China. The vast ground-swell of peasant discontent now has the effective leadership of students, professors, thinkers and *kanpu*. Formerly the lip-obedient people were curbed by mutual suspicion. The Hundred Flowers blew off the psychological lid. Since 1961 a new phenomenon arose which was unthinkable in the mid Fifties: open grumbling, argument and public rebuke of the Peking regime.

A genuine popular revolution, unlike a palace intrigue and *coup d'état*, always comes with painful slowness. It is born of deep misery and despondency. It comes only after long, soul-searching appraisal by the people of their hopes and despairs, their life and death. When conditions are not favorable, no amount of instigating or wishful thinking can make it succeed. When they are, nothing can stand in its way. The Chinese Communists possess the most effective terror weapons known to date: brainwashing, secret police and huge armed forces. But brainwashing has been over-rated, insidious as it is. It can easily change the victim's words and actions, but not his inner thoughts and convictions, especially if he uses Taoist resilience. The army and secret police are only as effective as the men in them. In China, many of these men are not only wavering, but actually siding with the peasants. When the chips are down, it is quite clear where the terror weapons, humans all, will veer. Their switch would irrevocably tip the balance. Weapons are a great help but not everything. Else the Bastille would never have fallen, Paul Revere's ride would have been in vain, and today's emergent nations would have remained colonies.

The trend of events in Communist China is now significantly clear. Up to 1957 the regime, using soft-hard tactics adroitly, was in firm control of the situation despite growing disaffection. The Hundred Flowers was the turning point. At that time in face of the overt criticisms the *People's Daily* mentioned two alternate remedies for the situation: "coercive remedy and dialectic (soft) remedy." It decided publicly to reject the coercive remedy because of "the danger of clear-cut opposition" (revolt). Five weeks later the regime was forced to switch to the harsh method. Since then it has been vacillating between soft and hard tactics, but each time the shift was forced by the people, who have seized the initiative.

Former secret police chief Lo once warned his comrades of the "counter-revolutionaries": "The longer they fight, the more skillful they become. When they strike, they usually strike at our vulnerable spots. No sensitive places in our government, army and Party are immune from infiltration." The *People's Daily* has also repeatedly admitted the serious probability of a successful revolution by the rebels: "It would mean . . . the heads of hundreds of thousands of (Communist) revolutionaries rolling to the ground. . . . Their number is not merely in hundreds or thousands. . . . If we think that they are satisfied with individual sabotage, then we are really too naive. Their aim is to topple the People's Republic." If this sounds hysterical, it is because the Communists have a nose for potential revolutions.

The real, stark mood of the people in Communist China was summed up in a public statement issued in October 1962 by some 130 college and high-school students, who escaped from Communist China to Hong Kong in the big refugee exodus in May that year. The statement says in part:

> We are a group of youths who recently left our hometowns and sought refuge abroad. . . . When the Chinese Communist regime was founded, we were all only children, ranging from high-school students to primary school pupils. Since then we have been receiving Communist education. To borrow an expression from the Chinese Communists, we can be called youth who "grew up in the Mao Tse-tung Era."
>
> However, as we grew up and our knowledge increased, we discovered that what the Communists said and did were completely opposite. The Communists know how to teach us to "hate the old society." But from our actual experiences, we hate this "new society" much more, because in this so-called "new society" the vast majority of people are suffering from cold and hunger, and are on the verge of starvation. The people have lost their freedom of speech, freedom of action and freedom of person. . . .
>
> Like our compatriots on the mainland, we have learned a firsthand lesson, that one should never entertain any illusions about the Communists. The basic Communist nature of enslaving the people at home and carrying out aggression against the people abroad will never change. We now offer this lesson, which we have learned at an excruciatingly painful price, to certain people in the free world who still entertain illusions about the Communists. . . .

This is the poignant voice of the young Communist generation. It has come from Poland, from Hungary, from East Germany, from Cuba and—in the exotic Chinese language—from Communist China.

By the end of 1962, Communist China appeared to be on the eve of a great storm. Amid reports of a fourth consecutive year of bad crops, food stock was steadily moved to centralized granaries, while rations were slightly increased. The population was exhorted to eat less and produce more. Some provinces reportedly refused to deliver grains to the central government.

Operations were suspended in 40 per cent of all heavy industrial plants and 60 per cent of all light industrial plants. Some 60 million farmers had converged on urban areas seeking food; and 30 million urban residents were being forcibly sent to the farms to "produce more food." The once systematic household control network began to loosen as hungry hordes moved back and forth. The regime on one hand was wooing old farmers, old professors, and modern engineers, and on the other ordering the "strengthening of military discipline" to supervise the demoralized soldiers "in and out of uniform." Regular troops marched into one commune after another to replace the unreliable militia. As the garrison troops became too friendly with the local populace, South Chinese troops were sent north and North Chinese troops sent south. Seven divisions of troops were moved into Fukien, opposite Quemoy and Taiwan, not to "liberate" Taiwan, but to guard against a Nationalist attack which would touch off a great explosion.

Shanghai passed the 1963 New Year under curfew, when the city buzzed excitedly with rumors that Red troops on nearby Chusan Islands had revolted. Defense works were built next to the Yangtze Bridge, as the official press reverted to talking of sharpening "class struggles" and refugee reports told of numerous bombings of mines, barracks, dockyards, railroads and bridges.

The Mysterious Absorption has worked. Souped up with ideological fuel and careening with hot-rod drivers, Peking's juggernaut is sinking by its own weight in the quagmire of Chinese resilience.

Meanwhile, the people of China are waiting—and waiting.

> *Nothing is weaker than water,*
> *But when it attacks something hard,*
> *Then nothing withstands it,*
> *And nothing will alter its way . . .*
> *This is paradox.* —LAOTZU

PART FOUR

THE TWO CHINAS

PART FOUR

XV

THE PRIVATE WORLDS
OF CHIANG AND MAO

HALF A CENTURY AGO DURING THE LAST DAYS OF THE MAN-chus, two Chinese youths snipped off their own queues. Theirs was a radical gesture portending the storm soon to sweep over China. Both young men were traumatically affected by the old dragon squirming in the new waves. In both, East and West, the old and the new, had met and clashed but never integrated. They were to become two mixed-up symbols of a mixed-up China.

Chiang Kai-shek and Mao Tse-tung are products of China's unique history, which in turn has been distinctively molded by them. Both are Chinese trained and Chinese oriented but their backgrounds are different. Chiang is of traditional Confucian China. Mao is of traditional popular China. Their personalities are also poles apart. Throughout these decades they have had their images glorified, warped, copied by friends, foes and plain ignoramuses. But images are deceptive. They do not reflect the obscure private worlds in which these men really live. To probe into the men behind the images, one must look for their peculiar frames of reference, patterns of behavior, sources of inspiration, idiosyncrasies, obsessions and grand dreams.

Chiang Kai-shek has been called a national hero, an agent of decay, a symbol of freedom, and a political corpse clinging to a lost cause. It is convenient to fall back on easy labels, but the real man is more complicated. Born in 1887 in the little town of Chikow in coastal Chekiang, Chiang is a descendent of scholar-farmers. His family was financially comfortable by rural China's standard until he was eight, when his father died. He was strictly brought up in the traditional style, first by his father, then by his mother, a woman of fine character and some learning. He studied classics in the local school, and by the time he entered the high school in nearby Fenghua, his study of classics, his innate seriousness and his poor but normal childhood had set his personality pattern. He was an extremely conscientious though not brilliant young man, strongly drawn to Confucian concepts in family loyalty and politics. But there were yet to be other influences.

Those were the years when China seethed under corrupt Manchu rule and foreign aggressions. At 18 Chiang cut off his queue, and voiced his desire to study abroad and become a revolutionary. In 1906 he entered the Paoting Military Academy, and was sent to Japan the next year. For four years he was a cadet in the Japanese Military College and a recruit in the Japanese 13th Field Artillery. He learned military science, associated with young Chinese revolutionaries in Tokyo, and became a favorite disciple of Sun Yat-sen. Like his generation, Chiang was intensely nationalistic, and later acquired Sun's political theory—a form of parliamentary democracy tinged with socialism.

When the Wuchang Uprising broke out on the Double Tenth, Chiang hurried back to China and became an active revolutionary. His attitude toward Communism began to crystallize in 1923, when he was sent by Sun on an inspection trip to Moscow. Upon his return Chiang issued a circular letter to his party's Central Committee. In the light of later events Chiang's letter was prophetic. It said: "The Russian Communist Party is not to be trusted. . . . Their so-called internationalism and World Revolution are nothing but Caesarism under another name, the better to hoodwink the outside world." The idealistic Sun, hungry for any outside help, considered Chiang over-cautious. Thus the Kuomintang began to play ball with the Russians and co-exist with the Chinese Communist Party. This political honeymoon fell apart in 1927 during the Northern Expedition when Chiang unseated the warlords, purged the Communists from the Kuomintang and expelled the Russian advisers. Since then, the Communists and the Nationalists have fought and talked peace with each other time and again—*ta ta, tan tan; tan tan, ta ta.* Mao grew in strength and finally drove Chiang from the China mainland.

Christianity also had an impact on Chiang's personality. Chiang was once married to a peasant girl through the traditional family contract, but their worlds grew apart when he became a radical revolutionary and the two were divorced. He met and fell in love with Mayling Soong, daughter of an American-educated Chinese Christian minister and sister of Sun Yat-sen's wife, who is now a vice-chairman of Communist China. In 1927 Chiang proposed to her. Her mother, a devout Christian, at first objected to the union because Chiang came from a Buddhist family. She asked if Chiang was willing to become a Christian. Chiang replied that he could not promise beforehand, but would study the Bible and accept Christianity only if he became a sincere convert. This completely disarmed the old lady who gave her blessings. Later that year the two were married at a church wedding in Shanghai. Eventually, after a diligent study of the Bible, Chiang was baptized. Ever since, no matter how busy, he has set aside half an hour each morning and evening for prayers and meditation. Wherever he goes he consecrates a room for worship.

Chiang's once looming and now receding image on the Chinese political horizon can only be appropriately appraised against his background and personality. He is a serious, conscientious, stubborn, aloof man anchored to Confucianism, molded by Japanese military training, fired by nationalism, and converted to Christianity. Beneath that veneer of Chinese reserve and modesty, he is as moralistic as a preacher and as inflexible as granite. From Confucianism and military training he developed an ardent belief in paternal government which demands unquestioned obedience to a benevolent authority. This residual Confucian political philosophy, reinforced by the circumstantial logic of a politically tumultuous China, is found even in many Chinese who believe they have completely absorbed Western democracy. In Chiang this leftover is especially strong. He is an ingenious manipulator of political personalities, a must in Chinese politics which are seldom run by the book. To control incompetent or untrustworthy generals, Chiang is known for by-passing normal channels and issuing "hand orders" to them on the battlefield, sometimes making a mess of the situation. Patiently tenacious on long-range goals but temperamental and autocratic on immediate issues, he is more proficient in making use of obedient bureaucrats than rugged individualists.

Chiang is personally incorruptible, although some members of his Kuomintang wallowed in corruption after World War II. He clings to the typical Confucian concept of a government by men who are governed by inner morals—a government by gentlemen. His speeches are heavily loaded with Confucian clichés, to which he is faithful and he expects others to be so too. In 1934 he started the New Life Movement, whose watch words were propriety, loyalty, integrity and honor. This simplified form of Confucianism, to an impatient new China set adrift from old values and searching for anything new-fangled, fell on deaf ears. The fact that Chiang always lives a materially Spartan and spiritually austere life while many of his subordinates went the other way is a great irony. It is also Chiang's personal tragedy.

Many incidents in Chiang's life indicate his tenacity and personal courage. The best-known is the Sian Kidnapping. A patriotic bitterness swept over China in the mid-30's after repeated Japanese aggressions, demanding a war against Japan. But Chiang believed that the internal Communist military menace should be eliminated before turning to a foreign war, and he defied public opinion on that point. In 1936 on a visit to Chang Hsueh-liang, the "Young Marshal," in Sian, Chiang was held captive by Chang who demanded that he stop fighting the Communists and start fighting the Japanese. Although his life was at stake, Chiang was fearless. After telling Chang that he should either release him or shoot him, Chiang refused to talk with his captor.

Although the whole nation was critical of Chiang's seemingly weak-kneed policy against Japan, strangely it rose as one man to show its loyalty and almost worship for him. Young students wept openly at the news of the kidnapping and community leaders all over China sent cables to the rebel leaders, warning that unless they released Chiang, "jade and rock will be burned together." Meanwhile, Chiang's diary was seized and read by Chang who came to realize Chiang's real reason for not fighting the Japanese at that time. Deeply repentent, Chang the captor surrendered to his captive and escorted him back to the capital.

For 24 years Chang was kept a virtual prisoner by Chiang. Contemporary historians are still unable to tell whether Chiang did this out of personal vindictiveness or the bitter regret that the Sian Kidnapping was the turning point of the Nationalist-Communist struggle, since after the incident Chiang was forced by public opinion to accept the Communists' United Front. Chang, however, was not otherwise mistreated. He was given a comfortable house and garden, allowed to play tennis, take walks, worship in Chiang's personal chapel, and do everything he liked —except leaving Chiang's vicinity. Chang regained complete freedom in 1960. By then he had become a Christian and scholar in Ming history. This case reveals a still unfathomed measure of Chiang's personality as well as unique contemporary Chinese politics.

During Chiang's captivity his first wife prayed to her Buddha that she was willing to exchange her life for his safety. Chiang was freed on Christmas Day 1936. On that day she was killed in Chikow in a Japanese bombing. Upon receiving the news, Chiang secluded himself for two days. Before he left the mainland, whenever he required deep thought or had suffered a setback, Chiang would go back to Chikow and take long, silent walks by his mother's grave.

Chiang's second marriage is an attraction between opposites. Mayling Soong, a charming, Americanized Wellesley graduate and fine Chinese painter, was not only instrumental in bringing

Chiang to Christianity but appears the only cursory link between the tradition-steeped Chiang and the West. Due to past imperialist aggressions, most Chinese had a strong anti-West feeling despite their desire to borrow from the West. The outgrowth of this feeling was a latent anti-missionary trend among some intellectuals and early Nationalists. It must be to his wife's credit that Chiang never grew into a rabid anti-Western nationalist. Instead, he grew to like foreign missionaries and educators. Against his Confucian grain and over the opposition of the zenophobic elements in the Kuomintang, he threw the lot of Nationalist China with that of the West. But like Mao Tse-tung, to this day he has never really understood the West, nor the West him. The old roots are too strong and the contacts are too limited.

This is Chiang Kai-shek, authoritarian Confucian, militant soldier, revolutionary nationalist and devoted Christian. Yesterday he was a national hero of all China; today he is almost a forgotten man licking his wounds on Taiwan. Tomorrow—if he lives long enough—history might take another look.

The private world of Mao Tse-tung, who looks like a grandmother, writes like a sage, sings like a poet and kills like a butcher, is as incongruous as Chiang's, but far more colorful and mystical.

In 1893 when Chiang was six Mao was born in Shaoshan, a village in Hunan. Hunanese peasants are known to be stubborn, impulsive and superstitious. Mao came from a family of rich peasants who owned three and a half acres of land. Compared to Chiang's family of small landed gentry, Mao's economic status was about the same although socially lower. His father, who had only two years of schooling, was a farmer and grain merchant who often beat Mao for being lazy and forced him to study the classics. Although Mao loved his mother, he developed an undying hatred for his brute of a father and often quarrelled bitterly with him. At eight he was sent to the village school which, like the rural schools of that time, dispensed Confucian classics with corporal punishment. During his teens, Mao's father married him to a peasant girl with whom Mao refused to live. Instead, carrying his bedding, he walked out of his home and went to study in the nearby Tungshan School. Upon arrival, Mao quarrelled with the janitor. Over-aged and with a hulking physique, Mao was mistaken for a bandit by the students, who raised an alarm. But despite his age, Mao was accepted as a student.

Mao's antipathy for classics caused him to escape into two non-classical, popular Chinese novels which he read avidly and repeatedly. The two historic romances, *Water Margin* and *Tales of Three Kingdoms*, were the sole source of Mao's childhood reveries and strangely, a principal inspiration for his adult actions. At Tungshan Mao became the unofficial story-teller and fascinated his schoolmates with episodes from his two beloved novels. They assumed such importance to him that he often argued heatedly with his history teacher who said *Three Kingdoms* was a historic novel. Mao said it was straight history. He tried to organize his schoolmates to get rid of the teacher and later the headmaster, who did not side with Mao. He wrote an appeal to the magistrate, demanding the ouster of the headmaster for his sacrilegious remark. When his schoolmates refused to sign the appeal, Mao got into a fight and became a social outcast among the boys.

Because of this Mao decided to leave the school and went to Changsha. When the 1911 revolution broke out he joined the revolutionary army for a brief spell. One day wandering aimlessly in Changsha, Mao met three young men in a pagoda tea house. This meeting, described by Siao-Yu, a close friend of Mao's from his school days, was to affect strongly Mao's life. Among the trio was loquacious Tan Wu-pien, whose remarks, that now the country was a republic anybody could be the president, fascinated quiet-mannered Mao. Mao asked if one wanted to be the president, must he study seriously and know much about foreign countries. Tan replied that learning was not essential, citing Chin Shih Huang Ti, Emperor Han Wu and Genghis Khan as great rulers whose learning was mediocre. Then Mao asked how one went about getting political power and defeating one's opponents. Tan said that one must ruthlessly attack one's opponents and organize a loyal political party for himself.

Eventually Mao wrote the classical poem *Chin Yuan Chun*, his most famous, comparing himself with the ancient emperors. Its second half runs:

> *Alas! Little literary splendor*
> *Had Emperors Chin Shih and Han Wu;*
> *Little poetic suaveness*
> *Had Emperors Tang Tsung and Sung Tsu.*
> *Epic hero Genghis Khan knew not*
> *But felling eagles with arrows.*
> *They are all gone!*
> > *For the romantic hero,*
> > *Look at today.*

Mao entered the Changsha Normal School where he graduated in 1918. Turning down an opportunity to study in Europe on a scholarship fund, he decided to learn more about China instead of dabbling in anything foreign. He worked as a stack clerk in the library of the National Peking University, where he became absorbed in Marxist books. During that period he was ignored by the more sophisticated city-bred professors and students.

When the Chinese Communist Party was founded in Shanghai in 1921, Mao was an obscure participant. Under Moscow-returned Chinese Communists run by the Third International, Mao spent seven frustrated and at times humiliating years as a junior leader. Following the Kuomintang-Communist split of 1927, Mao's guerilla group at Chingkiangshan, Kiangsi, was the only cohesive armed Communist group left in China. It grew in strength until driven by Chiang to the famed Long March. After a year of flight under unimaginable hardship, in 1935 Mao and his men finally settled in the loess caves of Yenan. From there he eventually emerged to become the master of the whole China mainland.

Mao's second wife, the one he loved most, was executed by a

Nationalist general in 1930 in a vendetta for the general's father, who had earlier suffered under the Communists. Mao divorced his third wife after the Long March and married a Shanghai movie actress in Yenan in 1939.

By nature Mao is sensitive, imaginative, meek-looking but covertly ambitious. His father evoked the rebel in him. His life is marked by rebellions against authority, first against his father, then against his teachers. As a Communist he more than once defied the Chinese Communist Party and the Third International. Peking's split with Moscow may be partly explained by his personality clash with Khrushchev. Perhaps the boorish, vulgar Khrushchev reminds Mao too much of his father. But Mao is no simple, defiant rebel. He knows how to wait. As an obscure Communist leader he was partly or wholly instrumental in toppling three supreme Party leaders, Chen Tu-hsiu, Li Li-san, Chen Chao-yu, and one powerful Red Army leader, Chang Kuo-tao. He can be extremely patient and shrewdly observant of his opponent's vulnerable spots, until the opportune time for a *coup de grâce*. This is due as much to his personality as to the books he treasures.

Among Mao's literary favorites the foremost are still the two historic novels he so loyally "defended" at school. *Water Margin* is a saga about 108 valiant outlaws during the Sung Dynasty who used guerilla tactics against the bureaucrats. *Tales of Three Kingdoms* is an epic of warring states in the 3rd century, about benevolent rulers, brilliant strategists, brave warriors and scheming plotters. It is a rich storehouse of heroism, betrayals, political and military ruses. Mao hates all Chinese philosophical classics except those of Hanfeitzu and Laotzu. Hanfeitzu's Legalist school condemns counter-revolution, glorifies war and is utterly totalitarian. Mao does not care for Laotzu's Taoist philosophy but is interested in Taoist paradoxes and tactics which he often quotes.

Mao's third favorite is probably *Tzu Chih Tung Chien*, a classical book on monarchist ruling technique and peasant revolts. He has also studied the writing of Suntzu, the 5th century expert in military and political ruses who may be called the father of guerilla warfare.

Among popular fiction, Mao also likes the prurient *Chin Ping Mei* (*Golden Vase Plum*), to which he frequently refers in conversation; *Hsi Yu Chi* (*Westward Travellogue*), about a Tang high monk's travel to India accompanied by a pig-god and a mischievous monkey genii; and *Liao Chai Chih Yi* (*Strange Stories from a Chinese Studio*), about tantalizing female ghosts and fox spirits which bewitch lonely scholars.

Mao's claim that he ran through six systems before hitting Marxism is specious. He barely skimmed over the writings of such thinkers as Adam Smith, Rousseau and Darwin. Due to language limitations he can only read Chinese translations. Chinese translations of Western philosophical works are many but few are really good. Many were based on Japanese translations. It is like reading Confucius' *Analects* in English. One merely gets the hang of it. Anyway Mao seemed to be groping for some coherent, self-contained thought system that would furnish all the answers. Marxism instantly clicked with him. Mao claimed he was converted to Marxism by three books: *Communist Manifesto*, Kautsky's *Class Struggle*, and Kirkup's *History of Socialism*.

The Thought of Mao Tse-tung, or Maoism, has tripped up quite a few Western analysts. Marx believed that capitalism would grow into imperialism, which would touch off a conflict between the capitalists and the proletariat with the latter seizing the power. Lenin altered Marx's theory by using intellectuals as professional revolutionaries to lead the proletariat. He thought such a revolution was possible in industrially backward nations, but distrusted the peasants because of their innate petite bourgeoisie nature. Stalin, not a theorist, used Marxism-Leninism for imperialist expansion. Mao has gone farther than Lenin by using peasants for his "proletarian revolution," because he could find no proletariat in China. Peasants, constituting 80 percent of the Chinese population, have been the occasional but violent force led by shrewd politicians for toppling dynasties in the past. Mao's dream of power and glory was initially, and perhaps now basically, tinged with feudalistic monarchism, as revealed in his poem matching himself against the emperors. In the 1920's rural China was seething with discontent against the combined evils of warlords, money-lenders and landlords. Mao realized that the peasantry was a vast potential.

Mao carried out a revolution flying the Marxist banner with a strategy never dreamed by Marx. For each of his problems, Mao would first reach his conclusion from his own heart, *then* get his major premise from Marxism, and scrounge his minor premise from some colorful Chinese historic episode. The whole thing is called Maoism. He uses a smoke-screen of dialectic clichés to hide his dichotomy. He virtually admitted this when he said: "We study Marxism, not because of its good words, not because there is any magic in it. . . . It is only useful." He relies more on his own idea that: "Every Communist must grasp the truth: that 'Political power grows out of the barrel of a gun.' . . . The whole world can be remolded only with the gun." This remark is typical of the prototype Chinese monarchist idea of *ta tien hsia* (fighting to rule the world).

Historically speaking, Mao is an extreme leftist radical; but politically speaking, he is an extreme rightist reactionary. In Communist terms, he has been both a dogmatist and deviationist, depending on the expediency of the moment. Perhaps Stalin's remark that Mao was not a genuine Communist was no deliberate lie. After Stalin's death Mao's ambition grew greater and his love for adulation bordered on the pathological. In recent years his build-up has been tremendous. The Maoists frequently use "*kung chen*" ("meritorious vassal") to praise model workers. The *People's Daily* once even praised the Party with the traditional monarchist phrase "*huang en hao tang*" ("bounteous imperial graciousness"). In 1960, 13 philosophers and social scientists in Peking issued this praise: "It is extremely difficult to explain in which particular directions Chairman Mao has developed Marxism-Leninism. Because first, Chairman Mao has comprehensively, systematically and creatively developed Marxism-Leninism in the directions of politics, economics, law, history, literature, art, language, philosophy as well as military science and diplomacy. Second, the Thought of Mao Tse-tung is extremely expansive and profound. We are daily and repeatedly studying it. The more we study the more we feel its richness and correctness. . . . The Thought of Mao Tse-tung is the compass for any and all tasks. With it, one knows the correct direction. Without it, all is lost."

Thus Mao has become the fountainhead of all wisdom—and more. He has been praised by Peking's new poets as "sun," "benefactor," "savior," "father," "Northern Star," "searchlight," "compass," "balsam tree," and "god of all gods." He is a poet possessing "literary spendor" and "poetic sauveness." Mao published 18 of his classical poems in a magazine in 1957, in the midst of an anticlassical movement, with a modest note expressing the hope that the poems "would not sow erroneous seeds." But the seeds thrived. Next year he published an anthology, adding three newly composed poems to the 18, entitled: *Chairman Mao's Nineteen Poems*, although it actually had 21. Evidently Mao wanted to imitate the title of a well-known classical anthology, *Nineteen Ancient Poems*. He must have been immensely pleased by this literary popularity, for a movement was started to study Chairman Mao's classical poems. Literary leaders vied with each other to heap praise on the poems. The Party secretary of the writer's association said: "Chairman Mao's contribution to poetry is a historic breakthrough in literature." Several other Communist dignitaries also published their poetic masterpieces. Mao even announced that socialist realism, hitherto the basic literary spirit of all Communist literature, was to be infused with socialist romanticism—whatever that means.

All this is quite un-Communist. Some Chinese critics said that it is a manifestation of Mao's secret yearning to appear sophisticated and erudite—a rebound from his earlier years when he was treated as a country bumpkin by the more blasé intellectuals in the National Peking University. Perhaps this is unfair, but it seems a logical explanation. Judging by purely literary standards, Mao is a jejune poet. He sometimes misuses inversion for the sake of rhyme, commits errors in tonal rhythm, and mixes up literary and legendary allusions. At times he borrows an entire line from an ancient poem with the change of a couple of words; or injects un-classical expressions strongly reminiscent of flower drum songs and popular fiction. There are quite a few classical poets in the Peking hierarchy, among them Marshal Chu Teh, Politburo member Tung Pi-wu, President of Supreme People's Court Hsieh Chueh-tsai, Marshal Chen Yi, Kwangtung Provincial Party Secretary Tao Chu and Vice-Governor of Kwangtung Chu Kuang. There are quite a few classical poets among the Nationalist leaders too.

It would be a gross simplification to label Mao merely a Communist. He is an erstwhile frustrated, ever ambitious and extremely shrewd politician deeply rooted in China's popular traditions. His subconscious hero image is a feudalistic emperor worshiped as much for his grandeur of power as for his poetic romanticism and sagacious philosophy. His father made him a rebel and Confucius-hater. Popular Chinese literature gave him a colorful vocabulary and rich imagery. Classical military strategists inspired him with battle ruses. Marxism gave him a banner and took away his conscientious scruples. Covert ambition plus success made him a tyrant. With all these, he has risen like an exotic comet over the international horizon to conquer 600 million Chinese and baffle the West.

Chiang Kai-shek and Mao Tse-tung have both remained extremely Chinese despite the impact from the West that produced a tumultuous China. Both have tenacious strength. Chiang's strength is Confucian, rock-like and based on inertia. Mao's is Taoist, water-soft and thriving on momentum. Chiang is a disciplinarian; Mao is a doctrinaire. Chiang knows nationalism and on that point he became a national hero. But he did not understand the fundamental forces playing on the confused chessboard of China. Mao made an apparently correct diagnosis of China's ailments. But he prescribed a wrong cure. It is still too early to appraise whose achievement has been greater, or whose failure will be more disastrous. But the time may come soon.

XVI WHICH CHINA?

TODAY'S SO-CALLED TWO CHINAS ARE AN EPHEMERAL DIS-
equilibrium which will vanish tomorrow. This in spite of the
earnest hopes to the contrary of some Westerners to freeze the
status quo. There will be an equilibrium someday—certainly in
our life time, probably during the coming decade, possibly soon.

When China became a republic in 1911 the only cohesive political group was Sun Yat-sen's young revolutionaries, many of them
overseas Chinese, some from the United States who had absorbed
Western democratic ideas. These idealists believed naively, as
many Westerners still do, that once a parliamentary democracy
was plunked down in a country, the system would run by itself.
But it was not to be so in China. Democracy bodily taken from
the West became impotent in this ancient land with its formidable
social institutions and deep political ruts. Against the firmly entrenched warlords Sun's unarmed party could do nothing beyond
shouting its idealism. His initial attempts to win over some generals merely resulted in a rearrangement of armed chaos.

Sun's appeal to the West for help was ignored by the powers
which had neither the desire nor the foresight to see a strong,
unified China. But Soviet Russia extended its hand. It had voluntarily renounced the unequal Czarist treaties and posed as a
champion of anti-colonialism. In spite of Chiang's misgivings, Sun
accepted Russian advisers and aid. Moscow sent Michael Borodin
to China in 1924 to reorganize the Kuomintang, hitherto a fra-
ternal party based on traditional morals and personal relation-

ships, into a mass party run by discipline and organization. Sun wanted only Russian help, not Russian ideology. He declared jointly with the Russians that Communism did not suit China. But Moscow had its private expectations. Sun's gullibility, though more excusable then than that of today's neutralists, opened the breach for Russian infiltration.

In 1921 the Chinese Communist Party was founded. Sun not only coexisted with it but let the Communists join the Kuomintang, believing he could keep them under control. This massive infiltration came to an abrupt end during the Northern Expedition when the Communists over-played their hand and alarmed the Kuomintang. The Communists fled to Yenan. They re-emerged in the late Thirties under Mao, capitalizing on popular anti-Japanese patriotism and forcing the Kuomintang into a United Front. Mao's real aim, as he told his comrades, was: "70 percent self-development, 20 percent compromise, and 10 percent fighting Japan." By V-J Day Mao's guerillas had grown both in strength and size.

At the Yalta Conference on February 11, 1945, Roosevelt and Churchill secretly agreed to Stalin's demands for Outer Mongolia's independence and the restoration of Czarist influence in Manchuria, including such privileges as leaseholds, joint control of railways, naval bases, and the right to move military equipment and troops to these bases. In June, China with United States assurances signed a treaty with Soviet Russia confirming these concessions. At the end of World War II Stalin marched his troops into Manchuria, dismantled all major industrial plants, blocked the entry of Chinese government troops, disarmed the Japanese and handed military equipment for one million troops to the Chinese Communists in flagrant violation of the treaty. Chiang made a strategic mistake by ignoring American advice and sending his crack troops into Manchuria, and then made another by following American advice and letting his troops be bogged down by two ceasefires. For two years the Nationalists and Communists sometimes *ta ta*, sometimes *tan tan*, while the do-gooder Marshall Mission, with a heart of gold and a head of wool, insisted on a coalition government. Eventually the Civil War became earnest. As a result Chiang is now cooped up on Taiwan and Mao is seated in the palaces of the Forbidden City.

The Kuomintang wrote several chapters in modern Chinese history. First it was a conglomeration of impotent idealists pushed around by warlords. Then it became an armed political party which unified the country. In 1928 it began a decade of unprecedented modernization which is now only remembered by historians. With technical aid through the League of Nations, the Nationalists pulled the ramshackle republic together with extensive reconstruction of highways and railroads, river control, forestation, rural rehabilitation, and measures to improve public health, industry and mining. Education was promoted with missionary help. Laws were passed to protect the "freedom of marriage" and equality of sexes, and to combat such traditional evils as concubinage, narcotics, infanticide and the sale of servant maids. Considering the ingrained social hindrances, the inadequate apparatus available, and the simultaneous threats of Communist subversion and Japanese aggression, the progress was little short of spectacular. In fact, it so alarmed the Japanese militarists that they moved to quash it.

During the war with Japan the whole of China rallied around the Nationalists, who successfully bogged down the Imperial Japanese Army and abolished all unequal treaties. Chungking was the symbol of patriotic nationalism. But from the end of World War II to the fall of the mainland, the image of the Nationalists changed drastically. Eight years of war resulted in economic exhaustion and Communist expansion. Chiang's preoccupation with military maneuvers left a clear coast for corrupt Kuomintang bureaucrats, carpet-baggers and unscrupulous merchants in the recovered territory. Inflation, speculation, corruption and subversion brought popular discontent. The extent of the corruption may be gathered from an exclusive story in Shanghai's *The China Press* in the summer of 1948, written by the author, who was then the paper's staff writer, and picked up by news agencies around the world. The story told of whole cases of bank-notes being moved away from Shanghai, presumably to the battle-fields as army pay, but mysteriously returning a few days later, still in whole cases, to be thrown into the already turbulent specu-lative markets. As much of the Nationalists' expenditures then went into soldiers' pay, and much of soldiers' pay went into mar-ket speculation, corrupt generals in one stroke shattered both the nation's economic and military situations. Except for a few pitched battles, much fighting was done with the under-paid, under-fed Nationalist soldiers one jump ahead of the pursuing Reds. Thus ended another epoch in China.

The Chinese Communists came into power at the most favor-able psychological moment. There was so much to be done; and they promised so much. The tragedy is that they overdid every-thing. China needed a strong government, so they supplied a total dictatorship. China needed incorruptible officials, so they pro-duced political robots fed on dogma and oblivious to human values. China was too lethargic, so they gave it never-ending shock treatments. China needed agrarian reform, so they killed off landowners and turned peasants into serfs. China needed mod-ern construction, so they built palatial buildings, unintegrated dams and leaking canals. China needed a good communication system, so they built bridges, highways and railways which are strategically significant but economically wasteful, and which often have to be rebuilt. China needed industrialization, so they lavished precious capital on heavy industry at the expense of consumer goods, food and human lives. China needed prestige, so they squandered food, resources and technicians on faraway emergent countries to pose as a rich uncle, while denying the poor people back home the essentials of life.

Under the mild social reforms of the Nationalists, defective outgrowths of old China were still many. Confucian platitudes were stultifying, so the Communists liquidated Confucius. Nepo-tism plagued China's business and political relations, so they scuttled the family. Old classics were too esoteric and time-consuming, so they substituted the vulgar literature of the illiterate. Education was not sufficiently widespread, so they used the right hand to teach confusing, unworkable alphabets for reading Party propaganda, and the left hand to burn books.

Is there *any* good that the Chinese Communists have done? A single act or a single program when isolated may have some value. A particular highway or dam or factory may work well. The children in a show nursery, the prisoners in a show jail certainly get good treatment. The literacy drive among the peasants at the beginning was something good in itself, until it was given up. But all such individually or temporarily good things when examined in the proper perspective become insignificant as far as the results are concerned.

The explanation lies not necessarily in the Communists' intention, nor appreciably in their competence, but mainly in the style, the pattern, the philosophy behind everything they do. When the dream of a fanatic idealist is so over-powering that he sets out to realize it with ferocious logic and brutal force, when the end justifies any means no matter how inhuman, untold suffering is often brought to millions. Such was the case with Hitler and Stalin; such is the case with Mao Tse-tung. The great tragedies in history were often wrought not by deliberate villains but by fanatical idealists. The irony is that the harm they did could never have amounted to major tragedies without the unwitting help of many gentle dreamers whose sole aim was a "better" world. History does not repeat itself. But fools repeat history.

Perhaps Mao Tse-tung honestly believes in his private escalator to utopia. In his incongruous world of mystical fiction, classical poetry and Marxist platitude, he may even expect all of China's problems to dissolve under Communism. Fourteen years of government by bloody circus, 14 years of fantastic experiments have proved the fallacy of Mao's dream. Today in Communist China there is universal slavery, which is deliberate, and universal poverty, which is unintended. Through oppression Mao planned to enrich the state by impoverishing the people. Through misrule he has impoverished the entire nation as well. Can an Instant Paradise be built for the next generation by killing off this one? Can it ever be built?

A shrewd appraisal of things to come could not be realistic without another look at the Nationalists cooped up in Taiwan. Too many today think Taiwan is a precarious island sinking under the weight of Nationalist troops and American aid. A close look at Taiwan today may shock the many who still retain the 1949 image of the Nationalists.

Taiwan (Terraced Bay), better known to the West as Formosa (Portuguese for "Beautiful Island"), is a balmy emerald isle in the shape of a tea leaf, with majestic mountains and swift rivers. It is about 100 miles from the China mainland and 200 miles north of the Philippines. Its total area, consisting of 78 islands, is 13,886 square miles, with a population of 11.2 million. Taiwan was a province of China until 1895 when it was ceded to Japan. It was returned to China after Japan's surrender in 1945.

During their 50 years of occupation the Japanese ran Taiwan as a typical colony, but ran it efficiently. As a colony Taiwan was deliberately developed as a factory backyard for Japan's industry. They built a fine communications network, developed agriculture and fisheries, but curbed its industry. They pushed literacy and primary school education but restricted college education to a small elite. At the end of World War II, due to Japan's draining of war supplies and Allied bombings, agricultural, industrial and power productions were reduced to 10 to 50 percent of their normal output.

The initial Nationalist administration of Taiwan was of the typical carpet-bagging type, so much so that a serious riot broke out against the mainlanders in 1947 and had to be quelled by bloody suppression. The provincial governor responsible for this debacle was fired, and later executed. Since the seat of the Nationalist government was moved there at the end of 1949, however, a significant change has been taking place.

Economic progress during the past decade in Taiwan is the

most spectacular in Asia. This is the consensus of specialists and economists from dozens of nations who have visited or worked there. A list of the island's accomplishments may sound like a Nationalist brochure, but the figures are not the mathematical rhapsodies of a mad statistician. They are checkable—and checked —by outside observers, including U.N. and U.S. organizations. And they are borne out by the casual observations or deliberate scrutiny of anyone who has visited Taiwan in recent years.

Genuine land reform, which the Nationalists should have carried out long ago on the mainland, now enables 86 percent of the farmers to own land. Landlords sold their land for grains and stocks in industrial plants, thus becoming a new class of people's capitalists. The Taiwan land reform is now the model for all Asia. This measure so encouraged the farmers that the per acre yield of rice has shot up more than 55 percent. By 1962 wheat production had doubled and rice production almost doubled that of 1949. The annual fish catch is more than double the record under the Japanese. Its rate of increase in recent years, according to U.N. reports, has been the highest in the world. Only sugar output has to be kept at the original level because of a lack of market.

In industry, fertilizer output is six times and cotton textiles 36 times the peak under the Japanese. Power capacity is double the Japanese peak, and consumption is more than five times that of a decade ago. Power rates are the third cheapest in the world. By the end of the war, 95 percent of the island's factories were destroyed by American bombers. But today Taiwan has 20,000 factories. During one decade, agricultural production rose by 75 percent and industrial production by 246 percent. In spite of the annual population growth rate of 3.6 percent, the per capita income has increased 400 percent at current prices. The average yearly economic growth has been 7 percent.

In 1960 the government accepted American advice and scrapped some 30 cumbersome laws, replacing them with a liberal economic law to attract international investments—considered the most attractive in the Far East. This was called by an American economist: "The greatest economic development in China since the abacus." Taiwan is one of the few Asian nations permitting complete foreign ownership of new factories. The Nationalists now have an increasing tendency to discard their mildly socialist state enterprise for a liberal competitive economy. Averell Harriman, U.S. Assistant Secretary of State for Far Eastern Affairs who visited Taiwan in 1962, later told the American Academy of Political and Social Science in Philadelphia: "The progress on Taiwan proves what the skills and hard work of the Chinese people can achieve in freedom."

Social reforms are equally remarkable. All civil servants and three-fourths of the industrial workers, fishermen and sugar cane farmers are covered by social insurance. The literacy rate has been raised from 65 percent under the Japanese to 75 percent. Under the Japanese 71 percent of the island's children aged 6-12 were in school. Now it is 98 percent. Then Taiwan had five institutions of higher learning; now, 27. The enrollment in high schools has increased seven times, and in colleges, 14 times. There were 91 medical institutions; now, 650. The number of doctors per 10,000 people is nearly seven times that of Communist China. The quality of educational and medical institutions, unlike those on the mainland, are on the Western level.

Visitors who retained the old image of China were mildly shocked by the prevalent prosperity as compared to other Asian countries. Most villages are electrified. New cottages have been built all over the countryside. Many farmers own bicycles and sewing machines. Soldiers, averaging 25 years old, are well-fed and well-disciplined. There are no beggars and little unemployment. An armed robbery is national news. Those most benefited by this new economy are native-born farmers and workers who constitute the bulk of the population. Next come the ex-landlords or new capitalists. Civil servants, teachers and soldiers are comparatively underpaid. The small elite who formerly had vested interests under the Japanese are the only group pining for the good old days. Higher education is now within the reach of most. Many college students are from peasant and laborer families. Many highway construction workers after saving for two or three years are able to marry a local girl and open a small shop. Taiwan's standard of living is second in Asia only to Japan's, and its overall growth rate has been one of the highest in the world. To make an absolute statement, the standard of living of the people is better now than at anytime in Taiwan's history, and better than any province on the China mainland during the past century. What a difference in world's history this would have made, if these programs could have been carried out when the Nationalists were on the mainland!

But not all is rosy. The economy suffers from deficits and slow but continuing inflation—a common ailment in all developing countries. This is due to the steady rise of the living standard and the cost of supporting 600,000 troops. Without American aid, the Nationalists could not have made such progress and still have kept a modern army in trim. But without the innate Chinese industriousness, the efforts of Western-oriented Chinese intellectuals and the growingly enlightened Nationalist attitude, no amount of outside aid could bring such an achievement.

The economic and social progress achieved in Taiwan are indisputably on record, though not yet widely reported. A nagging question to many is the political nature of the Kuomintang. Putting prejudice and wishful thinking aside, the Nationalist regime is neither a decadent dictatorship nor an American-made democracy. The average man in pre-Communist China was far more conscious of nationalism than democracy. His obsession was against foreign aggression. The privilege to vote and its consequential benefits only lurked at the periphery of his consciousness. The orientation of the Kuomintang and Chiang Kai-shek himself reflect this predominant trend. Actually the Kuomintang consists of various political shades. Mao Tse-tung once cautioned his comrades: "The Kuomintang is a party composed of miscellaneous elements, including the die-hards and the middle-of-theroaders, as well as progressives. The Kuomintang as a whole is not to be equated with the die-hards."

But there have been reactionary features in Kuomintang. This is due to three factors. First, China has had thousands of years of authoritarian—sometimes ineffective, sometimes tyrannical, often benevolent, but consistently authoritarian—government. This historic leftover is hard to erase. Second, the Kuomintang was patterned after the Bolshevik structure. The concept of the party as the sole patron of the government was instilled then, and has not yet been completely discarded. Third, the Nationalist government began as a military government to oust the warlords. In 1928 it settled down for a decade of national reconstruction, but it reverted to a militarist nature in 1937 upon the Japanese invasion. It is still on a wartime footing today because of the unfinished civil war.

Viewed against this historic background, the continuing though not thorough democratization in the Republic of China in Taiwan is significant. The National Assembly, which elects the president and vice-president, and the Legislative Yuan, were popularly elected in 1948, but have continued without new election. This suspension of new elections, made possible by legal gimmicks, is based on the *de jure* argument that the *de facto* loss of the mainland makes it impossible to elect new members and still represent the provinces. Although the Legislative Yuan gets no new blood, it is increasingly responsive to public opinion and often votes against bills and takes the government to task. Except the governor, all high-level provincial and local officials are popularly elected. The election turnout has usually been around 80 percent, another phenomenon never seen in the old days.

The Nationalists, formerly uninterested or even hostile to foreign investments, tourism, folk arts and traditional festivals, are changing this attitude. There are still curbs on the freedom of press, still covert hindrances to opposition parties, and still attempts by party hacks to cling to some of the old ways. But the growing influence of Western-oriented liberal intellectuals both inside and outside the government has been unmistakable. There is much bureaucracy, and some corruption. But the corruption in the whole of Taiwan is probably less than that in New York City.

The dominant figure of the Republic of China all these years has been the controversial Chiang Kai-shek, whose final evaluation rests with future historians, as the Chinese saying goes: "After the coffin is covered comes the final appraisal." What will happen to Taiwan when Chiang is out of the picture? The problem of succession appears quite certain. Chen Cheng, vice president and premier, will succeed Chiang as the president, with no appreciable change in the situation. However, what will happen in Taiwan depends far more on what will happen on the China mainland than on mere personalities.

These are the so-called Two Chinas. The Republic of China (Nationalist) is governed by a regime once incompetent and corrupt, now repentant and reforming. There, people have no luxuries but comfort, no complete democracy but basic freedoms. No historian can dispute the fact that the regime in Taiwan today is better than that of the Communists, the pre-1949 Nationalists, the warlords and the Manchus. Comparatively the people in Taiwan enjoy more democracy and prosperity than at anytime in China's history since the fall of the Ming Dynasty in the 16th century. Nationalist China with all its deplorable defects is at least free.

Culturally it is even more important to the Chinese. Communist China is no longer Chinese, just as Hong Kong, Singapore and San Francisco's Chinatown are not really Chinese. But Taiwan is intensely Chinese. It is not only a depository for the fabulous works of art and literature moved from the mainland, but retains much of the humanistic tradition in Chinese culture. The Chinese family remains the most respected sanctuary there. The political, economic and cultural pattern in Taiwan is jestingly called *San Chia* (three schools of thought): *Kung Chia, Lao Chia* and *Kwei Chia* (Confucianism, Taoism and Devil-ism). It is an imperfect but workable merger of Confucius, Laotzu and the Foreign Devil.

On the other hand, Communist China has been trying to obliterate all that is fine in the Chinese and Western heritages. It advertises a paradise but doles out slavery. There, hunger is a way of life; sleep is luxury; silence is crime; and love is depravity.

The Chinese in and out of China have to choose between the two existing regimes because of their compulsive need for cultural and ethnic identification. They have no luxury of choice, so the choice seems clear. During more than three decades of Nationalist rule on the mainland, there were no refugees besides several dozens of political exiles. But during the 13 years under the Communists, 3.5 million refugees left their ancestral land. This alone is one of the most dramatic plebiscites ever conducted.

In the British colony of Hong Kong, there is another dramatic demonstration of the people's feelings. Each year on October 1 (the Communist National Day), the five-star Communist flag is flown; on October 10 (the Nationalist National Day), the blue-sky-white-sun-red-earth Nationalist flag is flown. During the first couple of years the number of Communist and Nationalist flags was about equal. Then the discrepancy grew. By October 1961, street-by-street counting by the numerous units of a publicly organized flag-counting committee showed that the number of Communist flags had dwindled to 731, while Nationalist flags soared to 1,006,228. In October 1962, the number of Communist flags dropped to 478, while the Nationalist flags rose to 1,088,682. Almost all the Communist flags were flown by Communist organs, pro-Communist organizations and merchant houses trading with Communist China. The Nationalist flags were flown from private homes, hillside shanties, junks, sampans, cabs and the pushcarts of street pedlars—and the poorer the neighborhood the more numerous the flags.

This rare public political gesture of the inscrutable Chinese is due not so much to a love for the Nationalists as to a hatred for the Communists. It is analogous to the protest of the American who votes for one political candidate because he dislikes the other. The Hong Kong gesture, of course, has far more emotional depth because of the traumatic experience on the Chinese mainland. On Double Tenth 1956, the British officials there were shocked to discover this when a petty civil servant tore down two Nationalist flags and touched off Hong Kong's greatest peacetime disturbance. Some 50,000 enraged Chinese rioted for three days.

Physically, Taiwan is a puny chip off the block that is the China mainland. Its area is less than 0.4 percent and its population less than 2 percent of its massive Red counterpart. A superficial conclusion would be that whatever happens on Taiwan cannot make the slightest dent on Communist China. But psychologically, Taiwan is a sharp thorn in Peking's flesh. It offers an alternative to the millions of Chinese, including those overseas, who must identify themselves with a government. It shows that over-populated, economically backward China *can* feed the peasants well and industrialize with rational reforms based on the incentive system, without breaking hearts and necks. Taiwan is a pilot plant for the ultimate solution of China's vexing economic problems, and for other nations of Southeast Asia sitting on the fence silently but taking in every detail of the performance by the two Chinas.

Added to the psychological threat is a more solid threat to Peking. The youthful, well-disciplined, American-equipped Nationalist armed forces, completely different from the bedraggled Nationalist troops of the mainland days, are bigger than the armed forces of the United Kingdom or the two Germanies combined. It is the second biggest non-Communist striking force in the Far East, with the finest air force. Those who still retain the images of the Nationalist and Communist forces around 1949, and those who compare the two by weighing the hardware and human bodies, laugh at the Nationalist slogan of return to the mainland as a pitiful daydream. If the slow-poke analysts and pan-weaponists were correct, then Mao Tse-tung with his 5,000 rifles in Yenan could never have conquered China. If the population were solidly behind the Communist army, no outside force could ever dislodge it. But as things are, the mood of the people in China is such that they would welcome any outside "invasion," even one led by the Dowager Empress. This mood has been voiced by numerous refugees and demonstrated by several incidents virtually ignored by the Western press. Within four months after the Quemoy shelling, at least 11 peasant uprisings took place in the Amoy-Swatow area near Quemoy, touched off by rumors that the Nationalists were landing in the vicinity. These suicidal revolts by peasants armed with scythes, hoes and a few seized rifles do not prove the feasibility of such actions, but they reveal the immense probabilities in case an outside force does land in the coastal areas. In such an event, the response would come with the "force of splitting bamboo."

So while the rest of the world is using military pressure and political maneuvering to quick-freeze the two Chinas, both Peking and Taipei know how abruptly the present precarious disequilibrium may end. Taipei's open admission to such possibilities has been laughed at. Peking's secret admission has manifested itself in repeated attempts at the so-called "peaceful liberation of Taiwan." For Taiwan has become an intolerable threat to Communist China—not to its people but to its regime.

At first Mao Tse-tung believed and at least hoped that the U.S. would not interfere if he attacked the island. He repeatedly called for the "forcible liberation of Taiwan" and called Chiang Kai-shek a "traitor" and "war criminal." By 1955, when he realized he could not attack Taiwan without fighting the Americans, Mao changed his tune. "Traitor" and "bandit Chiang" became "the leader of Taiwan" and "Mr. Chiang." Through public flirting and private attempts to talk peace, Peking repeatedly put out feelers to Taipei, offering Chiang a cabinet post, the governorship of "autonomous" Taiwan, and suggesting a Nationalist-Communist "cooperation for the third time." Now that revolutions are fermenting on the mainland, Taiwan is a growing threat even without the presence of the U.S. Seventh Fleet.

For some inexplicable reason, the Nationalists have been merely issuing categorical denials of peace talks, without publicizing Communist peace overtures. Hitherto unpublished details of an episode may throw light on this situation.

In the summer of 1955, when the author was a Hong Kong correspondent for *Time* magazine, an acquaintance, Professor Tsao Chu-jen, confinded to him that he was acting as a bridge for Nationalist-Communist peace talks. Tsao had been a college professor in Chinese literature, a newspaper columnist, an unofficial aide and adviser to Chiang Kai-shek's son, Chiang Ching-kuo, when he was carrying out a reform in Kiangsi province, the author of many books including an unofficial biography of Chiang Ching-kuo, and one of the best contemporary Chinese writers of historical essays. Tsao had personally known many high Nationalist politicians but during the early Fifties his writing had veered toward the left. As a newspaperman's biggest problem in Hong Kong is rejecting misinformation and rumors, Tsao's remark at that time was not taken seriously. Several months later, however, a tipster supplied the author with details of a "definite" peace talk, naming Tsao as one of the intermediaries. Although the details sounded too fantastic, and many of them were later found to be baseless, the link to Tsao was significant.

The author approached Tsao, and at a series of furtive meetings Tsao guardedly revealed some details. Among the exhibits shown were his special travel permit from Peking and a letter in the well-known calligraphy of Shao Li-tse. Shao, a septuagenarian ex-Nationalist statesman and former Nationalist ambassador to Moscow, had become a captive member of the Communist Congress in Peking. Shao's letter discussed the peace plan in vague terms and added: "The XY route is definitely impassable." "XY route" was the code for "Two Chinas." Shao's letter was evidently inspired by someone high in Peking as he would never dare dabble in such an explosive issue on his own. In Tsao's conversation the name of Chiang Ching-kuo came up time and again.

Although fantastic peace rumors were circulating in London, Tokyo, Macao and Hong Kong at that time, what the author learned appeared something authentically big. The matter was discussed with the then Hong Kong *Time* bureau chief John Osborne, who immediately flew to Taipei to interview Chiang Ching-kuo. Young Chiang at first was reticent. After hearing Tsao's name, he produced four letters from his confidential files complete with postmarked envelopes. Three were addressed to Chiang, one to his confidential secretary, all signed by Tsao. The letters, dated from August 2 to December 30, 1955, repeatedly asked young Chiang to send a confidential representative to Hong Kong to talk with Tsao "for the sake of the nation and the race." They remarked that Tsao's previous letters had not been answered, that "opportunity is fleeting," and that he wanted to "submit important words personally at this critical time."

Young Chiang issued a statement: "The rumors published this week are malicious fabrications. . . . Communists are liars and devils. You cannot talk with the devil. It is my ardent belief that to solve the Communist problem, the only way is to eliminate Communism."

The Communists, using a traditional Chinese political approach, were trying to establish contact with Chiang Kai-shek through his son, who is Moscow-trained and has a Russian wife but is now an anti-Communist. Tsao was used as a bridge because of his personal relations with young Chiang and Shao. This incident, when viewed with the come-hither remarks made publicly to the Nationalists by Chou En-lai and other Peking spokesmen, falls into correct perspective. It also proves that Peking has definitely put out peace feelers to Taipei and that Taipei has ignored them.

A peace talk, if realized, would be the only feasible way for Peking to get Taiwan. Even if not realized, repeated rumors of such a talk could dishearten the Chinese populace and perhaps lure Washington to forsake Taiwan and play ball with Peking. This explains why these peace rumors were heard as early as the summer of 1955 and as late as the summer of 1962. Chiang Kai-shek, having repeatedly been a victim of *ta ta, tan tan; tan tan, ta ta,* is sadder and wiser. He just sits on the Grass Mountain in Taipei like a piece of rock, sticking to his tactic of "controlling ten thousand changes with unchangeableness."

While the feeling of the Chinese toward the Communists has completely crystallized, their attitude toward the Nationalists is more complicated. Generally speaking, the Chinese intellectuals who are influenced by Western democracy are more critical of the Nationalists than other groups. They would like a much more democratic regime, but they are reluctant to discard the Nationalists entirely and get something far worse—the Communists. This attitude is shared by practically all Chinese intellectual and community leaders, including the late Dr. Hu Shih, China's most famous liberal and frequent critic of the Nationalists. The more pragmatic Chinese peasants, who feel with their stomach and possess a more limited frame of reference, would choose the Nationalists outright, because their life under the Nationalists, bad as it was, was far better than under the Communists. Paradoxically this is true even for Chinese industrial workers—the proletariat. Today Hong Kong's factories have tens of thousands of Chinese workers who fled Peking's workers' paradise to a precarious foreign colony where they have found more food and freedom. They are among the most zealous hoisters of the Nationalist flag as a protest vote against the Peking regime.

Geographically speaking, the Chinese on the mainland, in spite of their memories of the past Nationalist performance, actually hope for a return of the Nationalists, for no other reason than that this is the only alternative in sight for continued Communist rule. This attitude strongly influences the population in Hong Kong. As the distance increases, the Chinese in other lands have less clearly defined preferences. Some Chinese who arrived in the United States before the Communists came into power prefer neither, because they are not forced by circumstances to make a choice.

This unique collective attitude of the Chinese leads to a strange phenomenon. There are many independent Chinese newspapers and magazines outside mainland China and Taiwan, reflecting the opinion of the majority of Chinese who love neither the Communists nor the Kuomintang. These publications are anti-Nationalist as well as anti-Communist. Criticisms against the Nationalists include their past mistakes and the insufficient freedom of speech in Taiwan now as compared to the West. Yet with few exceptions the most frequent and severe criticism against the Nationalists all these years has been for their failure to attack Communist China. Chiang and his Kuomintang have been lambasted for being satisfied with the local progress of their "little dynasty," for tamely submitting to American leashing of their forces, and for not actively rescuing the mainland people from the Communists. The term *chiang kung shu tsui* (performing meritorious service to expiate past sins) is repeatedly used by these publications to urge the Nationalists to ignore American restraint, carry out their back-to-the-mainland pledge, and by doing so atone for their past sins. Whatever the practicality of such an attitude, its emotional overtones are unmistakable.

The Nationalists appear eager to expiate their past sins by performing this meritorious service. Around New Year 1963, Peking and Taipei both announced that the Nationalists were landing and airdropping armed agents to prepare guerilla corridors in Communist China. Kwangtung peasants were pressed into anti-commando units and rewards were posted for exposing "enemy agents." All the nine major military regions held conferences to discuss measures against possible large-scale Nationalist landings.

The Chinese Communists came to power mainly because of the Chinese people's disillusionment with the Nationalists. It would be a great historical irony if the Nationalists someday should return to power on the mainland, because of the people's subsequent and greater disillusionment with the Communists.

PART FIVE

INTO DEEPER WATERS

XVII RUSE OF THE VACANT CITY

IN THE 3RD CENTURY, DURING THE VALOROUS ERA OF THE Three Kingdoms, lived Chuko Liang whose military genius is legendary. Chuko, commanding general of the army of the Kingdom of Shu, was trapped with only 2,500 of his troops at his advance base, Hsicheng, by an approaching enemy force of 150,000 under General Ssuma Yi of the Kingdom of Wei. Annihilation or surrender seemed the only alternatives. In a flash of desperate brilliance, Chuko threw open the city gates, furled all military banners and put some soldiers in civilian clothes to sweeping the streets near the gates.

Chuko himself, dressed in his favorite crane-feather cape and silk scarf, sat atop the city wall, flanked by two page boys holding a sword and a ceremonial duster. When Ssuma rode near the city wall he saw the unruffled Chuko smiling and plucking away at a lute. Chuko might be shaking in his clogs, but his stance was so bold that Ssuma, who had always respected Chuko's stratagems, suspected an ambush and ordered an immediate retreat. This is just what Chuko anticipated. He had hidden small bands of "pursuers" in the woods outside the city, who created a pandemonium by shouting, beating drums and gongs, and galloping to and fro on horseback. Ssuma's troops, fleeing from an imaginary trap, stampeded themselves into a disastrous defeat.

This *Kung Cheng Chi* (Ruse of the Vacant City) is familiar to every Chinese, especially to Mao Tse-tung, who once wrote his own turgid version: "The stage of action of the military expert is provided by objective material conditions; but with the stage set, he can direct the performance of many lively dramas, full of sound and color, power and grandeur."

All good military strategists in Chinese history loved *ruses de guerre*. They considered war in terms of a chess game. They much preferred to win not by head-on assaults, but by using feints, traps, bluffs, counterbluffs and similar tricks. Victory through brains rather than brawn was necessary to the weak and satisfying to the strong. The historic novel *Tales of Three Kingdoms*, Mao's favorite handbook of strategy, has hundreds of such devastating tricks. One is the Ruse of Bitter Flesh: a loyal official would be severely tortured, sometimes crippled, by his own people, then "defect" to the enemy camp where he would spill out false "inside information" or act as a spy. Another more familiar to the West is the Ruse of the Beautiful Woman: a tantalizing temptress would appear before the enemy leader to beguile and corrupt him.

For centuries such tricks have also been used by the Chinese in non-military areas such as politics, diplomacy, commerce and daily human relations. A few examples:

"Slapping one's face to pose as a fat man"—The face is slapped, either helplessly by others or deliberately by oneself, so that the swollen cheeks give the illusion of a fat, well-fed man.

"Much thunder, little rain"—Roar with loud threats and strike poses of imminent assault. If the opponent backs down, the bluffing works. If not, taper off with a drizzle.

"Using his trick as my trick"—Pretend to walk into the opponent's trap, after devising a trick within a trick to trick the opponent.

"Golden cicada shedding its skin"—When escape seems impossible, pretend that one is ready to surrender, then at the last moment slip out as a cicada sheds its dead skin, leaving the enemy holding the skin or the empty coat, as the case may be.

"Sound in the east, strike in the west"—If the move is in the west, make noise in the east.

"Tapping the side, slapping the flank"—If the opponent appears adamant, avoid direct confrontation but use subtle suggestions and psychological nudges.

"Hanging up the sheep head; selling dog meat"—This is the universal art of false labeling.

"Selling the aborigine's head"—Offering something worthless as a treasure to a gullible person.

The Chinese frown on a confrontation of naked force as uncivilized, and prefer what they call "intelligence jousts." Whether this means that the Chinese are devious or the foreign devils are simple-minded depends on one's point of view.

One of the favorite intellectual games in China has been "fooling the foreigners," mostly for fun, sometimes for profit. The number of faked Ming vases proudly exhibited in homes the world over must be making the bodies somersault in all the Ming tombs. "Fooling the foreigners," an innocuous Chinese recreation, has become a national enterprise under the Chinese Communists.

The most dramatic and brazen hoax perpetrated by Peking is the "conquest" of Mount Everest in May 1960. According to Peking's accounts, three of an assault team of four men who had little experience in mountaineering, after climbing continuously for seven days with a support group, scaled the last 220 feet to the summit from the hitherto insurmountable north side without oxygen masks—a physiological miracle. They forgot to bring a flashlight, or any liquid essential for high-altitude climbing, but did bring a flag and an 8-inch plaster bust of Mao Tse-tung to plant on the summit. Oddly enough, they brought a camera but took no picture on the summit. The expedition was said to have been prepared for five years, but at the last minute the team was still waiting for hastily made crampons. India and Nepal reported a blinding storm around Everest on May 25, the day they reached the summit, but the Chinese did not mention any bad weather. During the climb each time the flesh weakened, the spirit was strengthened by a discussion of the glorious Party. Judging from all these inconsistencies and the experience of the

Hillary team, Peking's conquest of Everest was a Great Leap Upward.

It is interesting to note that shortly before the alleged feat, Peking was involved in a territorial dispute with Nepal about Everest. The Nepalese premier said that one reason why Everest must belong to Nepal was that it had never been climbed from the northern side. A month later Peking announced to the world that this had been done.

On August 23, 1958 Peking started "much thunder" over the off-shore islands of Quemoy and Matsu and shot out 575,000 artillery shells within three months. Encouraged by panicky American and British public opinion, and anticipating a cringing United States and a crumbling Nationalist defense, Peking announced an impending landing and demanded a surrender from the Nationalist garrisons. But events turned out differently. The American government did not let go. The Nationalists not only clung solidly to those two little rocks, but their Sabrejets, manned by superior pilots, dealt a humiliating defeat to Peking's much-vaunted air force.

As a result, on October 6 Mao issued a "little rain" statement. In the name of the then Defense Minister Peng Teh-huai, he addressed "friends in Taiwan" and announced a week's ceasefire for "humanitarian considerations." It was followed by another ceasefire, which was later changed to alternate-day shelling. Westerners were puzzled, but to the Chinese it was a familiar ruse. Peking issued a face-saving statement to its comrades, unmistakably in Mao's earthy style: "Some Communists may not yet understand this for the time being. How come such an idea? We don't understand! We don't understand! Comrades, you will understand after a while." Being Chinese, the comrades certainly understood.

Peking relies on ruses for all situations. In late 1959, when it was wooing Nasser and trying to establish a radio station for its Hsinhua News Agency in Cairo, it sent four correspondents, bearing a gift to the Egyptian telecommunications bureau. It was a telegraph machine produced by the engineers of New China. Actually it was assembled from old American spare parts plus some Chinese-made parts and, by the time it was shipped to Cairo, it was rusty. Discovering this, the wily Chinese Communists in Cairo told the Egyptians that they wanted to postpone the presentation of the gift, because they wanted them to meet the two engineers who designed the machine. Meanwhile, two engineers were flown from Peking with the replacement parts. This episode was revealed by one of the correspondents who later defected in Cairo.

During the Hundred Flowers, Fan Yueh-hsin, Johns Hopkins M.D., revealed that provincial reports on epidemic outbreaks were kept secret in the Ministry of Public Health, "because if the number of cases since the Liberation showed an increase, this would affect the prestige of the People's Government." He himself in 1951 reported to the Ministry a suspected cholera case in Canton. The Ministry did nothing except pigeon-hole it for four years. Later the Ministry mentioned it in a report to the Sino-Russian Conference on Cholera, in order to show how thoroughly cholera-prevention work was done. At that conference, although a Chinese infectious disease specialist prepared a report on cholera treatment in China and the Russian doctors specifically requested information on the subject, the Ministry forbade the reading of the report, forbade the discussion of cholera by Chinese doctors, and forbade the presentation of any material about the pre-Communist years, saying: "Since 1949 there has been no cholera in China."

When Chou En-lai visited Burma in early 1961 he brought nearly eight million feet of cotton cloth as a lavish gift from bountiful China. At the same time, residents in major Chinese cities, who were already getting only a few feet of rationed cloth per year, were ordered to use "new techniques in tailoring" to save more cloth. This was a typical case of slapping one's face to pose as a fat man. So was the case of the delayed trains. In 1960 train schedules were bogged down by economic dislocation. But the *Peking Evening News* reported that thousands of delighted passengers wrote letters to the press, praising the frequent unscheduled stops of express trains, because this gave them the chance for calisthenics. The same paper in 1958 carried a detailed story about low wages, long hours and numerous industrial accidents suffered by Chinese workers in Hong Kong's Taiping Island Dockyards, owned by American capitalists. The story was most realistic, except that Hong Kong had no such dockyard.

Ruses are practiced for different purposes. One is to cover up mistakes. Another is to disguise a shortcoming into an item of prestige. And another is to stage a dramatic production solely for its effects on a selected audience. The most elaborate and ingenious ruse to fool the foreigners is Peking's adroit political tourism. During the mid-1950's some 5,000 tourists from 70 countries visited Communist China every year on conducted, all-expense-paid tours at an estimated cost of 1,500 United States dollars per person. Such visitors from Communist, non-Communist and neutralist nations include politicians, newspapermen, scientists, artists, writers, churchmen, educators, students and union men. Their itineraries are handled by the China International Tourist Service of the Ministry of Foreign Affairs, with the close collaboration of the Ministry of Culture and the all-important mass organization.

The well-trodden tourist path covers a number of typical show places, including a dozen coastal cities, industrial centers and a couple of hinterland cities. In Peking, the visitors can see the imperial palaces, the new government buildings, the Tien An Men Square, a model jail for political prisoners, a model village, the Fengtai Commune, a college near Western Hills, and the Great Wall to the north. In Manchuria they may see industrial plants, a model collective farm near Mukden, the automobile factory in Changchun, the Fushun coal mines, the Anshan blast furnaces, rolling mills and seamless tube steel plant, and Harbin's precision instrument and cutting tool plant. Further south they may view the Yangtze River Bridge at Wuhan, the great port cities of

Tientsin, Shanghai and Canton, and the romantic West Lake with its magnificent, renovated Lingyin Monastery. The more adventurous may be taken to see Mao's hometown in Hunan, the Nationalist wartime capital of Chungking, and the oil fields in Yumen.

All visitors are supplied with interpreter-guides whose knowledge of foreign languages is far surpassed by their political reliability. As soon as the visitors cross the borders, mostly from Hong Kong, they are showered with personal attention, hospitality and a crammed schedule for sightseeing, statistical briefings, interviews, conferences, dinner parties, a Chinese opera, and perhaps a shopping spree at a tourist PX where lacquer-ware, carved ivories, Tientsin rugs and silk embroideries are sold at ridiculously low prices.

These sights alone, however impressive, can only enrapture the most gullible. For an elaborate theatrical production, the *dramatis personae*, hundreds and thousands of them are sprinkled strategically among the stage props. Inmates in showpiece factories, communes, collective farms, and prisoners are a privileged lot so long as they play their parts. While most of them are forbidden to talk with visitors unless given permission, each establishment has a number of well-rehearsed persons designated to converse with the visitors. This is confirmed by the reports of many visitors who turned out to be talking to the same individuals in the same establishments and getting the same stories. In addition to these leading players, there is a reserve group in each place who may be chosen "at random" by the tourists if the need arises. All these actors—there is no truer term to describe them—can recite a staggering number of statistics and each has a tailored personal case history usually consisting of two parts: a sob story of hard times under the bad Nationalists, and the tender loving care of the Communists.

In industrial and commercial centers like Shanghai, a number of former prominent capitalists are domesticated in luxurious mansions with well-trimmed gardens, cluttered with refrigerators, pianos, Chinese curios and staffed with coteries of baby amahs, cooks and maid servants. These ex-capitalists tell the visitors of their joy at being robbed of their factories, and of their improved living conditions under a system that is supposedly antagonistic to capitalism. Two French industrialists, after listening to such a skit, gushed that if the French Communists should adopt a similar policy, they would have nothing against French Communism. French *savoir faire*, it seems, is no match for political *chinoiseries*.

To guard against the more astute visitors who may ask for undesignated spots, Peking has a defense in depth consisting of several "undesignated" cities and villages. In addition, in every tourist town there are "undesignated" sites not voluntarily offered to sightseers unless they ask. But sometimes slips are made. It was reported that once a European visitor asked to see a village "never been seen by outsiders." The Communists graciously obliged. There he was greeted by a village elder who innocently told him that he was the 100th illustrious foreign guest to honor that village. Another visitor discovered that in Mao's hometown, there were a number of Mao's "uncles" working in shifts. College professors are forbidden to communicate directly with people abroad. Professors of the Tsinghua University may talk to visitors, but not in English even though they speak it fluently.

Countless ruses are played on unsuspecting political tourists. During the early co-existence years, although most were converted into barracks, schools and granaries, a few mosques were renovated lavishly—in places visited by Moslem delegations from abroad. Shanghai's 1,000-odd Buddhist temples were reduced to less than 10, with the monks and nuns forced to marry or become factory workers. The famous Bubbling Well Temple was used as government premises. In the summer of 1952, when an important Buddhist delegation was to visit Shanghai, the *kanpu* there were suddenly moved out, and the temple was given a complete renovation. As soon as the delegation left, the bureaucrats returned. The same act was repeated in 1954 when the Dalai Lama visited Shanghai.

President Sukarno of Indonesia, one of Peking's co-existence targets, visited China in 1956. In Shanghai half a million students, workers and activists were organized and stationed all over the city as random crowds. They were told not to wear uniforms and badges but to appear in their best civilian clothes. They spent hours rehearsing spontaneous shouts of *"Bung Karno"* to please the playboy neutralist Peking was trying to win over.

All of Shanghai was shifted into high gear in 1954 for the visit of Clement Attlee. House fronts along Nanking Road, Bubbling Well Road and The Bund that would be seen by Attlee were repainted. Residents were told by the household police to dig out their most luxurious old clothes to wear for the duration. Attlee was housed in the 22-story Park Hotel instead of the usual place of hospitality, the Cathay Hotel. The latter, British property seized by the Communists, was scrupulously avoided so as not to step upon the imperialist toes of Her Majesty's Labor representative.

A few trained observers, while unable to penetrate beyond the elaborate stage props around them, were astute enough to see them for what they were. Swiss correspondent Peter Schmid said: "The visitor's only link with the government is the State Travel Bureau, which . . . functions with smooth efficiency as long as the visitor sticks to the beaten track; it breaks down completely as soon as he takes a single step off the tourist trail." French correspondent Robert Guillain of *Le Monde* said: "A more subtle 'curtain' never ceased to be drawn, cleverly and tenaciously, between me and China. Mark this well. There are 600 million Chinese, but in two months I was never permitted to speak with a single one in private. . . . I was never able to enter a house picked by myself at random. I never stopped at a factory, a farm, or any institution whatever without the visit having been arranged in advance. . . . Nothing is ever improvised. I wish to see a Chinese family? It is chosen for me, the hour, the locale, the car to go there. I would like to meet a Shanghai capitalist. . . .

He is chosen with care and, as I learn later, the same one whom twenty visitors before me have gone to see. . . . 'Come and see!' This invitation is one of China's most formidable weapons, a weapon which she uses with consummate skill."

James Cameron of the London *News Chronicle* also said: "And then one saw the simple peasant, chosen at random, and he was so palpably well rehearsed, one's questions faded away; one asked for a village and one found oneself in a place so immaculate that its roads were trampled smooth by the feet of endless delegations that had gone before." A European visitor was scheduled to see the Great Wall by car from Peking. When he asked to go by train the guide blandly replied that there was no railroad going there. When shown the railroad on a map, he said there was only a late train daily. When shown the schedule of daily round trips, he said the travel bureau never knew about this service.

Let the visitor abuse the hospitality by asking to see, not merely an undesignated village or prison but, say, the commune in Chungshan next to Macao, the Chingho Collective Farm near Peking, the city jail of Hangchow, a specific dam on the upper reaches of the Yellow River, the home of a worker he himself picks out in a match factory in Shanghai's Zikawei, or a rural area in Shantung or Honan hit by natural calamities; let him name names for a private interview with philosopher Feng Yu-lan, or Professor Liang Shu-ming, or purged Communist author Ting Ling, and the precision-run public relations of Peking instantly becomes inscrutable. The visitor might not be thrown out on his ear, for that would violate Chinese hospitality, but he would never get to see what he wanted and never get a Peking visa again.

Lord Lindsay of Birker, a Briton who had lived in China for seven years and worked with the Chinese Communists for four years during the war, accompanied Clement Attlee as his interpreter when the latter visited China. He should know China because he not only speaks Chinese but has a Chinese wife. Although once an enthusiastic admirer of the Chinese Communists, after his 1954 visit he implied that the regime was "an oppressive and unpopular government." In 1958 he and his family scheduled a trip to both Nationalist and Communist China, and received permission from Peking. Impressed by the Nationalists' economic progress, he said in Taiwan that here was "evidence to dispel the illusion of those who advocated Communism as the answer for underdeveloped areas." When he reached the Communist China border, he was refused entry without any explanation. The reason, in Lord Lindsay's own words: "The Communist action is an evidence to show how much they fear the people who know them well."

To the people who do not know them well, Mao Tse-tung has successfully elaborated the Ruse of the Vacant City into the Myth of Fabulous China. The theme is consistent but the variations are infinite. Mao may not have read Shakespeare but he knows that all the world's a stage, and his theatrical productions have received warm applause from some sophisticated Western observers.

XVIII

DRAGONOLOGY—THE GAME OF CHINA-WATCHERS

ONCE UPON A TIME TWO CHINESE VISITED THE UNITED States. Upon their return each wrote a report. One said:

> The American way of life is the most advanced, technologically, economically, politically and socially. The Americans have built their nation into a land of modern buildings, delightful homes and beautiful parks, linked with efficient, high-speed highways, railroads and air networks. Their standard of living is unsurpassed by any other nation in history. Everybody is well-dressed; everybody is well-fed; everybody takes vacations. Most homes have radios, television, washing machines, refrigerators, cars and other labor-saving gadgets. Stores are stacked with goods and restaurants are full of people. A month's relief money paid by the government to an unemployed worker far exceeds a year's per capita income in an economically underdeveloped country.
>
> The Americans are so democratic that anyone can criticize the president. Employers and employees call each other by their first names. People of all races and creeds are equal under the law. I saw no evidence of racial discrimination during my visit. There are 35 Negro millionaires in the country.
>
> The Americans give fabulous foreign aid to others without any strings attached. The percentage of the population with religious affiliations has risen from 10 in colonial days to 60 today. The doors of many homes are not locked. People leave money when they buy newspapers from unattended newstands. When a child is missing, thousands volunteer and sometimes risk their lives to search for him. Families spend their weekends together and magazine articles are full of togetherness and marital love. The country is full of museums, theatres, concert halls and research centers. A staggering number of people read newspapers, books, attend discussions, debates and adult education classes. . . .

The other said:

The American way of life is mostly propaganda. The United States is drowned in tidal waves of crime that grow year after year. The FBI reported that in 1960 an American woman was attacked every 34 minutes, and in 1961, 2 million serious crimes were committed. In the first half of 1962 in New York city alone, 25 crimes were committed every hour round the clock, and 20,355 criminals below the age of 20 were arrested. FBI Director J. Edgar Hoover said: "The massive avalanche of crime sweeping our nation is a shocking disgrace and a broad indictment of the American people."

American criminals have not only invaded night clubs, casinos, labor unions, college football, and boxing, but are getting into the stock market. They employ specialists, consultants, lawyers, prostitutes, triggermen who murder on contract, and pay off policemen, judges and Congressmen. Corruption is no longer what has been spitefully labeled an Oriental way of life. In Chicago and Denver, cops played robbers. Police brutality is described by the Civil Rights Commission as a "serious problem throughout the United States." A Congressman revealed that in West Virginia, vote-buying had been going on "for the last century." Voters sold their votes in exchange for cash and bourbon whiskey.

Corruption is not limited to the government. Rigged television shows involve many respected people. In New York city alone, thousands of academic theses are bought by college candidates from ghost-writing firms. Half of the students in a high school were estimated to cheat at examinations. Big corporations indulge in price-fixing, expense-account-padding and the use of prostitutes to entertain their clients. The well-known columnist Walter Lippman said: "America is beginning to accept a new code of ethics that allows for chiseling and lying."

Racial discrimination is prevalent. In the South, Negroes are terrorized by the Ku Klux Klan. In the North Negroes cannot find good jobs or rent good homes. Migrant Mexican farm laborers work like serfs. Puerto Ricans fighting for their independence once tried to assasinate the U.S. President, and another time shot five Congressmen while shouting: "Freedom for Puerto Rico!"

Youths and criminals are pampered, so that the people grow up defying parents, defying teachers, defying law officers. Old people, forsaken by their children and society, sit forlornly on park benches, or are put away in homes. Each year 1.2 million abortions take place and one out of every four marriages ends in divorce.

Americans know no nationalism. Each year they spend $4 billion more on fun than on national defense. Army reservists sent to protect Berlin from those who vowed to bury them, returned complaining that the crisis was manufactured by their own president. While the Russians were sending up twin manned satellites, American space program was held up by striking workers dedicated to more pay . . .

These are two hypothetical reports written by two hypothetical Chinese whose first-hand knowledge seems to give them an aura of authority. As they sound like U.S.I.A. and Tass releases, it is easier to impugn motives than to realize that the pair could be as honest as they are naive and ignorant. A lack of background knowledge, plus a misdirected eagerness for truth, can create distorted images from a pile of indisputable facts. This has been done by many non-Americans to the United States. It has especially been done to China, Nationalist and Communist, by non-Chinese observers.

Thrust into unwanted political intimacy with the rest of the world, Americans increasingly want to learn about other countries. But the American do-it-yourself chore takes up so much time that it encourages a think-it-for-me attitude. The trend of specialization favors predigested capsules of wisdom. Thus dragonology, or China-watching, became a fashionable new science.

Like any infant science, dragonology is a melange of truths, hypotheses, theories, tentative formulas and superstitions. Some of the Western dragonologists are excellent. But some are blundering amateurs or cynical quacks whose writing consists either of timid, non-informative intellectual acrobatics, or unguided emotional missiles that hit everything except the bull's eye. As a result, the overall picture of the China situation is incoherent. The experts disagree and the public is confused.

Many strange utterances about China are made by well-intentioned, honest people whose prestige and personal integrity are not equaled by their knowledge and judgment on the subject of China. U.S. Supreme Court Justice William O. Douglas said in Moscow after a camping trip in Outer Mongolia: "The Mongolians are a people who were crushed and walled off from the world by China for centuries. When they got their freedom, they turned West, and the nearest country was Russia." Mr. Justice Douglas of course would not have dreamed of making such a remark if his aides had learned something about Genghis Khan and the Yuan Dynasty before he chatted with his hosts in Ulan Bator.

Lord Boyd Orr, former head of the U.N. Food and Agricultural Organization and winner of the Nobel Peace Prize, visited Communist China in 1958. In his book *What's Happening in China?* he said he tended to take the most favorable view "so far as it seemed to be supported by the facts." So many things seemed to be facts that he saw no evidence of hunger and described glowingly the bountiful, weedless wheat fields, the well-stocked shops, the healthy, vigorous people, and the value of the backyard furnaces. As an international authority on food, he was convinced that Peking's claim of a huge food increase in 1958 was not exaggerated. But unfortunately soon after the publication of his book Peking publicly admitted gross errors in the very food statistics he believed in, thereby pulling the rug from under the venerable food expert.

After two visits, British correspondent Felix Greene in his 1961 book maintained that Americans are poorly informed about Communist China. Proceeding to inform them, he found that the communes were a spontaneous movement of the peasants, that women thought the public dining hall was a blessed innovation, and that he saw no signs of terror and no sense of fear. Some Chinese readers remarked that the book's title, *Awakened China: The Country Americans Don't Know*, should be changed to *Inscrutable China: The Country Felix Greene Doesn't Know*.

Edgar Snow, veteran China reporter, says in his 1962 book *The Other Side of the River* that on his 1960 visit to China he "diligently searched, without success, for starving people or beggars to photograph," and implies that stories of starvation in Communist China were due to "cold-war press indoctrination." This shows that either Snow has a boundless faith in a newspaperman's all-seeing eyes, or the many thousands of lowly Chinese refugees have been lying.

Jacques Hébert, a noted newspaperman who visited China in late 1960, in his interview with Montreal daily *Le Devoir*,

October 29, 1960, disputed the notion that Communist China was a police camp and the Chinese worked under force, because during his six weeks and 7,000 miles of travel very few policemen or soldiers were to be seen. In China, he said, people under 25 were enraptured with the regime, and everybody had enough to eat and received free medical care. He was impressed by the backyard furnaces and predicted, as implied in the title of his interview: "at the existing rhythm China may quite rapidly become the first industrial power of the world."

He deplored "certain aspects which we in the West would find revolting," such as the suppression of freedom and summary executions. But, he added: "In what measure have the Chinese ever had such freedoms?" The answer is that freedom in its most fundamental sense means the absence of restrictions. The Chinese Taoist-inspired concept of freedom (personal freedom) is in this category. Freedom is also defined as rights and privileges (political freedom). This freedom, more appropriately called liberty, is the concept generally used in the West and apparently the only concept comprehensible to this Canadian reporter. In pre-Communist days, the Chinese generally had more personal freedom but less political liberty than Westerners. Remarks such as this, that a foreign people do not mind brutal repression and summary executions because of their exotic taste, come either from palpable naiveté or intellectual imperialism.

This fallacy seems to have affected even some American men of God. Some American Protestant churchmen advocate United Nations membership for, and the recognition of, Communist China—a regime that has killed more Christians than all the Christians killed in the Roman arena. In advocating this, the Study Group of the National Council of Churches perhaps does not realize what an un-Christian reaction it has evoked among Chinese Christians. It is hoped that because of this the hitherto wonderful Protestant missionary work will not suffer too great a setback in the future in converting Chinese pagans.

Some dragonologists cannot distinguish between what is Chinese and what is Communist. The editor of a weekly in Chile after his visit explained at length the functions and advantages of the open-seat pants (pants with two lotus-leaf-like, over-lapping petals which can be opened quickly) worn by children in Communist China. His thoughtful comment: "The airy bottoms of the children thus are an expression of dynamic China under the Communist state." He did not know that open-seat pants are a residue of Imperial China, and have been worn by Chinese children for hundreds of years.

The Red Barbarians, a book authored by London newspaperman Roy MacGregor-Hastie, paints Mao Tse-tung as a superman. A *New York Times* reviewer found almost half of the names and dates were wrong, and in some places it followed very closely a history book published by the Chinese Communists.

The most flambuoyant dragonologist is Field Marshal Viscount Montgomery of Alamein, who after a brief trip to Communist China in late 1961 declared that there was no malnutrition in China, that Peking had no territorial ambitions, and that Mao was "the sort of man I'd go into the jungle with." In Hong Kong, where hundreds of hungry, sick refugees arrived daily, tempers exploded. The British-owned *China Mail* said: "Three weeks in China and he knows everything. Three weeks of plush carpet treatment, and he knows just what is happening in every isolated commune." Another paper said: "Someone once said that youth is the season of credulity. In view of Lord Montgomery's latest, that statement needs revising."

These and many other examples, mostly honest mistakes by honest observers, surround the China controversy with as much spleen as fog. It is, however, unfair to blame these dragonologists entirely. The confused farrago of opinions about China mainly stems from the often unconscious contrasts between the Oriental and the Occidental approach. This leads to the extremely important question of just how accurately the West has been judging the behavior, utterances and motives of the Chinese—the Communists as well as the people.

The crux of any assessment of China is not the quantity of information but the quality of interpretation. Among the Chinese stumbling blocks that trip up Occidental toes, the biggest is of course Peking's one-upmanship against foreigners. Another is its statistics, to which the Americans are the most vulnerable. In the United States the use of statistics is well developed and respectable. The Americans love to transcribe the indescribable into the measurable. They believe when something is expressed in figures it is classified, codified, categorized and made absolutely incontroversial. They use numbers to express anything from human intelligence to national vigor, from election fever to feminine pulchritude. The relentlessly Trendex-ed, Univac-ed, Kinsey-ed Americans seldom realize how many breath-taking figures and curves from Red China wear blatant falsies.

Too often an observer says: "There is no evidence that . . ." when he merely misses the evidence or is looking squarely at but is not competent to recognize it. He talks like a defense lawyer in a courtroom, when he should reason like a Sherlock Holmes, who combines intuition and logic into deductions that are often missed by others. The application of purely laboratory technique to complex human behavior, a dubious method of social sciences, has the danger of rejecting important evidence unintelligible to the observer or generalizing a situation from insufficient evidence.

The school of Instant Punditry also appeals to Americans, a society in a hurry. Disciples of this school would look at a fluctuating thermometer and report a change of seasons every hour on the hour. Then there is the Russian Rut, into which many a dragonologist slips. Too many, including some excellent Kremlinologists, treat the China problem as a simple variant of the Russian problem. The cultures, philosophies, agricultural and industrial conditions of Russia and China are poles apart. To predict that things will be so in China because they have been so in Russia is a use of intellectual crutches.

There are two other types of Western dragonologists who do more harm than good. One is the Armchair Pundit, who believes life can be understood through safaris to the reference library.

He dives and delves into books and documents, and fishes up logical bits that fit into a fallacious whole. Once he forms his theory he is impervious to evidence and eye-witnesses. He can recite enormous numbers of undigested facts, figures and quotes to prove his arguments about the Chinese, unaware that China is ancient and diverse enough to supply data for anyone to "prove" anything.

The other extreme is the Tourist Inspector, who feels that anything significant has to be visible. With the reasoning capacity of a news camera, he not only believes in everything he sees, but refutes anything he cannot. He is a push-over for Mao's lively dramas. He goes to Red China expecting to see savage Communists snarling at foreign intruders, and slave laborers in every street shuffling in chain-gang fashion. Instead, he is greeted by amiable officials full of humility, feted in fine restaurants crowded with well-nourished bureaucrats, led through magnificent palaces, lush collective farms and gleaming model factories. He converses "in person" (through official interpreters, of course) with happy, dedicated peasants, workers and penitent political prisoners of the happy, monolithic New China. He may even get a glimpse of Mao Tse-tung—a benign Buddha perpetually on the verge of invading Siberia or getting hopelessly enamoured with American aid and trade. After "viewing flowers on a trotting horse," the Tourist Inspector is honestly disarmed, bowled over. He returns with his eyewitness account of that exotic land, usually prefaced with the irrefutable remark: "I saw it with my own eyes," and concluded with a touch of subjective objectivity, that he saw no evidence that the natives are restless.

The Armchair Pundit admits the validity of reasoning but rejects that of perception. The Tourist Inspector admits the validity of perception but rejects that of reasoning. Both may be honest, but they overlook one fundamental factor in politics and human nature. No amount of hypothesizing, however esoteric, no amount of sightseeing, however close-range, can put the China picture in the correct perspective, if one is blind to the overpowering emotions of the silent millions who live and die under Communism. Without this empathy, ten thousand learned essays are but "scratching an itch from outside the shoe."

Western editors and the public have the romantic notion that once on-the-spot coverage is possible, the mystery-shrouded New Cathay will turn into a crystal-clear diagram. Perhaps someday the Bamboo Curtain will roll up and trained observers will be allowed into every corner of China. But even if Peking's ban on American newspapermen is lifted, there would be very little they could report. In an open society direct coverage is the best method. In a police state, the obvious is often missed by the eye, and direct coverage is only of supplementary value. During Stalin's reign of terror, most foreign visitors to the USSR brought back favorable reports and were hardly aware of the millions of kulaks dying of starvation and forced labor. During the Pacific War an International Red Cross representative inspected Japanese POW corps, blissfully oblivious of the living skeletons that were once Allied soldiers. Visitors to pre-War Nazi Germany brought back admiring reports. So did those to Castro's guerilla area before he became the "maximum leader." Tourists to Hungary on the eve of the Budapest revolt were unaware of what was coming.

In Communist China visitors not only miss the invisible truth, but are misled by realistic illusions. The record shows that visitors who did get in, including a few competent observers, missed practically every important story that has come out of Red China. Most visitors to China in 1954 were ignorant of that year's floods which covered one-tenth of the country's farmlands and displaced 40 million people. In 1956 an Indian delegation returned from Communist China, exuding admiration for its agricultural cooperatives and suggesting that India imitated the program. But even before the report was released, Peking admitted serious peasant resistance, and reductions in crops and livestock. In 1957 some China visitors described glowingly the fervent support of the Chinese youth for the regime. A few weeks later came the

Hundred Flowers, betraying the almost pathological hatred of Chinese youth for Communism. Sometimes even a Chinese may be misled. Novelist Han Suyin visited Peking in 1957 after an absence of 20 years and chatted with Chou En-lai. In her piece in the June 1957 *Holiday* she revealed a many-splendored thing: "Marx and Lenin appeared to me not as bearded political revolutionaries, but as philosophers voicing the sententious utterances of Confucian moralists." In her review of Simone de Beauvoir's *The Long March*, in the May 17, 1958, *Saturday Review*, she wrote: "I do not believe that a Communist tells *more* lies than does any other kind of official. There is, in fact, an outstanding tendency in Peking to try to tell the truth, painstakingly and punctiliously. . . . The Chinese revolution is getting more gentle and more reasonable." A few weeks after this review came the violent communes, the Great Leap and backyard furnaces.

Trained correspondents are usually unable to get significant news except for rare interviews with Communist dignitaries. The small group of foreign correspondents confined in Peking's diplomatic ghetto and permitted occasional restricted tours get far less than those stationed at the listening post of Hong Kong. Correspondents from France, Canada, Australia, England and Latin America have visited or been stationed in China. They have yet to bring out a good scoop. Those who believe that once American correspondents are allowed to enter they would learn "what is really happening in China," either consider the Americans supermen, or European and Latin American correspondents incompetents. Someday, if Peking dares to allow observers who know China intimately, who speak, read and write Chinese well, and ideally who look Chinese, then and only then can the truth be dug up through direct coverage. But that day is an enchanted, impossible day.

The free world, therefore, has to learn about Communist China mainly from its periphery. And there are many ways by which a research analyst or even a wire service correspondent can obtain a comprehensive picture with a wealth of details. The best available coverage is a combination of depth research of Chinese Communist publications, information from people coming out of China, and background knowledge of basic Marxism and the Chinese frame of mind.

Some tend to disregard completely Peking's publications except for its most sensational features. This is partly due to the propaganda nature of these publications, and partly to their dry, long-winded prose. But no matter how slanted and fabricated, this source material is indispensable. Peking's Hsinhua News Agency sends two versions of daily despatches abroad. The Chinese version has more details, and is more revealing than the English. Peking also allows the export of a few national newspapers but bans the rest. It floods Hong Kong with a thousand types of books, periodicals and pamphlets. Many of the banned publications, however, are obtainable from a thriving blackmarket in Hong Kong. These publications are eagerly studied by a number of research organizations, among them the U.S. Consulate General which funnels confidential reports to Washington.

Peking has internal Bamboo Curtains banning local newspapers of one area from going to another, except when subscribed to by Party organizations. These papers, including those from remote areas in Manchuria or Sinkiang, can be obtained in Hong Kong at costs up to 60 times the usual price. Party organs in Canton subscribe to these papers, which are immediately passed on to blackmarket couriers who buy off Party officials, customs inspectors and border guards. This has been going on all these years at the border of the allegedly incorruptible Communist China. By comparing the discrepancies in these regional papers one can often pinpoint an otherwise invisible problem Peking is trying to solve, or some event in one area deliberately kept from people in other areas. Even more fruitful than the area comparison is the chronological comparison of reports issued at different times on the same event.

Reliable news from Communist China seldom comes out fresh. What correspondents grab eagerly as spot news is usually official announcements and appointments whose significance, if any, sometimes cannot be grasped until reflected by subsequent developments. One often has to wait for months or even a couple of years to learn about some important events or to decipher their meaning. By then the public has lost interest, and information that should become headlines merely ends up in newspaper morgues. These are problems faced by even trained observers who know China and the Chinese intimately.

Much muddle about Peking's attentions and intentions comes from a language barrier which cannot be overcome—and at times is reinforced—by translation. The florid Chinese language, so delicate in nuance and rich with overtones, makes a "literal translation" into English an impossibility. One seldom gets identical impressions from an original Chinese text and its English version. A typical Peking policy statement is a conglomeration of Marxist dialectics and Chinese linguistic floss often deliberately made fuzzier for special effects. For Western observers this barrier is truly formidable if not insurmountable. It is public knowledge that very few Western visitors allowed into Communist China can carry out even a casual conversation in Chinese. In written Chinese, the problem is much greater. The Chinese language is so difficult to foreigners that, except for a few missionaries and some Japanese scholars, no Sinologist is known to have published a book or even an article in Chinese. There is perhaps not a single Western correspondent who can attend a Chinese meeting, listen to the confusing dialects and accents, and write a coherent report in English without falling back on English releases or their Chinese colleagues. The number of Western researchers and correspondents who can regularly and directly get information from publications in Chinese can be counted on the fingers of a single hand. It takes at least ten years of persistent practice and study to be proficient in Chinese. Those who zip through Army language courses in Chinese with flying colors, and claim they can coherently read a Chinese newspaper or intelligently converse with the Chinese are fooling themselves, if not others.

This situation is partly remedied by the translated material issued by the U.S. Consulate General and the U.S. Information Service in Hong Kong, using batteries of Chinese translators. The former translates some 42,000 words daily—about half a book. This daily avalanche, only a tiny fraction of the stuff Peking grinds out, discourages most readers except the most painstaking and those with time on their hands. Furthermore, most of it is straight translation, of little use to those who do not have the background to understand it. Much of the overtones in the original texts have been sacrificed through translation anyway. A couple of excellent English-language interpretative newsletters, the *China News Analysis,* for instance, are found in Hong Kong. They are of tremendous value to Western researchers but not made use of as much as they should.

Without an adequate background, the mere deciphering of Communist publications may turn an analyst into an Armchair Pundit, unless he puts his fingers, at least occasionally, on the pulse of people coming out of China. This important source supplies information on the daily realities usually not found in official publications nor known to visitors. However, these people are of varied backgrounds. Some are refugees permitted to leave; others have escaped across the borders. Some out of fear are reluctant to talk; others out of hatred exaggerate in their reports. Still others may give false praise because of hostages inside. Even those who talk frankly and freely may have lopsided views due to unconscious bias or limited experience. But if a large number of people from all walks of life and political shades are interviewed, a comprehensive picture emerges and individual inaccuracies can be easily eliminated. When this source material is correlated with a depth analysis of Peking's publications, unmistakable patterns, methods, styles and idiosyncrasies emerge to help the observer evaluate individual events and forecast trends.

A problem inherent in the interview method is that some Westerners assume that any Chinese would pour his heart out to a questioning stranger. The orthodox American reporting technique is effective on Hollywood starlets, Washington politicians and New York cab drivers. But it is often a dud with a naturally reticent people made more so by personal plight and fear. This is why some Western visitors to China who, against their own common sense, found themselves unable to disbelieve the incredible words of some individuals, labeling these words the result of "double-think," when they were merely double-talk.

This problem is present even in free areas like Hong Kong and the United States. A few years ago American immigration officers, when they asked Chinese students in the United States whether they were for the Communists or Nationalists, were astonished to find that many declined to answer. Those students were astonished that one should expect frank answers from such questions. Some years ago Peking started a campaign forcing families to write come-home letters to Chinese students abroad. The author was assigned by *Time* magazine to find some recipients of such letters in the United States and to write a story about them. He was told by a Washington spokesman of the Immigration and Naturalization Service that although many East European students in the United States had reported similar letters to the government, Chinese students would not even admit that they had received them. He said that another leading magazine had tried in vain to get such information, and expressed doubts that this attempt would succeed. Within a month, however, the author found in several cities a dozen reluctant, worried but talking recipients. It was the Oriental approach rather than journalistic prowess that did it.

Because indirect reporting on Communist China is a unique technique unintelligible to any except those who actually do it, news correspondents often fight a losing battle with their editors. Back home the editors, working in the normal journalistic way, expect the correspondents to cable them instant punditry for the next deadline. Out in the field the poor men, after staring disgustedly at realms of soporific translations, must brainpick American consular officials and browbeat Chinese leg-men for the impossible task of reporting a Peking statement or event, and footnoting it with a sagacious interpretation. Working against a deadline, newsmen rush in where the more knowledgeable fear to tread. Serious errors in assessment are thus made, and when these errors are picked up by the Armchair Pundits back home and touched up with scholarly respectability, the result is often a grotesque distortion that is reflected not only in journalism but sometimes in public opinion and foreign policy. Thus events which have cast unmistakable shadows come as pure surprise to the American press and government. This has happened with Vietnam, Laos, Cuba, the Congo, India and, of course, all these years with China.

Some competent dragonologists writing about Communist China are too shy to rely on their own judgment, because they believe their reports may not be accepted by the readers—and the editors—who have developed a conditioned reflex from the vast avalanche of interpretative writing on the subject. For example, up to 1959 the concensus was that Communist China was very strong and getting stronger. Some expressed admiration; others fear. Yet as early as 1956 most Chinese dragonologists outside the United States were predicting that things would not work out for Peking, that more harm than good was being done, and that even on pure economic grounds Peking was working itself into a disaster. Such views were scoffed at by most Westerners.

By the summer of 1962, however, symptoms from Communist China had become obvious even to the least informed. While a few China experts were still apologetically clinging to their original judgment and explaining that Peking's difficulties were temporary and would be solved soon, others conceded that conditions in China were much worse than they realized. Dragonologists in Washington coined the term "assessment lag" to explain away their own misinterpretation. It is not inconceivable that those who once attributed fantastic dedication and superhuman efficiency to the Chinese Communists may eventually jockey themselves into the new position that the Chinese are a ridiculously incompetent and backward people. This pendulum swing could happen when the incredible mistakes made by Peking are more widely known and believed. But it would be another extremist assessment that ignores the fact that it is the system imposed by an organized minority, and not the capabilities of the majority, that sets the style of a totalitarian nation.

The irony is that the rational and direct Western mind, which can reach stars many light years away to analyze their chemical composition, is bewildered and misled by the illogical, sophisticated mind of the East. The West's purely scientific yardstick gives strange readings when used on a too human subject. The abstract theories of political science are of little help in understanding the violent convulsions in countries like China—convulsions born of intense aspirations and disillusionments, of mangled lives and tangled emotions.

When all else fails, the Westerner falls back on the old cliché about "the inscrutable Chinese." But in the ultimate analysis, there is no such thing as an inscrutable people, only uninformed onlookers. For example, many Westerners think Mao is profound. To the Chinese he is merely complex. Many call him a poet and scholar. Yet if one knows a little about the Chinese milieu, Mao's utterances are just Marxist dressing mixed with so much Chinese corn. The minority of Western dragonologists who consistently put their fingers on the right spot carry no more weight than the amateurs, quacks and demagogues whose only qualification is that they are *not* Chinese either. In the cacophony of controversy and conflicting opinions, wisemen often sound like fools, and fools often sound like wisemen. Thus the experts quarrel, the governments blunder or are paralyzed by indecision, the public is confused, and the China problem remains an enigma.

XIX

SHADES
OF GENGHIS KHAN

COMMUNIST CHINA HAS THE HIGHEST RATE OF ECONOMIC growth, and the world's second largest and most dedicated army. It is itching to start a nuclear war, is ready to sacrifice half of its people, and will smother the rest of mankind with the remaining half. In a couple of decades, one billion Red Chinese will be trained to hate the United States, wrest mastery from the USSR, and become the greatest threat the West has ever known.

Moscow is worried about this yellow giant. It sabotaged the summit talks due to Peking's displeasure. It wanted the disarmament conference to forestall a Chinese nuclear bomb, and was uncooperative at it because of Chinese pressure. The yellow horde may soon swarm over and colonize the Russian oblasts in Asia. Hence the West in order to survive must be bold and imaginative. We should not be too nasty to Peking, lest we drive it back to Moscow's bosom. We should perhaps form a Russo-American alliance to defend White Civilization from the Yellow Peril.

Shades of Genghis Khan! There really is a Yellow Peril: when the yellow man turns Red, the white man turns yellow.

Each and everyone of Mao Tse-tung's grandiose dreams has become a clinical nightmare in the West. China casts a frightening shadow. But what is behind that shadow? The strength of any nation is gauged by its armed forces, its economy and its people. What is the real strength of Red China?

Militarily Communst China has a huge standing force of about 2.5 million. The air force has 50 fighter and 20 tactical bomber squadrons, with some 3,000 planes of which fewer than 2,000 are first-line combat planes, including more than 1,000 jets. The fighters include MIG-15's, MIG-17's, MIG-19's and probably a few MIG-21's. The bombers are mainly medium-range Ilyushin-28's and some obsolete long-range Tupolev-4's.

The small navy has one light cruiser, 4 destroyers, some 30 submarines of which about half are Russian medium-range W class, about 170 torpedo boats and gunboats, a few frigates and thousands of junks. It has no aircraft carrier and no battleship. It is essentially a coastal navy. The ground forces consist of 30 armies, falling into 120 infantry, 6 armored, 2 air-borne divisions, and a number of independent artillery and anti-aircraft units.

The overall picture is impressive in quantity rather than quality. Most equipment is supplied by Soviet Russia. Communist China can assemble airplanes, tanks, small ships, and produce out-dated rifles, machineguns, mortars and artillery pieces. It will not be able to build effective nuclear weapons and missiles by itself in the foreseeable future. It cannot produce airplane engines, nor reduction gears and clutches for modern marine engines, nor most of the alloy steels necessary for modern armaments. Even the shells lobbed on Quemoy were Russian-made. Its supply of aviation fuel is barely enough for operational training of the air force. Its supply of rifle bullets is so precious that in recent years they have seldom been used for target practice. It has some Soviet missiles, probably manned by the Russians. The radar network is spotty and the anti-aircraft system is weak, so that all these years Nationalist planes have been reconnoitering and dropping leaflets and food parcels over the coastal provinces with great ease.

Judging from the 1958 aerial dog fights over Quemoy, the wholesale defection of POW's in Korea, recent reports from refugees and Peking's guarded official admissions, the training and morale of the Red troops today are far inferior than those of the Nationalist forces. While the Red military force could create a serious problem in a brush-fire war in Southeast Asia, in a hypothetical war against the United States, Peking would be "hurling eggs at rock."

Economically, even if Peking's statistics are taken at their face value, Communist China is, as Mao put it, "poor and blank." Its construction and heavy industry are still negligible for a world power. On a per capita basis, the United States consumes 17 times more steel and 65 times more electric power than Communist China. The latter, with an area about equal to and a population more than three times that of the United States, has only 7 percent as many highways. Its railroads, of which more than 70 percent were built in pre-Communist days, are only two-thirds of what the United States had 100 years ago. Its estimated total number of trucks and buses is less than 10 percent of that of California. Its estimated total number of motor vehicles is less than Ceylon's, or less than one-fifth of India's, or slightly more than that of North Dakota in 1920. In 1950, the United States scrapped 32 times the number of motor vehicles owned by Communist China in 1962—most of these were inherited from the Nationalists. The oil produced in Communist China in the entire year of 1961 was not enough for two days' consumption in the United States. These are the economic muscles of Communist China.

Less tangible but more significant than economic strength is the human element. Communist China is ruled by the 17 million members of the Communist Party, the biggest in the world. About 80 percent of the members joined the Party after the regime came into power. The majority of Party members are therefore "rice Communists." But today there is little rice. Recently Peking admitted that 70 percent of its Party members were disappointed in the regime. What is the percentage now?

Party members constitute only 3 percent of the population, which is staggering. Population was a weapon of expansion in the days of Genghis Khan, when the strength of armies depended on the number of arrows shot from a human-sea. In modern warfare economic and technological strength count far more than population. In a food-short nation, population is a liability rather than an asset. The fear of an avalanche of Chinese overrunning neighboring contries is groundless; unless the emigrants were dedicated Communists, their leaving the country would only tip the balance against the Communist regime.

Although the popular fears of Communist China are unfounded, the regime does pose some serious threats to the rest of the world—threats generally overlooked. One is the Invisible Opium War. Peking exported 3,600 tons of opium and its derivatives in 1950, and by 1960 it was exporting 7,000 tons—more than double Great Britain's peak annual shipment of opium to China just before the Opium War. This output is ten times greater than the legitimate medical needs of the entire world. At least 65 percent of the world's illicit narcotics come from Communist China which, according to U.N. narcotics specialists, is getting an estimated gross income of one billion United States dollars annually, in gold and hard currency.

The dope is smuggled into Burma, Thailand, Hong Kong, Macao, Japan, the Philippines, Canada and the United States. Cuba has become a major transshipment point for Chinese narcotics. Dope addiction, which was unknown in pre-war Japan, is now a serious problem there. In Hong Kong, where the addiction rate has tripled in recent years, the British have a hard time fighting a reverse Opium War. A substantial amount of this dope gets into the United States as heroin which poisons innocent youth and promotes juvenile deliquency and vicious crimes. Peking's narcotics industry, efficiently carried out by carefully guarded state poppy farms and 21 special bureaus, is more than a big source of national income. It is also an ideological weapon. In Japan, dope is used to finance student riots and other activities of the Japanese Communists. In the United States, the impact of the dope on public morals is far more rewarding to Peking than the foreign exchange earned.

Another threat from Peking is its influence on opportunistic, underdeveloped nations which were given the idea that any country could leap into an instant paradise with great prestige, especially if it behaved like an international juvenile delinquent. This once ominous threat has greatly receded as a result of Peking's economic debacle, so much so that India dared to shove back in the 1962 border war.

This border dispute about the Ladakh area and the McMahon Line (never recognized by any Chinese government) was used only as an excuse by Peking. This is evidenced by the facts that Communist China in a 1960 treaty quietly yielded to Burma disputed areas comparable to those along the Sino-Indian border, and in a similar treaty in 1961 it yielded to Nepal some 300 square miles of disputed territory. In 1960 Peking indicated its willingness to recognize the McMahon Line, probably in exchange for India's support for its role as the Asian-African Big Brother, and for its participation in international events such as disarmament and summit conferences. But Nehru was too busy stepping into the limelight himself. This, on top of India's giving asylum to the Dalai Lama and the Tibetan refugees, so enraged Mao that he decided to chasten India, and to force it to practice what it had preached about its loyal friendship with Communist China. Mao, however, miscalculated because Nehru did an incredible thing—forced by public opinion, he resisted.

The question of whether Communist China may start a full-scale military adventure in Southeast Asia, against India, Pakistan, Burma, Laos, Thailand, Hong Kong or Taiwan, depends not only on its real strength, but also very much on its assessment of the West's determination. If it believes that an outside adventure will bring a spirited retaliation, it may generate much thunder at times but little rain. If it believes it can get away with it, an armed venture may be undertaken to divert attention from its domestic problems and prop up its lowered prestige.

A sane assessment of Communist China's internal strength, not its over-sized shadow, throws more light on its place in the international scene. The pivot of China's foreign relations is the Peking-Moscow axis, which has seen better days. Historically, there has never been any amenity between China and Russia.

After its birth, the Chinese Communist Party became the protegé of Moscow, which at first ignored Mao and cultivated its own Chinese Communist leaders. Stalin dealt with Mao only after the latter became the leader by his own efforts; even then he continued to consider Chiang Kai-shek as the real leader of China until the collapse of the Nationalists. Mao remembers all this, and perhaps with little ecstasy.

Russian aid to China has not been free. Some of the industrial equipment aid was originally stripped from Japanese-built plants in Manchuria at the end of World War II. Other forms of aid were mostly high-interest loans or the barter of goods, with the Chinese shipping raw materials to Russia at cut-rate prices. It was a double exploitation. Peking fought the Korean War for Moscow, but it had to buy the required military supplies from the Russians. This economic colonialism rankled in Mao and his men all along, but it was a price they had to pay.

After he came into Power, Khrushchev on his 1954 visit to Peking abolished USSR's special privileges in Manchuria reimposed by Stalin on Mao. But Mao did not seem to be moved by such friendly gestures. Instead, he was greatly embarrassed by the de-Stalinization which reflected unfavorably on his cult of personality. To make things worse, the personalities of Khrushchev and Mao seem allergic to each other. All this resulted in Moscow's considerable reduction of aid to Peking. Communist China's second Five-Year Plan got only token help from Russia. After the Hundred Flowers debacle, Mao journeyed to Moscow in November 1957, hoping to better the aid situation. Whatever happened at that meeting must have been unpleasant, for Mao returned to China in silent, cold rage. Soon Mao reacted on the rebound. He ordered the Great Leap, the communes and "Three Years of Bitter Struggle." Khrushchev not only refused to alleviate Peking's economic crisis, he also ridiculed the commune system.

The economic factor is perhaps the strongest one in the Sino-Soviet rift. The so-called ideological quarrel is a result rather than a cause. Viewed against orthodox Marxism and Leninism, both

Khrushchev and Mao are deviationists. Khrushchev, who would probably be a popular union boss or even a successful corporation president if he had been born in the United States, is a rightist revisionist. Soviet Russia is no longer a have-not nation. It is beginning to enjoy openly the decadent pleasures of capitalist society, even though it still uses Communist ideology to further its national power. The attainment of middle-class respectability often makes money look less evil.

Mao has been a zigzagging deviationist all his life. He used to be more of a rightist revisionist until 1957 when he became a leftist deviationist. Today Communist China—or rather Mao himself—is acting like an embittered poor man who feels the world owes him a living. This bitterness is vented upon Khrushchev, more for his stinginess to Communist China than for his talks of coexistence. Peking has no card to play against Moscow except one: ideological arguments. They are of mere nuisance value but the nuisance could be embarrassing to Moscow. Instead of giving in, Khrushchev retaliated with an economic boycott and a withdrawal of Russian technicians who even brought back blueprints of unfinished projects.

Peking temporarily knuckled under Moscow's partial boycott in 1961. Its domestic propaganda line changed from "opposing always leaning on others" to "opposing isolating oneself." All over China the Party promoted thousands of performances of a play based on the story of *"wu hsin chang tan,"* exhorting the people to sleep on straw, taste gall, swallow humiliation for an eventual revenge, but without saying against whom.

Mao realized that Communist China had to be an economic vassal of the USSR. Nearly 10 percent of Peking's investment resources and half of its foreign trade depend on the USSR, which spends less than one percent of its gross national product on all its foreign aid. If Moscow should enforce a total boycott, Peking's machine industry would be without spare parts, its atomic reactors would be without uranium, its planes, tanks, trucks and submarines would be paralyzed, and its whole economy, tightly geared to Russian aid, would quickly collapse.

Mao's temporary retreat, however, was soon negated by his growing resentment and rebelliousness against Khrushchev's boorish scorn. The quarrel got noisier. At the 1963 East German Communist Party Congress, the world witnessed the unprecedented spectacle of a public washing of dirty Red linen. But this was no novel emotional experience for Mao, whose fury was equally great when he defied his father and his teachers.

A rational appraisal is that notwithstanding the sound and fury, Mao would not dare to continue to defy the Americans, the Nationalists, the Chinese people, the Indians, *and* also the Communist majority. But he has not always been rational. For a man who believes in miracle farms, steel-making alchemy and instant communes, it is but one step beyond to believe that his "revolutionary optimism" can immunize him from imperialists, modern revisionists and nuclear warfare. However, the Mao-Khrushchev squabble is not necesarily a Sino-Russian split. The situation could change overnight if either one of them was out of the picture.

From Moscow's point of view, it would like China to stay Communist but to stay weak. This would be far better than a strong and headstrong Communist China. Peking's role as the Communist thoroughfare to Asia is greatly diminished now that the USSR has established direct rapport with Asian nations. Economically, Communist China is now a liability rather than an asset. It is far more profitable politically for the USSR to pour armament and other supplies to new bases like Cuba and Ghana than into the bottomless hole of Communist China which, once back on its feet, would certainly again swagger in the international arena, hogging the limelight from Big Brother.

The rest of the world, reacting to the Peking bugaboo, in its frantic search for solutions sometimes wants to try political gimmicks. One is the admission of Communist China to the United Nations. Proponents of this expect that once Peking sits in a UN chair, it could either be disciplined or flattered into reforming itself. But the UN Charter would have to be extensively doctored to admit a regime which not only fought against the UN, but tramples on human rights, practices slave labor and genocide, and floods the Free World with opium and heroin. Some talk compassionately that one should not "ignore 600 million people." But it would be quite a problem for the UN to represent the 600 million Chinese by taking in a regime which does not represent them. With all its lofty ideals, the UN sometimes resembles a bowler-hat version of the Chinese tea house—plenty of walla-walla* but little action. If Peking gets into it, the tea house might begin to resemble a circus, although Peking's performance would be on a more subtle level than shoe-pounding.

Another gimmick is the independence of Taiwan. On this point all Chinese—Communist, Nationalist and independent—agree: Taiwan is Chinese. The Chinese began to settle in Taiwan three centuries before Columbus set foot on America. They numbered 30,000 by the early 17th century. In 1624 the Dutch occupied part of the island. The Spaniards also occupied a corner of it for 15 years until driven out by the Dutch. In 1661 the Chinese general Cheng Cheng-kung (Koxinga) drove out the Dutch. For more than 20 years Taiwan was a political and cultural haven for a large number of Chinese refugees who fled the Manchus on the mainland. The Manchus finally reached Taiwan in 1683 and made it a prefecture of Fukien province the following year. In 1886 Taiwan formally became a province of China. In 1895 it was ceded to Japan following the Sino-Japanese War. The Allies at the Cairo Conference agreed that Taiwan was to be returned to China. This was done upon Japan's surrender in 1945.

Taiwan's population consists of three million Chinese refugees from Communism, eight million descendants of the Chinese settlers mostly from Fukien, and some 200,000 aborigines. The native tongue of Taiwan, or the Taiwanese language, is the Fukien dia-

---

* "Walla-walla" is Shanghai slang for noisy, spirited talk.

lect with some Japanese influence. When most people say "Formosans" they are unaware that they mean mainly the Fukienese and not the aborigines. The latter are the true Formosans or Taiwanese, just as the American Indians are the true Americans. There is a small group of disaffected Taiwanese, mostly Japanese-educated politicians and professional men who constituted an elite in the colonial days. Today the Taiwanese (descendents of original settlers) and the mainlanders (recent settlers) live with and marry each other freely. There *is* some Taiwanese resentment against the mainland "intruders," just as there would be native resentment if a quarter million Washingtonians and New Yorkers moved to Hawaii. The Taiwanese, unlike during the Japanese occupation, now own the majority of the island's private commercial and industrial enterprises. They constitute half of the Nationalist air force and one-third of the ground force, and have shown good fighting spirit defending the offshore islands.

There is no question that legally, historically and ethnically Taiwan is Chinese. It has never been a sovereign state, although it has been a Chinese province and a Japanese colony. China certainly has as much right to call Taiwan its own as the United States has a claim to Hawaii and Puerto Rico; and more right than Britain's claim to Hong Kong, India's to Kashmir, Indonesia's to Dutch New Guinea, or the Congo's to Katanga.

In the maelstrom of diplomatic gimmicks, political expediency, old prejudices and new fears, the party that carries the great and decisive weight in the outcome of the China situation is after all the Chinese people themselves. Others can only help or impede, but never alter the real wishes of one quarter of mankind. In this respect the United States plays an important role. Politically and ideologically, Peking needs an enemy who is wealthy and strong, who will not be belligerent and high-handed even when abused, who is indecisive, timid and shrinks the moment the other yells murder, and who is often hesitantly apologetic when he should be righteously indignant. The United States is the perfect, and the only, choice. If things are not overdone, the use of the United

States as a whipping boy by the Chinese Communists increases their prestige while guaranteeing immunity. It is no coincidence that all these years Communist China has staged violent anti-American campaigns, issued more than 200 "serious warnings" against alleged American aerial intrusions, yet never actually flung down the gauntlet.

Perhaps if Peking were to live its life all over again it would be less hostile to the United States—now that it realizes where the wheat comes from. But the clock cannot be turned back. Unless the United States government kowtows to the Peking mandarins, Communist China could not change markedly its anti-American attitude without losing its *raison d'être*.

There has been talk of United States recognition of Communist China. The logic is that with so many dead ends, let us explore a new avenue, let us find out what China really wants, let us talk and deal with it instead of pretending it is not there. Anyway, recognition does not mean moral approval. It seems an easy way out, an instant pill curing many headaches. Fortunately for the United States, this diplomacy by trial and error was never adopted. One needs not jump into the caldron to find out whether the soup is boiling.

As the Communist regime is actively loathed by the Chinese people, recognition by the United States, knowing the nature of that regime, would be morally repugnant to much of the Free World and a serious blow to the anti-Communist Chinese themselves. Advocates of recognition claim that it is absurd to ignore 600 million Chinese. But non-recognition, like the closing of consulates and the breaking of diplomatic ties, is a gesture of disapproval, scorn and anger against the government, not the Chinese people. At present the vast majority of the 600 million Chinese are battling against a regime under Mao, who is busily shuttling between the roles of savior and executioner. Thus those who advocate a "silent treatment" for the Peking regime or even a liberation of the Chinese people from that regime are, paradoxically, the ones who do not ignore the 600 million people.

The truth is that Peking yearns to be recognized by the United States. Next to getting the Nationalists out of Taiwan, it wants nothing more than United States recognition and a UN admission. Now more than ever Peking needs it to boost its sagging prestige. The Chinese Communists overtly attack the United States but covertly admire it for its wealth and power. Peking would scornfully accept United States recognition, if it were offered, and perhaps also do the favor of accepting American aid. First on the aid list would be food—food to beef up the Red Army and the Party. And if the American imperialists want to get rid of more of their surpluses, then even the Chinese peasants might get some extra rations after the state granaries were filled. With United States recognition, the greater insults Peking hurled out, the greater would be its prestige.

A lesson may be learned from Peking's treatment of Great Britain. London recognized Peking soon after Mao came into power in order to protect its colony of Hong Kong and its £300 million investments in China. But up to now, Peking has acted as if it does not recognize London. British diplomats in Peking can only get an audience with third-class bureaucrats of Peking's Ministry of Foreign Affairs, often after hours of waiting. The British Consul in Shanghai is completely ignored, often failing to receive letters addressed to him as "British Consul." Hong Kong is still British, only because its present status is more useful to Peking. As for the British investments, parent firms in England are still throwing good money after bad in their China branches, where the once proud British taipans are virtual hostages. What Peking really thinks of the British was candidly expressed by a Chinese Communist spokesman to William J. vanden Heuvel, President of the International Rescue Committee as he reports in *The New Leader*. The Communist said: "As for our relations with the British, we regard them as insignificant. The British are the tail to the American kite, always playing their game of trying for the middle ground."

What happened to India is even more enlightening. No government has appeased Communist China as much as Nehru's. In spite of this obeisance—or rather because of it—India incurred Peking's wrath and disdain for not being a complete echo. Mao Tse-tung probably has far more secret respect for Chiang Kai-shek than for Nehru. These are yet more proofs that with the Communists there is no middle ground—if you are not for them, you are against them. The United States will remain Red China's Enemy No. 1, even if Washington recognizes Peking.

Rightly or wrongly there is a belief in some nations that it is prestigious, and sometimes profitable, to abuse the United States. The popular impression is that the Americans so want to be loved that they will bribe others with foreign aid, tolerate in their foes what they condemn in their friends, talk tough but talk themselves out of a showdown. The truth is that the Americans are not really fools, but only good-natured, nice guys who bend backward to give everyone except themselves the benefit of the doubt. If pushed around once too often, they can be quite a formidable foe. The trouble is that this truth is not self-evident, thereby often inviting miscalculations by others, as when Khrushchev tried to install nuclear missiles in Cuba. This could be a great danger in international relations.

In the prevailing cold war, the Free World and the Communist bloc differ on many points in their thinking. To the Free World, each area, each incident, each momentary period is considered separately like chemicals isolated in test tubes. Thus on-the-spot judgments and step-by-step decisions result in what is called fire-brigade action. To the Communists, every tiny incident in every isolated hamlet is part of a global pattern. They sound in the east and strike in the west. They grab a foot when given an inch. Quemoy, Berlin, Laos, Cuba or India: each foothold gained or lost is an indication of the opponent's will or lack of will.

Many dream of relaxing tensions. But tensions, like fever, are a symptom rather than a disease by itself. Treating the fever without treating the disease that causes it will only make the patient more sick. A fact of life with Communism is that one sometimes has to act warlike in order to avoid wars. The dialectical tactics of the Communists thrive on tensions, conflicts, discords and suspicions. When they deliberately create tensions and conflicts, the West is forced to choose between brinksmanship and shrinksmanship. Everytime the United States is strong and firm, the Communists back down; everytime it is weak and hesitant, they get more ambitious.

In dealing with the Communist encroachment, some consider the contest mainly military. They believe the safest defense is nuclear deterrence and the best offense is dropping nuclear bombs on Moscow and Peking. Some consider it mainly economic. They believe that if enough American dollars are tossed into the under-developed, neutralist and deviationist Communist countries, peace can be purchased. But the world is not so simple that it can be set to rights with bullets or dollars. The problem of Communism everywhere is both military and economic, but it is also, and even more so, intellectual. In this battle for the mind, the Free World has hardly made use of its most formidable weapons. Communism's greatest power is in making people believe in a fallacy. To hit at its most vulnerable spot the Free World must expose this fallacy to people who have not yet lived under Communism, keep up the hope of those who have, and keep its own powder dry.

Specifically, the United States is a great threat to the Peking regime. The Nationalists are an even greater threat because they have turned out to be better agrarian reformers than the Communists, and because they possess a strong army which is *not foreign*. The greatest threat to Peking, however, is the Chinese people living under the Communist regime. This threat alone will eventually topple the Mao Dynasty, but not until the people have suffered long and painfully. The process could be accelerated if, say, an outside force is able to set off the vast explosive potential in the population. This force could be a military spearhead that sets the Red Chinese continent afire, or even strong moral backing from the Free World.

Some allies of the United States and some Americans themselves have criticized the United States policy of economically and militarily aiding the Nationalists, as if Washington were merely doing a favor for Taipei. In reality it is a two-way favor. Psychologically and strategically, if the United States wants to stay in the Far East, the island of Taiwan is its most crucial base. Its loss would shift the first line of defense back to Pearl Harbor. To maintain this base either as a defense bulwark or a possible offense springboard, the United States would have to garrison it with a large force. Many American boys would have to be sent overseas to risk their lives, and the anti-American feeling found in every big American base abroad would be generated.

But by aiding the Nationalists, the United States now has a modern fighting force of 600,000 in the China area, maintained at a fraction of the expense required for an equal American force, and ready to go into action if the necessity arises. The fact that these troops are Chinese negates any accusation of American "occupation" and the possible loss of many American lives. After all, the Americans cannot fight every battle in the world engineered by the Communists and carried out by the native people of each area. The job already done by the Nationalist army on Taiwan is seldom recognized. Through Peking's genuine fear of a Nationalist landing, it is tying down an estimated one million Communist Chinese troops on the mainland, who might otherwise be marching into Southeast Asia or Korea. Thus the real problem is not to economize by cutting foreign aid in the Taiwan area, but to find more such nations like Nationalist China, South Vietnam and South Korea to guard the frontiers of the Free World. The fact that these governments have serious shortcomings does not justify the strategic folly that the United States needs only pious allies.

Up to a couple of years ago anyone who said Communism in China was a passing phase was laughed at. Today this possibility can no longer be discounted. And those who are most afraid of it are the Chinese Communists themselves whose military and security measures along the South China coast in 1962 amounted to a slow-burning panic. In spite of Washington's public and private assurances to Peking that it will keep the Nationalist troops from attacking, Peking knows, if the Nationalists are allowed to attack by the U.S., or take the matter into their own hands, or drop large numbers of paratroopers on the mainland, what spontaneous combustion might be touched off.

If and when Communist China does collapse, the repercussions would be staggering. World Communism would suffer its greatest setback. It would be the first proof that a monolithic Communist regime is perishable—and can be toppled by its own people. This would equal the work of a million USIA's. All the promises and dreams of an Instant Paradise in China or anywhere else would sound absurd. Not only that. It would hearten the peoples enslaved by Communism. It would create tremendous chaos among the Communist rulers, with no risk of a nuclear war, because they would not know where or on whom to drop the bombs. It would certainly improve the Free World's situation in Southeast Asia, Berlin and Cuba.

The free world's secret weapon against Communist China is the Chinese people. The China situation, if manipulated with shrewdness and courage, could well be the Archimedean lever that moves the world back from the brink.

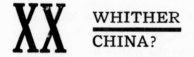

XX WHITHER CHINA?

IN 221 B.C. THE STATE OF CHIN VANQUISHED ALL ITS rivals and unified China, thus putting an end to two confused centuries of the Age of Warring States. The King of Chin proclaimed himself Shih Huang Ti (First Emperor) and appointed Legalist philosopher Li Ssu as his prime minister. He based his government on the premise that man was born evil and must be governed by the rule of law under an efficient, powerful state, exercising restrictions of liberties at home and armed conquests abroad. Thus the world's first totalitarian regime was born.

Chin Shih Huang Ti built the colossal Great Wall to defend China against the barbarians, turned feudal states into 36 centrally controlled prefectures, standardized coinage, language, weights, measures and even the axle length of vehicles, constructed national highways, seized all metal objects to melt into weapons, bells and statues, used slave labor to open virgin lands, built magnificent palaces and other mammoth constructions. To destroy Confucian classics and start history from himself, he burned books and buried alive 460 scholars who critized his regime. To build the Great Wall, 60 percent of the population was mobilized and three out of ten males were pressed into the labor gangs. Many thousands died under the ruthless task-masters and their bodies were buried in the Wall, which is sometimes nicknamed "The World's Longest Cemetery." Families were broken. People died of starvation and overwork. But the state of Chin, aware only of material gains and the power of the state, seemed to grow strong, monolithic and invincible.

One day 900 Chin soldiers headed by two petty officers were force-marching toward a destination when they were delayed by heavy rains. Under the severe Chin law the penalty for such a delay was death. In desperation the small band of peasant troops revolted. Within a month the rebels grew to tens of thousands, including 1,000 cavalry soldiers and possessing 700 war chariots. Peasants all over the country rose up in an overwhelming surprise attack on the government, characteristic of the unique mass revolutions that were to occur in China's long history. The reign of terror of Chin Shih Huang Ti, who expected it to last "for thousands and ten thousands of generations, for generations without end," lasted less than 15 years and collapsed spectacularly soon after the revolt.

It is an irony that Shih Huang Ti, in constructing the Great Wall to repel outside enemies, created a far more powerful enemy inside—the people.

Throughout her history China has had a number of despotic reigns. Each of these dynamic, ruthless regimes came after a period of decay and confusion. Each appeared strong and solidly entrenched, but each collapsed within a relatively short time. Each was succeeded by a long period of peace and prosperity. The best-known reigns of terror were begun by these tyrants: Hsia Chieh, 1818 B.C.; Shang Chou, 1154 B.C.; Chin Shih Huang Ti, 221 B.C.; the Sui Emperors, 589 A.D.; the Mongols, 1280 A.D. The periodic emergence of despotic regimes falls into a fascinating rhythm, occurring about once every seven or eight centuries. This is one of the unique features of the Dynastic Cycles of China.

After the collapse of the despotic Mongolian regime (Yuan Dynasty), China enjoyed a long period of peaceful resurgence under the Ming Dynasty, followed by a period of decay and confusion during the Ching Dynasty and the Republic. In 1949, seven centuries after the emergence of the last despotic regime, came the

Mao Dynasty—labeled by the Chinese as the only regime in China's history that out-Chins the Chin Dynasty. Will this unique Chinese pattern be repeated? Will the Chinese Communist regime, which has been ruthless and seemed strong and invincible, also disintegrate in the spontaneous combustion that is periodically brought by the Dynastic Cycles?

In 1957 a spontaneous, nation-wide revolution was almost touched off by the Hundred Flowers. It did not come off, superficially because of the subsequent repression, but fundamentally because the Hundred Flowers was initiated by the rulers, thus instilling an illusion in the ruled that they might get away with a verbal revolution. The existence of this illusion in 1957 revealed that in spite of popular hatred a genuine mass revolution was not thoroughly ripe because the people were not prepared to shed blood. If the Communists had shifted to a comparatively moderate and sensible policy then, their reign might have achieved some stability by now. In that case, perhaps a gradual mellowing of the regime and a gradual return of inherent Chinese traits might have resulted.

Instead, the Hundred Flowers was followed by a series of far-out measures that were tragically brutal and comically idiotic. The pathological reactions of the regime shattered any illusion in the people that they could change their fate without bloodshed, and at the same time created the classical atmosphere for revolution—universal poverty, hunger and repression. Peking's subsequent admissions of setbacks have been only a tactical retreat and not a change of philosophy. For Mao Tse-tung and some of his top Reds live in a mythical world of their own—an impossible mixture of Marxist materialism and Taoist transcendentalism —a world of semi-truths, pseudo-science and prefabricated emotions. Theoretically, they could still pick up the pieces if they make an about-turn. Practically, they are incapable of doing this. Politically, even if they were capable of it, a complete change of policy could not be made without almost immediate political collapse. In spite of their belated realization of past errors, hang-

ing on to the control system they have created, and thus protect-
ing themselves, is more important than the fundamental correction
of these errors.

Thus the direction Communist China is heading in the foreseeable future appears set. Peking will continue to admit past errors
in agriculture, industry, and political control, but the admissions
will be partial and the overall policy will go on. The economic
recovery will probably take half to a decade—if neither massive
Soviet aid nor disastrous leaps take place.

Politically, the regime will retreat—which will encourage overt
opposition, which will bring back repression, which will in turn
worsen the condition of the country and the people. The alterna-
tion of relaxation and repression may continue with an accelerated
rhythm until the precarious balance is upset. How this may
happen depends on many factors. An accident, an incident, an
otherwise futile riot may blow the fuse. It could be an outside
stimulus: a Maoist misadventure abroad, a Nationalist landing,
or any drastic international change. It could be something inside:
hunger and epidemics may result in nationwide chaos, with
revolting peasants joined by large-scale troop defections. Or,
before that stage is reached, some Peking leader, either a shrewd
politician or an ambitious general or a disillusioned Communist,
may stage a *coup d'état*. Or an explosion may be touched off by
another Hundred Flowers. It is possible that either Khrushchev's
or Mao's star will fall, or that Mao will capitulate. Communist
China may thus be economically bolstered by Soviet Russia, and
may appear somewhat stabilized. This, however, would only delay the inevitable end result of the broad political under-currents.
On the other hand, it is improbable but not inconceivable that
Mao may defy Khrushchev to the bitter end by throwing his
human and natural resources into a Quixotic siege—thus promptly
bringing about the bitter end. Any of these developments could
cause the Mao Dynasty to topple as suddenly as the monolithic
Chin Dynasty 21 centuries ago.

The most probable outcome, if the present trend continues,

would be widespread disturbances in Communist China, followed by a Nationalist landing or air-drop—with or without American help. Even though repeatedly criticized by overseas Chinese public opinion, the Chinese Nationalists will probably not make any move without Washington's concurrence. But if internal resistance on the mainland grows appreciably, the Nationalists would either have to make a move, or their political doom would be sealed. Judging from the mood in Taipei, they probably would. The Americans then would either have to support the Nationalists, or fight them to hold them down. If the Nationalists should air-drop or land large numbers of troops on the mainland, and hold a beachhead for even a few weeks, the response from the Chinese populace would be spectacular.

It is not impossible that Moscow would try to stop this revolution, which could be catastrophic to World Communism, but it is not likely. Soviet Russia could do little if the uprising were widespread. Nuclear bombs are impractical when a whole nation rises up against its own government. A million Soviet troops could be easily swallowed up in a vast and hostile China. It is conceivable that Moscow would not shed too many tears over the possible demise of the Peking regime, whose economic tribute, political cooperation and ideological importance have steadily decreased. Perhaps in the event of a collapse, Moscow might quickly occupy Manchuria and then deal from a position of strength with whichever regime that turns up.

The collapse of the Maoists would probably be followed by extensive food riots, and also the biggest lynching party in history. Tens of thousands, perhaps hundreds of thousands, may be slaughtered by the people in a cruel vendetta. Many innocent ones may be killed. The country may fall into a patchwork of small regions controlled by defected troops, peasants and indigenous organizations emerging from underground. This chaotic period would increase the population's physical suffering. It could be shortened by prompt action from outside: massive emergency food and medical relief and the maintenance of order by a well-organized *native* force. The only available means would be American food and Chinese Nationalist forces.

The outside world will be horrified to discover the state of things in China if and when the Communist government is overthrown. The extensively, perniciously damaged land will need decades for soil recuperation, reforestation, and correction of faulty water conservancy projects. Some of the industrial machinery will probably have been wrecked by the mob. Much of the jerry-built machinery will have to be scrapped anyway. Human damage will be found greater than material damage. Petty crime will be rampant. A centralized organ will have to be set up to help locate millions of missing and displaced persons. The population will be found suffering from serious malnutrition and disease. The most serious will be the deteriorated health of newborn babies.

Initial relief and rehabilitation, gigantic as they would have to be, will only be immediate measures. Long-term measures will be more complicated. Economically, post-Communist China would probably have to adopt a mildly socialist (as defined traditionally) system. Socialism may only bring mediocrity to a prosperous economy like that of the United States, but for an economically underdeveloped, and especially devastated nation, a certain amount of government control is needed to put the economy back on its feet until it can thrive by itself.

Politically the cry will be for democracy. The Chinese wanted personal freedom but never bothered to protect it by participating in the government. Today through its total deprivation the Chinese under Communism have learned how precious democracy is. They have learned that if they do not run the bureaucrats, the bureaucrats may run them. This lesson has been learned at a high price. A future government in China—a totally new or a reformed Nationalist, or a reformed Communist regime—most probably would have to stay in power via the ballot box. It would have to be more democratic than any previous Chinese regime in order to satisfy the people.

It is not impossible that the next regime in China may be in the hands of some Communists who will have toppled the Mao Dynasty. If this is the case, the regime would have to be democratic in nature as well as in name. The hated Communist label would have to be discarded. It is also possible that the Nationalists may help when a spontaneous uprising occurs, thereby regaining its power on the mainland. This, however, would not guarantee their continued power after the initial military phase, unless the Kuomintang, even with all its improvements today, is greatly reformed. It should weed out most of the incompetents and professional hacks, and absorb new blood and youthful talents. The concept of the party as the sole patron of the government must be abolished once and for all. Above all, complete freedom of press as practiced in the West should be permitted. Judging from the overwhelming desire of the Chinese everywhere, the real question is not whether China would be again under Kuomintang misrule, but whether the Kuomintang would be able to identify itself with the awakened wishes of the vast majority. If it can, it may survive as a major political party. If not, it may fade from the picture completely. This is a problem not for the Chinese people, but for the Kuomintang itself. Thus the immediate problem for democracy in the early stage of a post-Communist China appears comparatively simple.

The real problem is long-term, as a strong will for democracy does not guarantee success. Most problems of democracy appear to be political but are actually social. Democracy is not just a parliament or a constitution. It is a national way of life born of a specific physical environment, the manners and mores of the people, and the ideas of their thinkers. It is tailored to the entire social, economic and cultural structure. Democracy as is known in the West is the product of the Roman Law, the Magna Carta, the Boston Tea Party, the Fall of the Bastille, the Industrial Revolution, of Jean Jacques Rousseau and John Locke and Thomas Jefferson and Abraham Lincoln. This traditional soil, plus such prerequisites as relatively high literacy and the absence of violent upheavals, make democracy work in the West because it is indigenous.

But democracy has not done too well in other areas. The fact is that Western-designed democracy cannot take instant root in countries like the socially underdeveloped nations of Africa. It is even more difficult in countries like China, where society has over-developed in quite a different direction. Nations going through violent transitions often can only be held together by some form of centralized regime or by dominant personalities. Until very recently the West seldom realized this.

The fact that China's traditional way of life is engulfing Communism does not guarantee that it will not engulf any other political system. There are traditional traits in China's heritage that work against democratic practices. The Chinese value highly their traditions of *chien jang* (humility and yielding to others), tolerance, patience and the non-interference in others' affairs. No matter how virtuous and capable a Chinese may be, he would always say that he lacks virtue and capability. This humility is a sign of cultivation by which others judge him. It is unthinkable that any Chinese political candidate would boast of his virtues and talents as in the West. Anyone doing this would be laughed out of the political arena by scholars and peasants alike. The pure individualism of the Chinese also works against democratic practices; the Chinese work well individually but not as a team. They hate to interfere in "idle affairs." Public spirit and civic pride are difficult to grow in such a soil. Thus many of their personal virtues become public vices in a democracy.

However, there are traits favorable to the basic spirit of democracy. It is a strange historical accident that in China's kaleidoscopic history, democracy as it is known in the West has never been indigenously conceived. In China's 50 centuries of monarchism there were a few tyrants and many incompetents, but also many benevolent rulers. Since the days of Confucius the concept of the government had been the rule of divine right with the emperor given a mandate by heaven to govern the people. But this mandate had a rider: heaven listens to the people. If the people suffer, the emperor's mandate is automatically rescinded by heaven, and the people have the right to revolt. This has happened many times, but each time an emperor was overthrown, the people would habitually look to a new emperor. The parental government concept of the Chinese means government of the people, for the people, but *not by* the people. A famous classical poem expressing the carefree joy of the Chinese peasants says in part: "I work when the sun rises and rest when the sun sets; What is the emperor's power to me?" It reflects the ideal Chinese political concept in which a government does not meddle in people's affairs.

Chinese tradition has other features favorable to democracy: China has had no hereditary aristocracy and feudal system for more than 2,000 years. China has had no serfs, big landlords or monopolistic capitalists as known in the West. The reason why the basic democratic spirit of the Chinese has not worked out is because it was never developed to the ballot box. The problem is how to create a political system democratic in essence but indigenous in application, and one that suits modern conditions, too. The failure of democracy in China during the past 50 years is due to the failure to realize this problem. Partly responsible for this were the Nationalists, who at first thrust a Western parliamentary system into the alien soil, then reorganized the Kuomintang on the Bolshevik pattern. Partly responsible were the Western do-gooders whose attitude was to feed others democracy even if it choked them. Thus a so-called coalition government was naively and militantly forced on China after World War II, adding political to military and economic chaos. In 1962 it was again forced on Laos where it will not work either.

Most responsible for this failure, however, were the Chinese people themselves, who were almost entirely nationalistically oriented. The vast majority neither understood nor cared for democracy. The intellectual minority on one hand rightly criticized the Nationalists' undemocratic traits, on the other did not work—or did not know how to work—for democratization themselves. They did not care to vote, did not pay income tax, did not help with political tutelage and economic improvement of the peasants who, after all, comprised the bulk of the populace. The disparity in political concepts between the peasant majority and the intellectual minority was a major factor in democracy's failure in China. Furthermore, although the May Fourth Movement was an inspiring awakening of China, its shortcoming lay in the total discrediting of everything old—good or bad. Thus old values were discarded but new values adaptable to the basic soil did not grow. The vacuum created sucked in Communism.

The development of a creative democratic system applicable to the Chinese soil is therefore of paramount urgency. Equally urgent will be the simultaneous development of a new national personality adaptable to modern democracy. For without a new personality China cannot have an effective new political system. In this respect China's experience under Communism will not be totally without benefit. Besides the intense craving for democracy it evoked, the Communist regime has also coached the Chinese in how to be disciplined. The Chinese are usually hard to discipline by others even though they can be very self-disciplined, since the Chinese control mechanism is inside rather than outside the individual. Another good result is that spiritual values, challenged seriously during times of trouble, have been stimulated into a new life. Heroism, sacrifice, loyalty, compassion, love, and belief in God have already surged up quietly and stanchly in Communist China. They will be openly cherished when freedom is regained. Western missionaries may make many converts when they resume their wonderful work there.

The old days will never come back intact and some of the nostalgic past will be lost forever. But the basic Chinese outlook will probably return: that in spite of strife, life is full of contentment and meaning. The Chinese will continue to enjoy quiet pleasures, noisy festivals, good food, affectionate friends and close families. But they will want to vote.

China will need new leaders who understand China itself as

well as the changing world around it; who see the undesirable traits in Chinese tradition but are proud of its fine heritage; who are humble enough to borrow from the Western way of life without aping its shortcomings as well. This will be a serious problem as it has been a controversy among the educated Chinese all these years. The biggest group, who may be called the substitutionists, would like to substitute Western culture completely for Chinese culture. They treat science almost as religion, ape everything Western, and often are ashamed or scornful of anything from traditional China, including even Chinese furniture, architecture, clothing and folk arts. The second group may be called the traditionalists, who cling desperately to anything Chinese, belittle and fear anything Western. The third group may be called the infusionists, who want a merging of the East and West, generally Eastern philosophy and Western science.

The lack of an integrated approach toward this clash of cultures has created many bizarre phenomena in China, such as chanting Buddhist monks and wailing mourners in a Chinese funeral procession followed by a brass band playing "I Wonder Who's Kissing Her Now." It is neither possible nor desirable for China to be entirely cut off from its heritage, or for it to ape the superficial features of the West. Many fine Chinese traits should be retained, such as patience, tolerance, humility, individualism, contentment, sense of humor, love of peace, love of family, inner morals, and harmony with nature and man. After all, there must be some intrinsic value in a society that has produced almost no alcoholics, no juvenile delinquents, no psychopaths, few spinsters and divorcees, a society that makes old-age a time to look forward to rather than to dread, and enables a people to weather terrible misfortunes as well as sudden successes.

The shortcomings in the Chinese culture can be remedied by an infusion of the best values from Western, and especially from the dynamic American, culture: aggressiveness, competitiveness, pioneering spirit, rule of law, the sense of civic duty, social consciousness, *esprit de corps,* and the dogged probing in physical sciences that brings power and wealth to modern nations. After all, there must be some intrinsic value in a society that in only a couple of centuries became the greatest nation on earth, with its people enjoying unprecedented political liberty and material wealth.

On the other hand, Western civilization, with its technological development far ahead of humanistic progress, also has its own peculiar shortcomings. Over-emphasis on the measurable and the visible creates the fallacy that all things can be worked out by recipes and formulas, that all eventualities can be anticipated, that intangibles do not matter, and that man is so rational that his primitive emotions play no role in his objectivity. Juvenile delinquency, alcoholism, crimes of violence, psychoses, divorce, and the despondency of old-age may remain serious social problems so long as it is believed that they can be remedied by legislation, medication and couch consultation instead of by something from within. These problems arise in the West partly because social institutions try to take over too many family functions, just as once other problems arose in China partly because the family tried to take over too many of the functions of society.

It is no coincidence that the deficiencies of the East are the strengths of the West, and vice versa. The aggressive Western culture, without borrowing a little mature wisdom from the East, may develop into a civilization of affluent hysteria. The serene Eastern culture, without borrowing a little youthful effervescence from the West, may stagnate into physical senility. Perhaps, by borrowing a little from each other, the two cultures need not each grope for novel solutions to its peculiar problems.

This does not mean that the Chinese should chew gum and copy the American Constitution; or that the Americans must practice shadowboxing and Zen Buddhism. The spirit is often more essential than the form. The West has borrowed many things from China: first important inventions as previously mentioned and items in gracious living like venetian blinds, bonzai and toothbrushes; then such ideas as insurance, grain storage, impeachment and civil service examinations. The current emigration of Chinese refugees from Communism has already resulted in some discernible cultural influences. The exit of a large number of attractive, svelte Chinese women has brought about a craze for Oriental fashions, especially the tantalizing *cheong-sam* (sheath dress). Many of the best Chinese chefs are now bringing authentic, delectable Chinese cooking to the world's gourmets. Sophisticated, highly educated Chinese, who never cared to stay abroad in the old days, are settling down in the world's major cities, giving a new perspective to the world's image of the Chinese. It is not inconceivable that someday the West may want to borrow the more profound features of the Chinese culture to enrich its own. China will certainly have great influence on the rest of the world, an influence quite different from the Yellow Peril.

Unless the nations of the World can minimize their economic discrepancies, discover a common social frame of reference, and develop an earth-wide culture, violent political upheavals may continue even if Communism should disappear one day as Nazism did, because other systems and other philosophies may breed wars and suffering. In a world thrown into obscene intimacy by modern communications, goaded by a shrieking tempo and scared of its own technological ingenuity, this can easily happen. The best solution is a vigilance against all fanatical dreamers and glib prophets who peddle instant paradises at the expense of freedom, decency and love. History does not repeat itself. But fools often repeat history.

One fine day, when the world is truly under the rule of law, then perhaps it may advance to the rule of propriety. Then man will be governed not by extraneous systems but by something from within. Confucius once envisioned such a world. But he was way ahead of his time—and ours.

BIBLIOGRAPHICAL NOTES

DUE TO THE AMOUNT OF DOCUMENTATION THIS BOOK CONTAINS AND the degree of its condensation, I felt that listing every reference individually would interrupt the text with thousands of footnote numbers and expand the book to an unwieldy size. Since this book is primarily meant for reading and secondarily for reference, I decided to list all important reference sources in a catch-all Bibliography here.

This has several advantages. For instance, each of seven chapters in Parts Two and Three contain more than 200 reference sources, many of which, however, are from identical publications. Also, a number of statistical figures in Chapters V, VI and VII were obtained from two to some 20 different sources and worked out by myself. An adequate footnote in such cases would be virtually impossible.

More than 80 percent of the factual material in the book has been taken directly or indirectly from recorded Chinese Communist sources and, in the majority of cases, based on the original Chinese texts. This is especially so with important official statements and opinions, such as the Hundred Flowers quotations. These primary source materials were available to me during my years of residence in Hong Kong and my information-gathering trip there in late 1959, from special libraries in the United States, and from my news contacts in Hong Kong. Paraphrased Chinese passages and English translations (including official Peking translations) have been used only when the Chinese texts were not available.

Among the non-Communist publications, valuable help was received from these excellent, independent Hong Kong publications: *China Weekly, China News Analysis,* and *Modern Critique,* all research periodicals; and *Truth Daily* and *New Life Evening Post,* both dailies.

CHINESE COMMUNIST PERIODICALS

Archeology
Book Reading
Chang Pei
China Agricultural Journal
China Forestry
China Reconstructs (English)
China Workers
China Youth
Cultural Objects
Current Affairs Handbook
Economic Research
Electrical Engineering
Food Grain
Geographical Knowledge
Geology Monthly
Heavy Machinery Monthly
Historical Research
Hsin Hua Semi-Monthly
Ideological Front
The Journal of Peking University:
    Humanitarian Sciences
Liberation
Liberation Army Warrior

Linguistic Research
Literary Gazette
Literary Study
New Construction
New Harbor
New Industry and Commerce
People's China (English)
People's Literature
Philosophical Research
Planned Economy (now merged
    with *Statistical Work* as *Planning and Statistics*)
Planning and Statistics
Poetry Magazine
Red Flag (or *Hung-chi*)
Science Journal
Statistical Work (now merged with
    Planned Economy as *Planning and Statistics*)
Study
Water Conservancy and Power
Women of New China
World Knowledge

CHINESE COMMUNIST NEWSPAPERS

Anhwei Daily, Hofei
Canton Daily, Canton
Changchun Daily, Changchun
Chekiang Daily, Hangchow
China News Press, Peking
Daily Worker, Peking
Fukien Daily, Foochow
Honan Daily, Chengchow

Honan Peasant Daily
Hopei Daily, Paoting
Hsin Hua Daily, Chungking
———————, Nanking
Hupeh Daily, Wuhan
Inner Mongolia Daily, Huhehot
Kansu Daily, Lanchow
Kiangsi Daily, Nanchang

Kirin Daily, Changchun
Kuang Ming Daily, Peking
Kwangsi Daily, Nanning
Kweichow Daily, Kweiyang
Liaoning Daily, Mukden
Liberation Army Press, Peking
Liberation Daily, Shanghai
Nan Fang Daily, Canton
New Hunan Daily, Changsha
Northeast Daily
Peking Evening News, Peking
People's Daily, Peking
Reconstruction Press, Kweilin
Shansi Daily, Taiyuan
Shensi Daily, Sian
Sian Daily, Sian

Sian Industrial-Commercial-Economic Evening News, Sian
Sian Masses Daily, Sian
Sin Wen Pao, Shanghai
Sinkiang Daily, Urumchi
Szechwan Daily, Chengtu
Ta Kung Pao, Hong Kong
————, Peking
Teachers' Daily, Peking
Tsingtao Daily, Tsingtao
Wen Hui Pao, Hong Kong
————, Shanghai
Yangtze Daily, Wuhan
Yunnan Daily, Kunming

* * *

Hsinhua News Agency releases

CHINESE COMMUNIST BOOKS (Chinese)

Ai Ssu-chi. On Historical Materialism. Peking, 1951.
Archeological Acquisitions in the New China. Academy of Science, Peking, 1960.
Chao, Yi-wen. The Industry of New China. Statistical Publishing House, Peking, 1957.
Feng, Yu-lan. First Collection of Essays on the History of Chinese Philosophy. People's Publishing House, Peking, 1961.
———— Looking Back at Forty Years. Peking, 1959.
———— Second Collection of Essays on the History of Chinese Philosophy. People's Publishing House, Peking, 1962.
Liang, Jen-tsai. Economic Geography of Kwangtung. Peking, 1956.
Liu Shao-chi. How to be a Good Communist. Peking, 1951.
Mao, Tse-tung. Selected Works (4 vols.). Peking, 1951.
Soil Conditions for Better Harvesting of Wet Rice. Academy of Agrarian Science, Peking, 1959.
Soong, Ching-ling. Struggle for New China. Peking, 1952.
Ten Glorious Years. People's Publishing House, Peking, 1959.

CHINESE COMMUNIST BOOKS (English)

Chen, Po-ta. Mao Tse-tung on the Chinese Revolution. Foreign Languages Press, Peking, 1953.

Chen, Po-ta. *Stalin and the Chinese Revolution.* Foreign Languages Press, Peking, 1953.

Chou, En-lai. *A Great Decade.* Foreign Languages Press, Peking, 1959.

A Guide to New China. Foreign Languages Press, Peking, 1952.

Hu, Chiao-mu. *Thirty Years of the Communist Party of China: An Outline History.* Foreign Languages Press, Peking, 1951.

Mao, Tse-tung. *Selected Works* (5 vols.). International Publishers, New York, 1954-1962.

Ministry of Agriculture. *People's Communes.* Foreign Languages Press, Peking, 1960.

Reform of the Chinese Language. Foreign Languages Press, Peking, 1958.

State Statistical Bureau. *Ten Great Years: Statistics of the Economic and Cultural Achievements of the People's Republic of China.* Foreign Languages Press, Peking, 1960.

NON-COMMUNIST PERIODICALS (Chinese)

China Weekly, Hong Kong
Freedom Front, Hong Kong, (discontinued)
Modern Critique, Hong Kong
New Life Evening Post, Hong Kong
Truth Daily, Hong Kong
The United Journal, New York

NON-COMMUNIST PERIODICALS (English)

The China Mail, Hong Kong
China News Analysis, Hong Kong
The China Quarterly, London
China Reporting Service newsletters, Hong Kong
Chinese News Service releases, New York
Current Background, Hong Kong
Current Scene: Development in Mainland China, Hong Kong
Far Eastern Economic Review, Hong Kong
Free China Review, Taipei
Hongkong Tiger Standard, Hong Kong
The New Leader, New York
Problems of Communism, Washington, D.C.
South China Morning Post, Hong Kong
Survey of China Mainland Press, Hong Kong
Time, New York
U.S. News and World Report, Washington, D.C.

NON-COMMUNIST BOOKS (Chinese)

The Book of Changes (I Ching)

The Book of History (Shu Ching)

Chang, Kung-tao (ed.). *The Death of Chen Han-po*. Freedom Press, Hong Kong, 1952.

Chang, Ta-chun. *Who's Who of Communist China*. Freedom Press, Hong Kong, 1956.

Chao, Tsung. *Literary Scenes on the Mainland*. Union Press, Hong Kong, 1959.

Chao, Yung-hsin. *Railroad Construction in Communist China*. Union Press, Hong Kong, 1954.

Chen, Han-po. *How I Worked as Mao Tse-tung's Secret Agent*. Freedom Press, Hong Kong, 1953.

Chen, Shu-fang. *The New Marriage Law of Communist China*. Union Press, Hong Kong, 1953.

Cheng, Chu-yuan. *An Analysis of Communist China's First Five-Year Plan*. Freedom Press, Hong Kong, 1955.

—————. *The Slave Labor System of Communist China*. Freedom Press, Hong Kong, 1952.

Chiang, Kai-shek. *China's Destiny*. Chungking, 1943.

Chien, Mu. *History of Chinese Thoughts*. Kao Yuan, Hong Kong, 1957.

Chow, Ching-wen. *I Act as a Witness for History*. Modern Critique Institute, Hong Kong, 1959.

—————. *Ten Years of Storm* (original Chinese version of the English edition). Modern Critique Institute, Hong Kong, 1959.

Chu, Pu-fu. *The People's Police in Red China*. Freedom Press, Hong Kong, 1955.

Chuangtzu. *The Book of Chuangtzu*.

Confucius. *The Analects*.

—————. *The Doctrine of the Mean*.

—————. *The Great Learning*.

Fan, Ya-kang. *A Brief History of the Chinese Communist Party*. China Problems Research Institute, Hong Kong, 1955.

Hsia, Yung-po. *The Story of Repatriated Students*. Asia Press, Hong Kong, 1953.

Hsiao Ping (pseud.) *Illusion Pursuers* (original Chinese version of Robert Loh's English edition *Escape from Red China*. Coward-McCann, New York, 1962). Union Press, Hong Kong, 1959.

Hu, Shih. *Outline History of Chinese Philosophy*. Chuanshang, Shanghai, 1930.

Hu, Yueh. *A Critique of Historical Materialism*. Freedom Press, Hong Kong, 1951.

Kan, Yiu-lan. *Mao Tse-tung and His Clique*. Freedom Press, Hong Kong, 1954.

Ku, Kuan-chiao. *Thirty Years of Chinese Communism*. Asia Press, Hong Kong, 1955.

Kung, Chu. *The Red Army and I*. South Wind, Hong Kong, 1954.

Laotzu. *The Book of the Way (Tao Te Ching)*.

Lei, Chen. *Collected Essays on the Finance and Economy of Taiwan*. Free China Institute, Taipei, 1957.

Lei, Hsiao-tsen. *Thirty Years of Turmoil in China*. Asia Press, Hong Kong, 1955.

Lo, Kuan-chung. *Tales of Three Kingdoms*.

Pa Chin. *Home*

Sma, Lo. *Eighteen Years of Struggle*. Asia Press, Hong Kong, 1952.

Sun, Yat-sen. *Collected Works of Chung-sen* (4 vols.). Shanghai, 1927.

Sze, Nai-an. *Water Margin (All Men are Brothers)*.

Ten Years of Communist China. Union Press, Hong Kong, 1960.

Three Hundred Tang Poems.

Ting, Li. *The Militia in Communist China*. Union Press, Hong Kong, 1955.

Tsao, Chu-jen. *On Chiang Ching-kuo*. Chuang Ken, Singapore, 1954.

Tsao, Hsueh-chin. *Dream of Red Chamber*.

Wu, Cheng-en. *Westward Travelogue*.

Non-Communist Books (English)

Barnett, A. Doak. *Communist China and Asia*. Harper, New York, 1960.

Boyle, Samuel E. *The Church in Red China: Lean to One Side*. Hong Kong, 1950.

Lord Boyd Orr and Townsend, Peter. *What's Happening in China?* Doubleday, New York, 1959.

Buck, John Lossing. *Chinese Farm Economy: A Study of 2866 Farms in Seventeen Localities and Seven Provinces in China*. University of Chicago Press, Chicago, 1930.

——————. *Land Utilization in China: A Study of 16,786 Farms in 168 Localities, and 32,256 Farm Families in 22 Provinces in China, 1929-1933*. The Commercial Press, Shanghai, 1937.

Chen, Chi-yung. *Fool in the Reeds*. Rainbow Press, Hong Kong, 1959.

Cheng, Chu-yuan. *Income and Standard of Living in Mainland China* (2 vols.). Union Press, Hong Kong, 1957.

Chiang, Kai-shek. *Soviet Russia in China: A Summing Up at Seventy*. Farrar, Straus and Cudahy, New York, 1957.

China Mainland Today: Communist-Controlled China as Foreign Visitors (and as *Foreign Residents*) *See It*. (2 vols.). Free China Review, Taipei, 1957.

China Yearbook (formerly *China Handbook*). China Publishing Company, Taipei.

Communism in China. Union Research Institute, Hong Kong, 1959.

The Communist Bloc and the Western Alliances: The Military Balance 1962-1963. The Institute for Strategic Studies, London, 1962.

Cressey, George B. *Land of the 500 Million: A Geography of China.* McGraw-Hill, New York, 1955.

A Decade under Mao Tse-tung. Green Pagoda Press, Hong Kong, 1959.

Doig, Peter. *A Concise History of Astronomy.* Chapman and Hill, London, 1950.

Government of India Planning Commission. *Report of the Indian Delegation to China on Agrarian Co-operatives.* New Delhi, 1957.

Guillain, Robert. *600 Million Chinese.* Criterion, New York, 1957.

Greene, Felix. *Awakened China: The Country Americans Don't Know.* Doubleday, New York, 1961.

Hsieh, Alice L. *Communist China's Strategy in the Nuclear Era.* Prentice-Hall, Englewood Cliffs, N.J., 1962.

Hsu, Francis L. K. *Under the Ancestors' Shadow: Chinese Culture and Personality.* Columbia University Press, New York, 1948.

Hu, Chang-tu. *China: Its People, Its Society, Its Culture.* HRAF Press, New Haven, 1960.

Jaegher, Raymond J. de and Kuhn, Irene Corbally. *The Enemy Within.* Doubleday, New York, 1952.

Kung, Henry. *Asia's First Republic: The Story of China 1912-1961.* China Publishing Company, Taipei, 1961.

Laotsu. *Tao Te Ching,* (translated by R. B. Blakney). Mentor, New York, 1955.

Lederer, William J. *A Nation of Sheep.* Norton, New York, 1961.

Li, Choh-ming. *Economic Development of Communist China.* University of California Press, Berkeley, 1959.

Lifton, Robert Jay. *Thought Reform and the Psychology of Totalism: A Study of "Brainwashing" in China.* Norton, New York, 1961.

Lin, Yutang. *My Country and My People* (rev. ed.). John Day, New York, 1954.

Liu, F. F. *A Military History of Modern China 1924-1949.* Princeton University Press, Princeton, 1956.

Liu, Shaw-tong. *Out of Red China.* Duell, Sloan and Pearce, New York, 1953.

Moraes, Frank. *Report on Mao's China.* Macmillan, New York, 1953.

Orleans, Leo A. *Professional Manpower and Education in Communist China.* National Science Foundation, Washington, D.C., 1961.

Overstreet, Harry and Bonaro. *What We Must Know About Communism.* Norton, New York, 1958.

Provincial Government of Taiwan. *Achievements of the Taiwan Provincial Administration.* Taipei, 1961.

Research Backgrounder Series, Hong Kong
   China's Land Problem Series (5 vols.). 1960-1962.
   Current Scene: Reports on Communist China. 1961.
   Directory of Chinese Communist Leadership. 1960.
   Standard Translation of Chinese Communist Terms. 1960.
   State Farms in Communist China. 1962.
   The Young Communist League, 1959-1960.
Schmid, Peter. *The New Face of China.* Pitman, New York, 1959.
Siao-Yu. *Mao Tse-tung and I Were Beggars.* Syracuse University Press, Syracuse, 1959.
Snow, Edgar. *The Other Side of the River: Red China Today.* Random House, New York, 1962.
————. *Red Star Over China* (rev. ed.). Garden City, New York, 1939.
Statistical Abstract of the United States (annual). Bureau of the Census, Washington, D.C.
Stevenson, William. *The Yellow Wind.* Houghton Mifflin, Boston, 1959.
Taire, Lucien. *Shanghai Episode.* Rainbow Press, Hong Kong, 1958.
Tang, Peter S. H. *Communist China Today* (2 vols.). Praeger, New York, 1957.
Thursfield, H. G. (ed.). *Brassey's Annual, 1961.* Macmillan, New York.
United Nations Statistical Yearbook. U.N. Statistical Office, New York.
Walker, Richard A. *China Under Communism.* Yale University Press, New Haven, 1955.
Wan, Yah-kang. *The Rise of Communism in China, 1920-1950.* Chung Shu, Hong Kong, 1952.
White, Theodore H. and Jacoby, Annalee. *Thunder Out of China.* William Sloan, New York, 1946.
Wilson, J. Tuzo. *One Chinese Moon.* Hill and Wang, New York, 1959.

INDEX